BRIEF EXTRACTS FROM NOTICES
of
Previous Editions of this Narrative.

The Times.—"The Queen has been pleased to confer a Civil List Pension on the Rev. J. Inches Hillocks, author of 'Hard Battles for Life and Usefulness.'"

The Contemporary Review.—"His Battles differ from most others in that they have been struggles for usefulness as well as for life."

The Athenaeum.—"Difficulties faced with courage and constancy."

The Spectator.—"Told with much sympathy and force, and in a very kindly, charitable spirit."

The Scotsman.—"From first to last the narrative is full of genuine interest. . . In certain respects it is superior to what even a Dickens or a Trollope could paint. Whosoever wants to deal with the lowest class of our overcrowded towns in a practical way, will find this work full of interest and instruction."

Dr. Smiles (Author of 'Self-Help').—"One of the most encouraging and exhilarating books I have ever read. Self-Help with God's Help can do much."

The Glasgow Herald.—"A very remarkable volume. The lesson it teaches is a far higher one than the Proverb 'Honesty is the best policy.' . . . His descriptions of London life are written with great force."

THE CHRISTIAN.—" Mr. Hillocks' life is full of eventful success and consecrated energy ; a career devoted to the highest and truest interest of mankind. . . . . His life will be studied with pleasure, so long as an interest is felt in an earnest, religious man of parts, character and courage, doing battle against impediment and wrong."

THE CHRISTIAN WORLD.—" Mr. Hillocks has raised himself to usefulness and esteem, where he is able to do much for the service of others, not by his active efforts only, but by the example he furnishes in his own person of what can be accomplished by a brave heart and determined will."

THE CHURCH REVIEW.—" He proves not his descent from Norman blood, but his incontestable right to have his name inscribed on the roll of Hard Battle Abbey."

THE FREEMAN.—" A Record of the highest worth. Mr. Hillocks is one of God's Heroes. A man inspired by a noble purpose, loving sympathies, and invincible resolution. The book will be an incentive to multitudes."

THE UNITED PRESBYTERIAN MAGAZINE.—" Struggling upward to the usefulness of a ministerial life, he has been fitted to become helpful to many."

THE ILLUSTRATED LONDON NEWS.—" Mr. Hillocks has overcome difficulties, and we laud him. He has toiled to save souls, and we honour and thank him."

THE BRITISH MEDICAL JOURNAL.—" As was natural to be expected of a minister of religion, Mr. Hillocks' observations are largely tinctured with a condemnation of sin and vice. The work to which he has devoted himself with so much self-sacrifice does far more to lift the humbler of our fellow-creatures to the dignity and comforts of life than any number of Acts of Parliament."

THE SCOTTISH REVIEW.—"The incidents, struggles and acts of genuine heroism the volume records make it at once interesting and inspiring. Whatever Mr. Hillock's theology may be, his religion is manly and Christ-like."

PUBLIC OPINION.—"Mr. Hillocks' earnestness is an indication of the true renunciation of self. It is such men as this Author, who can alone help to lay bare before the public mind our awful surroundings."

THE METHODIST TIMES.—"His battles have been fought with trust in God, and a desperate determination not to be beaten. The record is graphic and thrilling."

THE ENGLISH CHURCHMAN.—"His has been a career of patient endurance and of a struggle for knowledge and right against the might of almost insurmountable difficulties, more striking than we ever remember to have seen before.

THE COURT CIRCULAR.—"Mr. Hillocks' 'Battles for Life' began in motherless babyhood, and his 'Battles for Usefulness' have been fought in the slums of London. He is worthy of any one of Dr. Smiles' heroes. His enthusiasm never makes him unjust. Though decidedly evangelical in his opinions he is no narrow dogmatist. His preaching runs evenly on the lines of doctrine and duty."

THE SWORD AND TROWEL (*Rev. C. H. Spurgeon*).—"He began life as a Dundee weaver toiling for bread. Bye-and-bye he weaves another web, his whole nature acting as the loom; and then with his homespun he covers many a brother's nakedness. . . As champion for the oppressed poor he has done his best for reform and benevolence."

THE BRITISH QUARTERLY REVIEW.—"He gave himself to the service of the poor, first in Scotland, and then in London, with a rare consecration, unselfishness, and religious enthusiasm."

THE FAMILY CHURCHMAN.—"Mr. Hillocks' life has been 'No mere May game, but a battle and a march.' His simple and unaffected heart throbs with an unceasing love of God."

THE COURT JOURNAL." Mr. Hillocks is a person of genuine poetry, and of great zeal and energy. He is just the sort of man to forward any cause that it pleases him to undertake. Nothing daunts him. He is ever prepared to struggle with difficulties."

THE NONCONFORMIST.—"We are much impressed with the earnest endeavour of the Author to devote his life wholly and entirely to public good. This is the one great object of his life—the amelioration of the physical and spiritual condition of the poor. The compensation he obtained for injuries received in the terrible Railway collision, which nearly cost him his life, provided him with the necessary funds to work gratuitously for years in the heart of London. His experience will be of great value and real interest to all intelligent Christian Workers."

THE MONTHLY REVIEW (of the Y.M.C.A., London.) "It is most gratifying to note how true worth is noticed by our beloved Sovereign. Mr. Hillocks has been further honoured by Her Majesty with a Civil List pension. This shows the high esteem in which he is justly held by the highest in the land, by reason of his devoted life-work among the lowest.

Yours faithfully
J J Hillocks

HARD BATTLES

FOR

LIFE AND USEFULNESS

BY THE
Rev. JAMES INCHES HILLOCKS,

AUTHOR OF "MISSION LIFE IN LONDON," "THE GENTLE PRINCE," ETC.

IN TWO PARTS.

THIRD EDITION.
Revised and Illustrated, with Portrait.

"His motto through his severe life struggle has been the very brief but most pregnant sentence—'I'll rise again!'—expressing in one terse phrase his energy as a Man, and his hope as a Christian."

LONDON:
HOULSTON AND SONS,
PATERNOSTER SQUARE.
1889.

PART FIRST.

BATTLES TO LIVE AND LEARN.

𝔇edication.

To JAMES COX, Esq., Ex-Provost of Dundee.

My Dear Friend,

"Kind words can never die." I felt their beneficial influence when, as "The Young Weaver," I was employed by you in what was then the small village of Lochee. They are associated with the early days of my preparation for the work to which God has since called me. Though you did not then know it, they encouraged the young lad to persevere in the midst of great difficulties. They came from your worthy brothers as well as yourself, and I rejoice to learn that the same kindly spirit is manifest in the large and enterprising firm of which you are the eldest member.

This of itself would have induced me to dedicate to you these Battles to Live and Learn. But there is more. I am addressing one who himself has risen to Christian Usefulness as well as to a high social position. It is no small honour to become the Chief Magistrate of one of the leading commercial centres of this great nation, but to me the thoughts that surround the words "Christian Usefulness" are much more attractive. This shows we are one in mind and heart.

In all good work, yours faithfully,

J. I. HILLOCKS.

CONTENTS.

Chap.		Page
I.	My Parentage	9
II.	My first Three Years	14
III.	The next Six Years	21
IV.	Thrice Saved on one Sunday	27
V.	Glancing Upward	33
VI.	Some Ups and Downs	39
VII.	Mental and Physical Distress	49
VIII.	Hard Work but Nothing for it	54
IX.	From Home and Back	61
X.	Some Steps Nearer the Mark	70
XI.	Making the Best of my Position	76
XII.	Pressing Forward and Breaking Down	81
XIII.	Some Important Side Incidents	88
XIV.	Round and Back to the same Point	97
XV.	Another Round of Events	105
XVI.	More Turning Points	115
XVII.	Almost Lost in Edinburgh	121
XVIII.	Sowing some Seed	132
XIX.	Stepping Stones to London	140

SEE INDEX, END OF THIS PART.

INTRODUCTION.

BY THE REV. WALTER C. SMITH, D.D., LL.D.

Under the name of an INTRODUCTION, I am not to give a criticism of Mr. Hillocks and his work. All I would do is simply to commend the narrative as giving a vivid picture of a human soul fighting an unusually hard battle, and using the lessons of his own experience to help others, who, like himself, have a stiff fight to maintain. It is in this respect that the man is to me especially interesting.

We have in these days many biographies of people who had perhaps as great hardships to face, and who met them with equal courage, and who conquered fortune in the long run and died millionaires. I am interested in the struggles of such men, but quite indifferent to their success. The moment they begin to prosper, the thoughtful reader begins to yawn. Of what consequence is it to any one how many thousands a year they made, as compared with the dauntless hearts they had in the days of their adversity? Their battle was something, but their victory, if that was all they aimed at, was not worth the cost.

Mr. Hillocks' story reads a very different lesson. He was not one to make a great fortune—was not shrewd in business, or clever in speculation, or lucky in investing when he happened to have a trifle to invest, which was not often. But, from the beginning, while he struggled honestly to maintain himself, he at the same time was trying to do some good to others. His schoolmastering, his drug-selling, his missionarying among the poor, all were directed to the same end, to raise himself only by raising the poor round about him. And now, in his latter years, his only wealth is a burden of care for the London poor; yet he is rich, if you could but see it, in the kindly feelings and abundant labours which he expends upon them. He, too, has conquered fortune, for he has won the place and power to do the good which it was in his heart to do. That is true success, and he fought gallantly for it.

I took it on me to recommend that he simply tell his own story, leaving the readers to make the reflections for themselves; but my excellent friend has been too much accustomed to preaching to carry this out entirely, but what comments there are in this volume do not mar the unity of the book.

What may be thought of his opinions I do not know, but his experience of life, the facts that have come under his eye, and have been carefully noted by him, will be found helpful to all his fellow-workers, and should stimulate others to go and do likewise.

His book was not written for literary purposes; it is a plain story, and makes no pretence to be anything else. As such, I recommend it to all who are interested in the heroism of humble life, and the success of benevolent work. It is a story of one who had a hard battle for existence, and also for faith, and who is still fighting on, that the battle might be made somewhat easier for others. It never loses its interest, therefore, because each success only leads on to new effort.

TO THE READER.

HAVING read the explicit INTRODUCTION by my sympathetic friend, the Rev. Dr. Smith, you will require very little from me by way of preface; but I may tell you that, in issuing this edition—as it was in regard to the other editions—I would fain expect a favourable reception. I do so from the generally admitted fact, that "the tale of a human life has to every human being a deep interest." After all it is this that touches the heart, that stirs, and may inspire the soul. And, doubtless, this is done all the readier if the thread of that life has upon it several hard knots. In that case the coils are likely to be taken up readily, and traced from end to end. Hence, notwithstanding my shortcomings, I venture to hope for a measure of continued interest in these Hard Battles for Life and Usefulness.

I am aware that it is a risk for even the best of pens to write in the first person, but this is necessary in autobiography. In all such cases the "I" must lead; but then it is possible that in the "*I*" the fact and thought expressed may be as true and kindly as can be found under the wing of the "*We.*" It is not said that this is always the case; all I look for from you is to remember it is possible, and my opinion of you is that you will suppose the best.

Again, I have no wish to banish from my mind the truth contained in these words: "It is a hard subject for a man to write about himself. Naturally it grates on his own heart to say anything of disparagement, and it as naturally grates on the reader's ear to hear anything of praise from him; and this becomes the more marked when the state of the heart as well as the course of life is referred to."

The man who writes to praise himself is sure to miss the mark, and serve him right. But it may happen that those who are inclined to suppose the best find that what looked like praise had not been given by the writer as such. Be that as it may, speaking for myself, my simple object has been to state facts in relation to other facts, *not* as praise, *nor* as blame, but simply as *facts*.

I need scarcely tell you I am not without decided opinions on the general topics of the day—social and political, philanthropic and religious. Naturally, I was inclined to sustain them when called up by the incidents recorded; but I have refrained from this course because of the space it would require, but chiefly because to have done so would have broken up the narrative. In this edition I have followed Dr. Smith's advice more implicitly; but (D.V.) I shall make up for this in the Sequel, which I hope may soon follow. I think of the proposed Sequel because, as has been said, my "personal knowledge and considerable experience might become helpful to other Christian workers."

May our Heavenly Father—who has so graciously sustained me in the midst of all these battles, bless the book. If He does, as I believe He will, then this effort to acknowledge His great goodness and loving mercy will not have been made in vain.

J. I. H.

Eden House, 127 Stoke Newington Road,
London, N., *December*, 1888.

BATTLES TO LIVE AND LEARN.

CHAPTER I.—MY PARENTAGE.

MY parents belonged to "the Peerage," but it happened to be "the Peerage of Poverty." By those who know no better than to regard poverty as a crime, this may be looked upon as so much against my parentage. *The paternal side.* But there are other thinkers who are not so foolish. To this they do not say "Amen," preferring to take a true, just, and common-sense view of things, poverty included. What I mean is simply this: Though my parents found it hard to make both ends meet, they lived to be useful in their day and generation. They were amongst those who honestly work for their daily bread, who believe that work is honourable.

My grandfather, on my father's side, belonged to an almost extinct class who were designated "Small Manufacturers." That is, those who themselves did not object to weave whilst employing other weavers. On the principle of "live and let live," the employed and the employer were mutual helpers, comfortable and happy. A sudden and short illness cut him off in the prime of life, leaving a wife and two children, both sons, to mourn his loss.

Whilst yet mere boys, the lads went to sea. Their mother died a few years after, and the elder son died early in manhood, while the younger, my father, was pressed into His Majesty's Service, and so became "a Man-O'-War Sailor."

At heart, as well as by descent, he was a patriot; but, like all manly men, he hated tyranny. Finding that he could no longer endure its crushing pressure, he deserted, but only to be brought back. He was willing to serve, and he said so. Fortunately for him, up to this time, his character stood A 1 for activity and bravery, being also regarded as a "Superior Seaman." He was sent to another ship, and there, as at first, his heart went with his work. He continued to be one of the many who successfully defended our "Isles of the Sea" till "the peace" was proclaimed, when he was discharged. But, rightly or wrongly, this act of desertion, though persistently provoked, stood against his name and prevented any recognition of the many years of faithful service to his country.

Having no home, he, like many more at that time, became as a vessel cast adrift, not only without anchor, but also without a haven for which to steer. Forfar was his native town, but no mother was there to keep the light in the window. He returned to Dundee, resolving to make that sea-port town his future haven.

But he soon found that the vicissitudes of many climes, exposure to unhealthy conditions, and the long strain of a hard life, had greatly impaired his naturally robust health and remarkable strength. In time this so told upon him that he resolved to give up the seafaring life. Still he was not without the manly hope of being able, in a measure, to fight his way honourably through life. After a little rest, he became a hand loom weaver. And, comparative youth being still on his side, he was eventually able to rejoice in a partial return of his native vigour. Supposing that he could hold his own in life's battle, he thought he would get on all the better if he had a "helpmeet."

The maternal. My father was happy in his choice of the precious woman who became his wife. It was a love match. In loving care and thrift, she was all he could desire. She was "a wife at home," and all that these four words happily imply.

"I knew her well," said an elderly friend to me some years ago. "She was a nice, bonny body. Neither short nor tall. Slender, yet well-formed. Her face was sweet, and her ways were winning."

I often look upon this simple photo. Others entered more into details than this friend, particularly my father. From him I learned that my mother was a good housewife, godly and kind, earnest but cheerful, gentle and quiet, cleanly and tidy, a loving wife and an affectionate mother.

Hence, to say that my father was worthy of one so pure and bright—having such inbred characteristics, so womanly and so Christian—is to say much, but not too much. And I am sure you will not be astonished at my being thankful to God for such parents. Without doubt, I owe much to them.

Of course, as admitted, much of this I have from hearsay, but it is not less true for that. I also learned from the same source that this happy couple—happy in God and in each other—were lovers of the sublime and the beautiful, and that the locality of their humble home, together with their strong desire and pleasing habit, favoured and fostered these refining emotions. They had but little time for the cultivation of their tastes and desires in that direction, but they lived near to the fields, not far from the woods, where possibly they had their walks even as before their marriage.

As then, they loved to see the elegant forms and smell the sweet perfumes of the wild flowers and budding plants of reviving spring. No poet loved the seasons more than they did. To them each season had something worthy of notice, something beneficial. But it seems that spring had the largest share of their admiration. Their delight was to watch the gentle but irrepressible growth of the herbs and flowers and trees, the green sprouts and tender blades, and fleecy clouds smiling down upon the bursting buds. They felt and enjoyed the soft sweet influence of the warm sunshine, the silvery water, the refreshing air, all luminous with tender beauty—

> "A bursting into gladness,
>   A waking as from sleep,
> A twitter and a warble
>   That make the pulses leap,"

calling forth that sweet felicity which grateful admiration is sure to bring. In all this, above and around, they saw the goodness of the beneficent Creator, providing for our pleasure, as well as our maintenance in this recovery of life, which, only a few weeks before, seemed to have been lost. And as a rule, such walks led up to the singing of the grand old song—"Praise God from whom all blessings flow."

Thus they lived, in their humble home, a quiet but useful life, kindly and neighbourly, but never forgetting their hearth. *A life given and a life lost.* They were blessed in the gift of a beautiful boy, but he died suddenly before he saw his second birthday. However, this bereavement was soon considerably modified by the birth of a lovely girl. For almost two years after, this was a home of earnest labour and happy contentment.

"I am now so strong. A little turn in the open air does one so much good," said the mother as she returned one day after one of their short walks. "True, one can work with renewed vigour after a few minutes' relief," chimed in the father—the click, click of the shuttle preventing the conversation from being continued, for that shuttle went all the swifter to make up for the short time spent in the pleasant walk.

"It was our last walk," my father would sorrowfully say, referring to this incident, and what followed. Frequently he spoke to me about these things.

"Matters went on much as before, till the seventh of April, the day on which you were born."

Emotion became so strong in him as to prevent him saying it then, but I afterwards learned that mine was a sunny birthday. "For a fortnight all went on well. Hope too beamed brightly whilst hearty thanks were returned to our heavenly Father for life given, and life spared, but soon the bright prospects vanished. Whilst our fondest hopes were being not unreasonably fostered, my grateful joy had to give way to deep sorrow. Your mother died on the twenty-first day after you were born."

Referring to this event in "Life Struggles," my late sympathetic and generous friend, the Rev. George Gilfillan, author of "The Bards of the Bible," truly said, *The loss of a mother.* "The loss of a father is painful, but the loss of a mother is even more painful. The father dies, and the protection of his roof is withdrawn, but that might have been a shelter for indolence. The fatherless boy is compelled to go out into the world; and as all his retreat is cut off, he is thrown on his own resources; and his powers, as if inspired by the spirit of the departed sire, develop rapidly into maturity, while his energies enable him to surmount difficulties, and attain heights at which he himself becomes astonished. But the death of a mother takes away an important shield in the battle of life; and the motherless combatant is much more likely to be defeated. At all events, the ills of life are almost certain to fall fast around him."

Chapter II.—The First Three Years.

It was at "Bonny Dundee" where these events happened, and I am proud of my native town. It was not a city about sixty years ago, neither was the Chief Magistrate called "My Lord Provost," but history testifies that long before that date, Dundee had been the scene of important and never-to-be-forgotten events. In these I am deeply interested, but none of them can be more interesting *to me* than that April morning which enabled me to enter on the stage of an endless life.

Dundee about sixty years ago.

It is not exactly known to a year when this took place; yet, judging from my father's reasoning on this point, and what he frequently repeated—it must have been either in 1826 or 1827, most likely the latter year.

One thing is sure, Dundee was not the same sixty years ago as it is now. Every intelligent reader knows the honourable position that energetic city now occupies, therefore I need not at present do more than mention that some aged Dundonians, who were lads when I was born, have told me that then Dundee had some of the most primitive districts. Such, for instance, as that then called the Blackscroft—which might have been called "The Alsatia," without the special wickedness of the latter. At that time, too, another rather queer district was the quiet antique region then called the Bonnet Hill, now the Hilltown. At the top of this hill, the surrounding district was almost rural, and tenanted chiefly by handloom weavers. Here my parents then lived. The house is yet specially noticeable by means of what is called an "Outside Stair." It was in this house where I first saw the light of day.

His Birthplace.

Here, too, my father continued for some time weaving on the ground floor as was usual. Having lost the best of all nurses for his children, the mother, he had to pay for two, as well as provide for himself—no easy task, for the loom was the only means of income—and weaving was then on the wane; but he faced all difficulties with a brave heart. He might have said, "It never rains but it pours," for that was true in his case; the birth of a son and the death of the mother within one month. These events filled all around with compassion. The father now felt as if enveloped in one of the blackest of clouds. The cheering hope of his heart, the precious partner of his life, gone. And what of their helpless children, the mitherless bairns?

The mitherless bairns.

My sister was strong for her age, having had two years of motherly care. She too was comparatively fortunate in the woman who undertook to see to her simple wants. But with me the case was far different. Some wet-nurses are so very kind that they become real foster-mothers to those placed under their care. Mine was the reverse of this. Those who knew me in infancy told me that the sad results of her shameful neglect and heartless conduct—together with her systematic drugging during the time I was *in her keeping*—made me a weaker child at the end of two years than I was when my mother died.

The *end* of these two years was an important period in the history of my struggles to live. If I had been inclined to die, my excuse for doing so was at hand; but I was *not* inclined, and my heavenly Father, as well as my earthly father, had resolved that I should not die then. Still the natural tendency of the treatment to which I have referred was to stunt my growth, and pave the way for numerous diseases which followed in rapid succession.

Another mother.

The claims upon my father were many compared with his income. But somehow he made out to have a small balance in his favour. My sister gave him little trouble for she was well cared for and continued healthy, strong, and rosy. It was my condition that troubled him most, though he was kept in ignorance of my sufferings and danger. Alone, and all but helpless, he thought of trying to mend matters by dividing his responsibilities with a second partner in life. This he did, and, almost immediately after, I was taken to the new home.

Referring to this second marriage, my father was heard to say, more than once, "It enabled me to take my children home, and if I had not done so, then, the lad would not have been alive now."

It was after I was taken home that the sad results of the ill-treatment of the wicked nurse became fully known. And no doubt, in the providence of God this was the means of saving me from an infant's untimely grave. As it was, my almost hopeless condition led to frequent visits from the tender hearted. But some who came were more inquisitive than sympathetic.

"It would be well if God would take the child to Himself," said one of the latter. All knew what that meant, but my father still hoped, even against hope.

"The boy is so weak that he cannot be reared. And even were that possible, he must be a helpless object for life. He never can get strong. He must be a living trouble to those who have charge of him."

Such was the opinion of another of the visitors, and in this not a few agreed. But all this ended in securing for me more and more of that fond endearment which only a loving father can give. It must have been an interesting sight to see the sailor-weaver gently and softly wiping his tears of affection from the pale face of his baby boy. He felt sure that God knew best what to do. His prayer was that he and my step-mother might be enabled to do their best for my preservation and comfort, as far as possible in a poor man's home.

The new nursery.

God followed His own plan without taking any unusual course. He blessed us as we were. He neither took me right away to heaven, nor did he remove me to a large and comfortable mansion. As you will see, if you read on, He, in this case, as in other cases—saw the end from the beginning.

My new nursery was a wonderful room. It served as the parlour, the kitchen, the breakfast, the dinner, and the supper room; as the sleeping apartment, and all the rest. The roof was low, and the windows were small. Of course, I do not remember, but I think I must have been greatly amused at life as I saw it here—particularly after I was strong enough to look around me, and intelligent enough to reflect on what I saw. Perhaps, I need not tell you there was no affectionate and faithful nursemaid to anticipate my wants, and kindly attend to my comfort—no cook glad of the opportunity to come with beef-tea—no housemaid to make any unnecessary visits to the nursery with coals, and catch the coveted smile for the attentions and favours of opulent cradle-dom. I knew nothing of these, but then I did not miss them. It would have been unreasonable on my part to have expected all the indescribable manifestations of the pathetic patience of my mother, had she been there. The other duties of the busy household took up the time generally spent in bestowing adulation on babies whose lines have fallen in pleasant places. Nevertheless, the change to my new home was favourable. Now I had a better blanket, and it was clean—a better pillow, and it was soft. I had also room to stretch out. It must have been more comfortable and cosy to me to have the pillow turned, not to speak of an occasional kiss from a loving father.

It must have been very pleasing to me when the Doctor said I might be daily lifted from my cradle, and placed in a child's chair by the fire-side. This was a change in the right direction. When all is well, a child, *Doing three things almost at once.* two years old, is plump and generally smiling, a delight to look upon. But, even after almost another year was added to this, I had not approached that desirable condition of childhood. But what was regarded as more astonishing by those who did me the honour of a little attention, was the fact that as yet I had never laughed right out, never spoken, never walked a step. But I, at last, was able to make up for all this, and almost at once, just after I had seen my third birthday.

One day, sitting at the fireside as usual, I observed the water in the tea-kettle boiled over, the fizzing commotion caused me to laugh heartily. The next day the consequent astonishment was increased when I spoke a few words to my sister. And more so, when, a day or so later, I made a successful attempt to walk.

As might be expected, these incidents caused much talk in the neighbourhood, particularly by those who had taken a special interest in me since I was brought home to this nursery.

"He may win the battle yet," said one.

Chapter III.—The Next Six Years.

But this home, even such as it was, proved to be much better than no home and no help. Now there was the presence of kind hearts and willing hands, these do much, in a measure, to make up for the absence of desirable comfort. This is evident to the thoughtful and grateful, the real peerage of poverty, that, in the providence of God, there is generally compensation somewhere, if we could only look for it from Him, and see it when it comes. God never leaves the poor.

Pressed into service.

In all this we had room for thankfulness. My parents were thankful because I was growing in strength, and I was glad for the same reason, and because it was now possible for me some day to be helpful in my humble way. That was not long in coming to pass. All too soon I was willingly "pressed into service."

And this met with a reward of a kind. Some children of tender years, like some of our children of mature years, are as fond of high sounding titles as fashionable young ladies are of stylish bonnets. If I had been among the first, I had cause for joy. From the beginning I had titles thrust upon me without having to pay for them, and that is more than some of our "great" Ph. D.'s, LL.D.'s and D.D.'s can say. Before this I had my W.B.—"the Wonderful Bairn," chiefly because of the threefold incident just recorded. My B.L. came in this way. Those who at last, but reluctantly, admitted that God was right in sparing me, and that "I might yet become a man," accompanied their admission by a saving clause, "If he only got out and about." Well, I did get out and about a little, and the fresh air not only imparted increasing strength, it also caused a natural glow of health to tinge my cheeks, and by those who were glad to see this I was called "the Bonnie Laddie."

On first thoughts, it would seem almost silly even to mention such childish things, but when they remind me of how God and His poor work together, I do not think the life of childhood is so silly as some imagine. At least the remembrance of these things has urged me to helpfulness on behalf of children.

But I must return to the narrative, and tell you that this pleasing rosy tint, which every loving father and mother delights to see on the cheeks of their children, soon disappeared after I was pressed into service, to help as much as I could, and more than I was well able. Of course there were fault finders in those days, and some of them were not slow to give "a bit of their mind." Everyday we find people who must be ever talking about other peoples' business. As is generally the case, they talked without knowledge. They did not know the impelling cause was this: My dear father was poor and often ill.

The work assigned to me was that of a *winder—winding pirns*, or filling the bobbins, by means of a wheel. I was not tall enough to reach the spokes by which it had to be turned. But this difficulty was soon obviated by cutting shorter the legs on which the wheel was supported. As the *winder*, I was placed at the back of my father's loom to supply him with *pirns*. There I sat driving away as light-hearted as possible, and those who came to see me felt so amazed that they gave me my L.W., the Little Wonder—I was so young and so little.

Craving for mental food.

But titles are empty things. At least they did not satisfy me. I thought of other things. The advantages of fresh air and joyous recreation. Their happy results—that of sustaining the physical health and lightening the spirit of the young—were, till now, almost absent in my case. I felt dissatisfied for the first time, but it was more with myself than with my circumstances. True, I was feeling the effects of a growing physical weakness, but it was not that which troubled me most—though certainly it is an unpleasant feeling. However, my pale face suggested to my father the *necessity* of a little open air exercise. This was kindly offered to me in the *gloamins*, and this gift of a few spare moments became a little ray of hope. Though not so well attired as the better-to-do boys and girls, they at once took to me kindly; and hence these fortunate breathing moments became a great source of pleasure—like a sudden burst of sunshine in April, I revived. And my new young friends were helpful.

Still healthful and pleasant as all this was my dissatisfaction increased. The presence and speech of my playmates reminding me that I needed some school education, some mental food. It is strange, even in young life, how one step leads to another. Not long before this my father found he could speak to me as a kind of a companion. He took a delight in telling me about places and habits abroad. This information, fresh in my mind, I carried to my young friends. They were delighted, and asked many questions in connection with their geographical lessons. Hence, at the end of a game, we clustered round to talk, and so on till my company was courted by the more cultivated and refined. But whilst all around me could, after a manner, do something in regard to the three R.'s, I knew nothing of either.

"Oh to be able to read," said I to myself, thinking what a benefit it might be to me.

For the time this was my strongest desire. And soon after it was greatly strengthened by a domestic incident—the receiving of a letter by my stepmother from some relatives in America. Those relatives said they loved me. They also promised to send for me *when I was big*. The Americans like big people and big things, and perhaps that accounted for the saving clause which gave me not a little trouble. At last I became so uncharitable as to suppose they knew I never would be "big"—at least they never sent for me.

But though I did not then get to America, I at last got to school and was glad, for this was the height of my ambition.   *Three months at school.*

Those who are in the habit of abusing the poor—and there are too many given to that exercise—are ready to blame them for many things, and one is "the ignorance of their children." But they do not know the difficulties which then stood in the way of poor parents gratifying their desire to send the children to school. First, all possible labour was so much needed as a means of keeping starvation from the door. Again, the school-fee, however small, was not easily raised. And then the books needed became a great hindrance; at least this was so with us. But the effort was made. And that was to me an important day on which I received my A B C card. That morning, with heart light as a lark, I left for the humble seminary to become a pupil.

"Bode a silk gown," says the proverb, "and you'll get a sleeve." I did not get my longed-for gown, but I got pretty well on for the sleeve, soon becoming master of the Alphabet, and that was a gain. In time, I could rejoice in my "Primer." Of course there were no School Boards then, nor any "Standards" as we have now.

I liked the teacher's wife much better than the teacher himself. She was a gem of a woman, full of calm dignity and common sense. She loved me and encouraged me, and I have been all along susceptible to kindness. And glad was I to be able to be one of those who rendered her the last service she needed on earth. In the teacher there was too much of what is now called "the old school"—too much of what is still in the new school. He was a physical force man, to the pain and sorrow of his pupils. At first, I was frightened like the rest. But when he was enraged beyond measure, I sought refuge under the care of his good wife. Yet passionate as he was, he never even threatened to punish me. Why? I know not, save this—I was obedient and industrious. But I was sorry for the rest. He went the length even to pat me on the head in a fondling way, and prophesy that I would soon be the best scholar in his school.

I went to school for several reasons. One was to become a scholar; another was, in the hope of becoming a teacher. This I took to heart, to try to follow all that was good in my teacher's wife, and to avoid all that seemed evil in him, particularly his ungovernable temper. Even then I could foresee the injury done to all concerned whenever physical violence became the order of the day. Good boys were made bad, and the bad were made worse. One day I found myself mentally making this promise, "If ever I become a teacher I shall never follow the violent mode of *teaching*."

"If," yes. This was a bold conjecture, but, as I soon was led to think, was soon driven out of it. Circumstances over which my father had no control—and against which it would have been foolish to contend—seemed to go against any such possibility. To me the home lessons were easy, and this gave me time to do what I could at the wheel during the evening. And such was my progress, by the end of the third month, that my teacher pronounced me "ready for the Bible and Collection"—two of the most advanced of his reading classes.

This news I brought with glee. But it meant new books and an increasing fee. These my father could not afford. Still I was grateful for what I had learned, *Improving the little.* and so were my parents. And after-events proved that these three months at school were not fruitless. Better a little than nothing. And besides, I had received the key. Having mastered the Alphabet, what may we not obtain?

This, or something like it, urged me to improve the little I had received; and that by the help and advice of my father. Of course, for a time I could not, in my reading, go much beyond children's story books—such as I could get for a chance penny earned by helping any of the neighbouring weavers. This not only retained, but improved my ability to read. No miser could hunt for gold more keenly than I tried, as time permitted me, to follow "Jack the Giant-Killer," "Cock Robin," "The Babes in the Wood," and such like nursery tales.

From these stories I advanced to other reading requiring more thought, and in which the words were much longer; but my father assisted me in their pronunciation. At first this consisted of tracts, such as "The Monthly Visitor." Then followed selections from religious books, such as "Baxter's Saints' Rest." At last I was urged to try the short paragraphs in the newspaper The end of it was my appointment to the office of "family reader." In time my labours in this direction extended to the workshop, and this rubbed off the bashfulness, so that I was able for " Our Sunday Evening Reading," leading up to a new title for me, namely, "*The Young Minister.*"

Then—as in several places in Scotland even yet—the chief services for public worship on Sunday were held in the forenoon and afternoon. This left the evening to be disposed of as the head of each house might direct. In our home, Sunday evening, as a rule, was spent in a way which was helpful not only to us as a family, but also to others who were pleased to assemble with us. Reading and conversation were the means used—the chief part of the former lay at my door. God blessed this mode of increasing our knowledge and fostering piety. It also encouraged the hope, that the time might come when there would be a reality in the title my humble part suggested. The light and joy thus received, as well as imparted, have been, and still are, of service to me to-day. Young as I was, my heart was refreshed as well as stirred. My mind, too, must have been in a measure invigorated and enlightened. At all events, my experience then and since has led me to put great value on a good tract.

CHAPTER IV.—THRICE SAVED ON ONE SUNDAY.

THIS was fast rising, but it was before a sudden fall. Like our first parents I was tempted, at a time when least expected. Like them, too, I fell, because of disobedience.

Though a liberal in politics, my father was a conservative in religion. That is a conservative in the true and best sense of the term. In this matter, he was inclined to be severe, keeping close to the letter of the law. He was, as his forefathers were, clear, simple, genuine; exact as to truth, and rigid as to right. He was a Puritan of the Puritans; and as such governed himself, and tried to lead others, his household included. He was what some sneeringly call "a Sabbatarian." He regarded the first day of the week as holy unto the Lord, a day for worship and edification. And, on that day my parents attended public worship *time about*, the one keeping the house and children, whilst the other was absent.

Those of us children who had not clothes sufficiently good, remained at home, but never so far as I can remember, without the advice to "Remember the Sabbath day to keep it holy," and not to go beyond the outside door. Perhaps, if we had lived in the country or in some self-contained house, it might have been easier to obey. However, one Sabbath morning I foolishly, if not wickedly, disobeyed to the danger of my life.

On that day, not long after my father had gone to the morning service, I left our room, and went to the common landing or passage. I was in possession of a half-penny, a greatly prized store for a poor boy. At least, I thought so much of it that I showed it to some boys, who were older than

About to sink in the deep.

myself, and whom I met in the passage. I was the richest of the lot, and of course, my company was courted. Boys are so like men, in evil as well as in good ways. And, by an eloquence worthy of a better cause, they succeeded in drawing me out, taking me from home. We stopped not till we arrived at the harbour. Here they offered to give me a sail in a boat moored to the steps which led to the water, if I gave them the halfpenny. This offer I accepted, but would not pay till I had had the sail. The intention of the boys was to let me out the length of the rope, and then pull the boat back to the steps; but a stranger boy present was stronger and more wicked than the rest, and having no interest at stake, he pulled the rope from them and threw it into the water. The result was, I was soon drifting helplessly out with the tide, and was approaching some of the most dangerous places, when, almost paralyzed with terror, I was picked up by some men, who seeing my danger, had made haste to the rescue. A policeman was ready to seize me when I landed. He laid hold of me and threatened much, but I told my simple story, and he let me off with a harsh warning and a very hard kick, both of which I took with the best possible grace, and ran off, thankful that I had escaped a watery grave.

Whirling in the air. The boys with whom I had bargained, had run at the approach of the policeman; but as soon as they saw I was clear off, they made up to me, and demanded the fare. I could not see that it was fair, to pay for being nearly drowned, so I kept my halfpenny and made for home. But when I arrived at the top of the lane which led to our house, I was afraid to go further. By this time the people were returning from public worship, and in order that my father might not see me, I went beyond our lane. This afforded a favourable opportunity for the boys with whom I had left home. They followed me, and strange to say, I kept to the bad company—or they to me—like the drunkard to his glass.

I was able to reason somewhat, at least I knew I had done

wrong in breaking my promise to a kind father, and going so far astray. And yet in this state of anxiety, and with good resolutions in my mind, I did not then return, but went still further away. At last we came to an entrance to a field, in which a large number of very rough carters were grazing their horses.

What a scene! I think I see it yet. Some of the men were sleeping on the grass, some were drinking, some were dead-drunk, some were fighting, some were playing at cards, others at pitch-and toss, and almost all who could open their mouths were cursing. I learned afterwards that this was the fearful way in which these men passed their Sundays during the summer months, and that in Scotland.

From childhood I admired the grand and beautiful in nature and art wherever I saw them. Here my eyes were fixed on the horses, many of which were the opposite of handsome; but among them was one beauty, and upon it I gazed with admiration. My mind must have been filled with such thoughts as spring into being when contemplating the graphic and glowing description of the horse in the Book of Job. The lovely creature on which I feasted my eyes was called "Missie." She had just been banished to the cart because of her "vices." Her owner had been gambling, and had lost all, glad of even a halfpenny that he might "try his luck" once more, and having heard of mine, he offered me a ride on "Missie" if I would give the copper to him. Fascinated with the beautiful animal, I consented. Greatly delighted, but very timid, I was helped upon her back, when the owner gave her such a smart cut with the whip, that in a moment I was thrown whirling in the air, so high that those who were looking on did not expect to pick me up alive, fearing my neck would be broken by the certain fall.

I was very much hurt, but not so much as was feared. Deeply repentant, I made my way homeward as soon as I was able to creep along, supporting myself by resting my hand against the low dyke or wall which bounded the field

Hanging over a precipice.

on the left side of the wood. Some of the boys followed me, and by their advice we took what they called a near cut. When we approached the " braes "—that is, the cliffs which towered above the banks of the River Tay, one of the lads threw a stone from the top of one of the cliffs. This startled a soldier who, with his sweetheart, was reclining on one of the slopes below, near to the river edge. Of course he must be gallant, so made great efforts to overtake us. My companions were about as fleet as he was. This enraged him all the more. I saw him coming, but being crippled I could not run from what I supposed to be a red-coated fury, so I thought of dodging him, by crouching behind a furze bush, near to the face of one of the rocky precipices. But imagine my alarm when, just as he passed, I began to slip down. Perceiving my danger, I called for help, but the soldier went on in pursuit. Clinging to the slippery grass as well as I could, and finding myself nearing the brink, I called again as for life, but no person was near. Fortunately, I was barefooted and the bended root of the bush happened to be so placed, that my toes entered the bend. Being thus assisted, I held on desperately, waiting the soldier's return. He, at no small risk, and with considerable ingenuity, succeeded in bringing me to the pathway. Another moment, and I would have gone to pay the penalty of Sabbath desecration.

I told the soldier all that had happened to me on that day. He wept, even before his sweetheart, who, by this time, had joined us. Seeing this proof of a tender heart, I thought he might become an effective advocate, and asked him to accompany me home, and to intercede for me. He complied with my request, and I had no occasion to speak. My parents were grieved because of what I had foolishly done, but glad because I had been so mercifully preserved.

Hanging Over a Precipice.

Chapter V.—Glancing Upwards.

As kind Providence would have it, our good minister paid us one of his frequent and helpful visits soon after this merciful preservation. He was always welcome to our humble home, but this time I felt rather queer—asking myself several questions, such as, Has he heard of it? Will my father tell him? What will he say to me? At first, I felt inclined to try to find my way to the door; but he had not been long seated before he asked me to come to him and take my usual place—between his knees.

The minister's visit.

As he frankly admitted, he came to our house for his own sake as well as for our good. His aim in the first case was to have a talk with my father about life on the sea. For though our home was far from what some would call poetic, yet my father was full of poetry when he grew warm in his graphic descriptions of the varied incidents of the dreadful days of his early manhood. It was the same poetic nature welling up in him that led him in after days to frequent the neighbouring fields and green lanes. And it was the same love of the sublime, as well as the beautiful, which was manifest in his vivid details of sea-faring life as he had seen it. In spirit, too, he remained the British Tar, feeling he was all the more a man when, in such conversations, he was reminded of what he, with others, had done for his country's safety, that he had been one of the many who had made our bulwarks terrible. All this was known to our minister and was delighted in by him. He was noted for his eloquence as well as his kindness. And it was noticeable that on the Sunday after a conversation with my father the eloquent preacher was almost certain to paint, in glowing language, some grand or terrible picture as a thrilling and telling introduction to a powerful sermon.

But it is only just to the memory of the good man to add here, that no minister was more faithful to his duties as a pastor than he. At that time a minister's visits, especially the stated visits, were generally regarded as very solemn occasions. Something like fear laid hold on old and young alike. But this was not our experience in regard to our minister. He gave no cause for this. Still, every attention and possible reverence were paid by us to his message which was generally addressed to us young ones. And what he said had a lasting influence. He did not frighten us with hard questions, but spoke of Jesus as "the children's Friend" in such a way as to make us feel he was sent by that Friend. Even yet, I think I feel his kind hand laid softly on my head, while with the half-bent fore-finger of the other hand he would gently press up my chin, until my eyes met his. Then with a smiling face he would look on mine and say some cheering word to me.

And certainly this visit did not differ from other visits of the same kind. The only difference lay with me. On former occasions I was ever a careful listener. Often did I repeat to myself the story of storms. But not so on this occasion. The thought of the recent transgression shut my ears, and my heart kept thump, thump, thumping. I felt ill. He noticed it. This led to an explanation of the whole case by my father. At first, this made me worse; but the minister was equal to the occasion. There was not a sign of harshness, neither in the reproof nor in the warning. The advice, too, was seasoned with love. It was the very thing I needed, just as if God had told him what to say.

At the Sunday School. Every day and every act of kindness on the part of my father, and such as that shown by our minister, sent my transgression deeper into my heart. Young as I was, I could see that the disobedience and blame were all on my side, but I also felt that the preservation and praise were all on God's side. My sorrow was deep, and my gratitude was sincere. I prayed for forgiveness and promised much, but it was sometime before my former peace of mind and repose in my heavenly Father returned. This was not until in child-faith I could see Him, and look upon Him, as my Redeemer, Preserver and Guide.

Next in point of benefit from the minister's visits was my becoming a Sunday school scholar. And this took place soon after I was the happy possessor of my first Sunday suit of clothes—in which I went to our Church happier than any king could be.

By this time Gilfillan had become the minister of "our Church" known as the School Wynd United Presbyterian Church. On that Sunday he preached "A Sermon to the Young," but there were others present, and no doubt he meant to have something for all ages—strong meat for men and milk for babes. At times he was "grand and powerful," so my father said. Then I was not able to see the beauty. It was a long way above me. But he did not forget us young ones. I think we had the best share of the good things, and in this sense I was greedy of gain, eager to get as much as possible. As a baby loves the natural milk, so did I love this sermon when I understood the preacher. When he was simple he carried me with him and I was glad. If I may judge of the influence of that sermon on my young mind and my after life, it must have been a treat, sweet and refreshing. He closed by giving an advice which became very important to me—that all the young hearing him should attend some Sunday school.

This advice I at once followed, to my lasting benefit and great joy. The Sunday School to which I went was held in the same school-room to which I went with my A.B.C card. The same teacher was not there, but his dear wife was, and she was glad to see me. As when I first entered the Week Day School, so on going to the door for the Sunday School—I was shy and timid. But my mind was filled with hope as well as fear; and my hope became livelier as the good superintendent came to me in a very winning way. After he had asked several questions, he kindly took me by the hand. Oh, such a kind hand his was. His love came right through it to my heart. He gently led me to what he considered the class best suited to me, said some kind word and then left for his own class.

No doubt, he did what was best, but I would rather he had taken me with him, possibly my teacher was good in his way, but my heart followed the loving smile that first imparted the courage which enabled me to enter. In a comparatively short time, I rose from class to class and reached the goal—to be in the superintendent's class. To him I listened, and through him, under God, I had a life-giving look at Jesus, such as I had never seen before. What a delight! I wept for joy.

I should also say here that this Christ-like superintendent was the late David Robertson, Union Grove, Dundee. To him I afterwards dedicated a little book on the Sunday School. This I did in gratitude for his kind encouragement, fatherly care, and precious teaching; also in memory of the happy days, and some of the dearest and sweetest associations giving lasting joy to the grateful soul.

Rising in the labour scale. I think no lad could be more grateful. Grateful to God for all His mercies including His wonderful preservation of my young life; grateful for all His blessings including the Sunday School. Now my cry was to be ever able to love and obey God better day by day, to be stronger in Him and more able to resist temptation; to be saved from evil and lifted to good.

Though I was only on the threshold of life, I had been favoured with another upward step—every step turned out to be a step upward. This one was on the labour ladder. Between these two memorable Sundays—that in which my disobedience had brought so much suffering, and that in which I was advised to go to a Sunday School—I was permitted to ascend from the *wheel* to the *loom*. I had not then read of

"The Banner with the strange device, Excelsior!"

but, somehow or other, the inspiring spirit which these words indicate took hold of me quite early in life. Ever since I can remember, I felt I must not only push *through* life, but *rise* as I went along. In this case, my joy was not so much because I had escaped the dreary toil of the weary wheel, as that I felt I was rising to increasing usefulness, to be more helpful to my poor dear father. And then there was the natural and pleasing feeling which the boy enjoys when he thinks he is becoming a man.

It was true, I felt my physical deficiency—shortness in stature—stood against me. But, as at the wheel so at the loom, this difficulty was at once met. "Where there is a will there is a way," clogs were nailed to the upper part of the treadles, and by means of a suitable erection, I could reach the yarn and cloth beams. Indeed, in a very short time, I could make the shuttle fly, and weave as much as others who were much stronger than I was.

This being the case, I was of more money value to the family, and this did not come a day too early. By this time, and sometime before it, my father had been suffering more than usual from the effect of a constitution shattered when in the prime of life. And besides his having become an almost helpless sufferer, there was the domestic depression which often follows the honest poor when they feel they have come down in the world—if such a phrase can be used in connection with those who in the sense of riches have never been up in the world.

For all we had passed through, unknown sufferings—arising, at times, from semi-starvation—we were regarded as the better to do of the well-doing poor. Even our minister was not made aware of the trying straits to which we had been often put. The depth of our poverty—and the consequent distress—was only known at our fireside and to God. If we children were often without shoes, our feet, like our hands and faces, were clean; and, though sometimes without cap or bonnet, our hair was tidy. All that nature gave us was made the most of, and hence we were generally admired. Whatever white things the girls had, they were often washed in the night-time, dried and ironed in the morning, and this pointed cleanliness gave a sprightliness to their natural beauty. All this lifted us up in the eyes of others, and no doubt kept us up in our own eyes. To help in all this was one reason why I aspired to the loom, even before time. I was glad I persevered and succeeded. You will understand the joy this gave me when I tell you that from the beginning I have never been happier than when helping others.

Chapter VI.—Some Ups and Downs.

ONCE up and twice down. How long can the strongest and the highest stand that? I cannot say. This I know, my three upward steps were soon beset with difficulties, some of which were new. Still these very difficulties became my instructors, even when the *Downs* were quite as frequent as the *Ups*.

Our new abode.

Because of my father's long continued illness we had to think of a cheaper home in what was then considered the neighbourhood of Dundee, but which is now a portion of it, and is called the fifth ward. I mean Lochee, which was then a village, the High Street of which was exactly two miles from the High Street of Dundee. In Lochee the house-rents were considerably lower, but the houses were correspondingly inferior. It was to one of the inferior class we removed—rather than incur debt. Let me try to lead you, in mind, to the hut-home wherein, for years, we tried to live, and in which I tried to rise.

The village had three main roads, with several streets—rather streets in prospect, like Washington—branching off them. Now the streets are more numerous, and almost every one is crowded. But the roads are there still, only not so marked as then. What was called the Quarry Road bounded the village on the north. That passing through the centre in a zig-zag way was known as the Mid Road. The other, the straightest, was called the South Road. And about midway on the south side of that road was what was at that time designated the Rotten Row—five or six low-roofed, thatched "houses," at the back of which was "the burn."

One of these "houses"—the second from the west end of the Row—became our home. There was no attic, but there was a ground floor in more senses than one. It was about a foot lower than the ground in the front, and of exactly the same material, hardened by a little clay. When the space within the four mud walls was empty, you might have seen seven windows—seven openings surrounded by as many shaky frames into which some knotted green glass was set. The back wall was favoured with four of these, the front having three, and a door.

By means of a careful arrangement of the furniture we at first divided this space into two "apartments." One was called "the shop"—that which had the two back and the two front windows opposite each other. Here the four looms were placed. The other apartment was called the kitchen—a general name for washhouse, dining-room, dormitory, or any other use to which it might be applied.

In this arrangement my parents saw at least one defect. They missed the convenience of a "But and Ben"—that is, two adjoining apartments, the "Ben" being the best furnished, the tidiest, and generally kept for visitors. A little ingenuity and re-arrangement, however, secured this needed apartment. At night time it served as father's and mother's "bedroom." In the day time it served as a place of retirement for those who wished to be alone, or to have a quiet talk with a friend. Really when all things were set in order—as they generally were on Saturday for Sunday—the aspect was not so offensive as one might suppose. Most prominent to view was what was called "the curtain bed," which had been a very grand one in its better days, the four polished posts almost reaching to the rafters. There too was "the *timmer* bed" (the wooden bedstead), the lids of which were kept shut to try to exclude the tow-dust flying about everywhere from the wheels and looms in the adjoining workshop. And within a foot or so of this bedstead was a chest of drawers, minus most of the handles. And, close by, was a roughly finished *dresser*, a kind of sideboard, over which, resting against the wall, was "the plate rack," with some necessary crockery. It was made of white wood, and was, by weekly scrubbing, kept white.

Here we settled down, content if only we could keep the wolf, hunger, from the door. No easy task, but we did our best to face every difficulty as it came. As before, and of necessity, much depended upon myself, still I was as willing as ever.

My study.

My "easy going loom" soon became a matter of talk among our new neighbours. The little contrivances which led to this comparative "ease" were invented from time to time because I was far from being robust, and because I was anxious to accomplish as much work as possible each day, of quite sixteen hours, from six to ten, sometimes earlier and later. And, besides, I wished to think as well as work, and had my books so fixed that I could glance at them occasionally.

It was not long before I got into my former regular order, imposing upon myself a given portion of work every hour. As a rule, that portion was finished before the time was up—which spare time I devoted to reading, five minutes more or less. When the last of these spare seconds was gone, the click, click of the shuttle was heard as before.

At ten p.m. I retired to my "Study," tired enough. It was the apartment at "the other end," that just referred to. There, at the front of the "drawers" already mentioned, I took my stand—the top of this piece of furniture served as my "desk." On the top was a small variety of books, mostly second hand—some School Books, the Life of Dr. Franklin, Dr. Channing's Self-Culture, also a number of tracts, political and religious. Health and circumstances permitting, I might have been seen there till mid-night, reading, casting up figures, or writing, when all others were asleep.

Certainly these were "Hard Battles to Live and Learn," but there was no repining. If such was necessary to gain the same end, I would do so again. The desire was equally strong with the desire to live, and this combined with the wish to become more and more useful helped to drown the pain whatever its cause, and the least measure of success imparted gratitude as well as pleasure. And for all the hardships we endured, this home, and our efforts at mutual help were not a bad school in which to be trained.

On this spot a new, and slightly improved house is built. And in memory of these days and efforts, it was, by the builders and workmen, named "Hillock's College."

Seeking relief in rhyme.—My Mammy's Awa. Before we went to Lochee, one of the forms of affliction which followed my ailing father was rheumatism, and to this our new home gave renewed energy, if not new life. Of course, this made bad worse—worse as to pain, and worse in regard to the family wants. But I remained wonderfully strong for my years—a strength which was severely tested. Of this you may judge when I tell you that for weeks not a penny was brought to the home saving what my loom produced, and that during some of these saddest days of want and woe, I have had to work for four-and-twenty hours on end upon a few spoonfuls of pea flour made into what we called *brose*. Often did I think that this remarkable power of endurance was more than my own, given specially from above. At all events, it enabled me to finish the web and get some money, and so save us from pending starvation. It was truly sad to hear my father groaning under pain, whilst the helpless ones were crying for bread.

And then the time came when I, too, suffered from weakness. This was also followed by that strange feeling which springs from the sad experience of the fact that "Hope deferred maketh the heart sick." At times the cloud of adversity became so dense that the silver lining was scarcely visible, and despair almost succeeded in several attempts to get the upper hand of hope. But even in such cases the looked-for assistance came in ways not thought of. For instance, nothing could have been farther from my mind than to think of my step-mother as in any way adding to our want of the necessities of life, and yet, somehow or other an idea took hold of my mind that my sufferings would not have been so great had my own mother been alive. The pressure of

The Rotten Row, Lochee.

poverty is the father of many an inconsistency. Poor people under the crushing power of dire calamity sometimes think and say and do things they never would have otherwise thought of.

I had frequently given way to verse-making, and this generally gave a kind of relief. Being so young these efforts were childish, though some of my more appreciative neighbours said they saw in me a coming second Burns. This has not come to pass, nor is it likely now. Still each rhyming fit was more or less reviving.

One of the days in which I tried to spare a little time, I sought the quiet—such as it was—of a quiet nook, and there wrote a few lines under the heading, "My Mammy's Awa." Years after these lines saw the light of day in a rather out-of-the-way manner. Perhaps they should be given here:—

> Cauld, cauld is the day, the frost nips my wee face;
> I'm heartless an' sad, how waefu' my case:
> On my bare wee leggies the bitin' winds blaw—
> Oh, hoo is a' this?—My Mammy's awa'.
>
> Baith laddies an' lassies are happy an' gay,
> They rin to the school, an' then to their play
> But I maun rin errants 'mang frost, sleet, an' snaw—
> Oh, hoo is a' this?—My Mammy's awa'.
>
> They a' get braw claes, an' their heads fu' o' lear,
> To mak' them a' great, if God should them spare;
> But nae schoolin' for me, nae learnin' ava—
> Oh, hoo is a' this?—My Mammy's awa.'
>
> Yet onward I'll push to get lear like the lave,
> I'll ever be active, determined, and brave;
> Though hard be my fate, it safter may blaw,
> For God will prove kind, though Mammy's awa'.

This was one of our many dark hours before the dawn. Being cold and hungry, almost to fainting, I felt an awful sinking feeling, but, reviving, I once more took heart again, remembering the couplet, here slightly modified,

Up in mind.

> "Despair of nothing good you would attain,
> Unwearied diligence your point will gain."

And this I kept before me. Even when things were at the worst, I looked for the silver lining, though, like angels' visits, the bright hours were far between, yet each one gave me a little lift. In most cases—though as you shall see not exclusively so—the silver lining came in the form of my father's partial recovery, after some long illness. In his generous nature, he was anxious as soon as possible to relieve me of what *he* called "the burden," which *I* never regarded as such, that of being "the family helper." As soon as he was able to work, he was sure to manifest his gratitude by bestowing on me some consideration. Looked at by ordinary eyes, it was never much taken by itself. It could not be much. It was a case of doing what he could, and affection, with God's blessing, magnified, if not multiplied, the gift.

Some one has said, "Give a boy the alphabet, and you give him the key to every library." As you know in the midst of no ordinary difficulties my father gave me the alphabet and a little more. May I not add, Give a boy a sixpence and that might start him in life, if he applies it to a good purpose, as is likely, if he has an ambition above a confectioner's shop. I speak from experience. On one of the occasions of my father being able to resume work, he gave me a sixpence weekly. This was truly a bright sixpence. How little helps the poor when timely given. To me, that little coin emitted a charming ray of hope. It warmed me all over so pleasantly. On it I read the words, "It is possible." It gratified a longing desire to get the aid of the living voice to tell me if my advances were real. It cleared my way to the Evening Classes.

Meantime, I continued my habit of learning while working, my books and tables, printed or written, being so fastened as to give me the opportunity of glancing at them, when I desired. The mental faculties and the physical powers worked nicely together. Now, perhaps, even more than before, my heart was in every effort, and every day brought me "nearer the mark."

Nor was this all. In prosperity as well as in adversity, I began to feel something like the emotion which comes when we realise the saying, "It never rains, but it pours." So I thought, when, some time after, my father made another offer of a more extended nature to me—namely, that I should pay so much for my board, and have whatever was over with which to prosecute my studies. How kind! What a stimulus! When I had saved enough, I went to the day school, eking out my savings by weaving in the evening—preparing my lessons in the morning. This was a joyous time. The sunshine was beautiful. Hope rose as my knowledge increased. It was difficult to make up leeway, and cope with those who had been at school for years, but that difficulty was soon overcome. And besides, as events proved, I was fortunate in my teachers, each one seemed to have a better heart than the other; and then they had ability as well as heart. They were not only interested in their pupils, but they also freely expressed themselves and their gladness, when they saw any special signs of rapid progress. To me this was encouraging. I was always human enough to take kindly to kind words when I knew they came from honest hearts.

But all this proved to be too much for my bodily health. While I rose mentally, I fell physically. This did not come without cause nor without warning. Any one save an enthusiast, might have known that this learning and weaving, weaving and learning, were too much even for a strong lad. I heeded not, but pressed on, till nature, in the proper exercise of her lawful authority, arrested me as a lawless offender. *Down bodily.*

If I had been anxious to grumble or to plead excuses, and overlook my own errors, such as going beyond all bounds, mentally and physically—I might have blamed circumstances over which I had little or no control. I might also have attributed my illness, at least partly, to my being surrounded by some of the most dangerous atmospheric elements compressed in a small, low, damp abode. But I preferred to plead guilty, and accept the consequences. If I had been wise enough, I would have known that nature never hurries, that she accomplishes her work little by little.

Several times I had been laid aside for a few days, but this time it was for months, and the alarming illness became the talk of the village. The doctor who was first called to see me, being a true man, confessed that the complaint was baffling his skill. He asked that the assistance of another doctor be secured at once. Daily, and sometimes thrice a day, they consulted. Still as grave doubts were yet entertained of my recovery, they brought with them a well-known physician from Dundee.

It was an anxious time to my parents. At last, however, the combined skill of the three doctors, under God, began to manifest itself in a favourable form. In the end I rallied, to the surprise of all concerned; but, oh, so weak and weary—for months unable to walk.

Chapter VII.—Mental and Physical Distress.

"He is as one risen from the grave," said the aged physician to the other doctors, as he left after the close of the last consultation in regard to my prospects of a complete recovery. And these words brought before my mind many thoughts in relation to my Inner Life. *Re-reading the Bible.*

Being thus marvellously spared, I should have been happy as well as grateful, but I was not happy, having for a time lost sight of the blessed source of happiness.*

It was months before I was able to resume work, but that time was spent to profit. The doctors were one in the opinion that all books of a *scholastic* nature should be kept from me. To this I consented, but leave was given to read any ordinary book. This was fortunate, and at once I took to the Bible, and found it fresh as ever, interesting as ever, profitable as ever. It really seemed to me to be fresher and more interesting than before. At least, I drank deeper and deeper from this well of living water.

If I were to say anything here to those who wish to train the young in the truth as it is in Jesus—judging from my own experience—it would be this: The Bible first, theology next, if needed.

Now—no doubt much better than before—I could see the soundness of its maxims, the wisdom of its precepts, and the importance of its commands. Its poetry was more attractive than its philosophy; and its history, its journeys and biographies, gained from me more time than its prophecies and doctrines. I felt a pleasure which I cannot describe, a grateful emotion too

---

* It is a sad story, but I have promised (D.V.) to give its light as well as its shadow in another volume.

strong for words, when, again, in the Book I found lessons suited to my age, instructions adapted to my condition. Often did I read the 23rd psalm, the Sermon on the Mount, and the 17th Chapter of the Gospel according to John—each time with special pleasure and much profit. With a hearty enthusiasm, and the tears of gratitude streaming down my yet pale cheeks, I was able to join in the sentiment contained in the Hymn beginning

> "Holy Bible, book divine,
> Precious treasure thou art mine."

Other Books. This was a blessed time. My gladness seemed to lessen the pain of body, and give me new strength. And then I was favoured with a reading of other books. The choice of books is an important matter to those who desire to make a good use of "the key that admits us to the whole world of thought and fancy and imagination." One has said, "Choose well, your choice is brief but yet endless." This is applicable to those who have the means of having a plentiful supply of books of all sorts, but especially to those who find it difficult to procure any. In such cases, as it was in mine, what a blessing that the best Book, the Bible, is about the cheapest. But this blessing was, at this time, greatly enhanced by the kindness of some new friends who came to inquire concerning my health.

One friend lent me the history of Sir William Wallace. And this I read with great interest. The impression it left on my mind was lasting. The earnest patriotism of the Scottish hero, wrought like a charm on me. Before I had finished the reading of the book I felt the full force of the poet's words:—

> "At Wallace's name what Scottish blood
> But boils up like a spring-tide flood."

Another friend lent me a copy of "Burns' Life and Works." A book of quite another stamp, but no less fascinating. It made me laugh and weep, and laugh again. It went into my soul, and my soul went into it. If ever I wished to be a poet, it was then, willing if only able to evince a tenth part of his rich genius. I had no desire ever to possess the physical strength of Wallace, but I longed for the power of the poet. There was such a charm in all he said, that I was almost falling in love with his errors. Happily, I had experienced the religious feeling so eloquently, graphically, and trustingly expressed in his immortal "Cottar's Saturday Night." I had also seen and suffered from the hypocrisy which quailed under his withering satire, and perhaps this made me rather ready to swallow his bitter things. I almost worshipped the poet, but I wept for the man.

Another friend presented me with a copy of the "Scottish Worthies." This also roused my emotions; I soon found myself wishing I had lived in the days of these worthies, and witnessed their heroism. But the book was so well written that I could live the whole over again. Their many heroic deeds, their strong hearts and noble aims, their indomitable resolution and wild enthusiasm, stamped an impression upon my mind that will ever remain. Their glorious deeds won my admiration, and their intense sufferings awakened my sympathy. Often did I pause and tremble when reading the stirring records of the savage and stern times. What a glorious idea, thought I, to see the rich and poor, the learned and unlearned, asserting their right to think for themselves, rising in fearless honesty of conviction against oppression, and bravely vindicating to the death the liberty of conscience—to see them manfully paying the stern penalty of their burning love for eternal truth; to see them "pressing onward red-wat shod" to victory or death; to see them dying in the sure hope and sweet peace of believing.

To have missed these renewed readings of the Bible and the reading of these other books would have been to lose not a little of what has been useful to me. *First lessons in the laboratory.* All, with God's blessing, combined to lift me up again. And by the time I was once more able to try the loom, I felt prepared to face pecuniary difficulties which stood like so many lions in the way before me. But, strange to say, these lions disappeared one after the other, almost as soon as they came in sight.

I got stronger and abler for work sooner than could have been expected. Without attempting to build any theory upon the fact, I cannot help recording it here; namely, almost all the time I was thus laid aside, my father was better able to work than he had been for a long time before. Not only so, he continued better some considerable time after I was able to work. This was a source of joy to all of us. It also enabled me all the sooner to pay off the extra domestic debts contracted during my illness.

The only other lion remaining in the way was the doctors' bills. Having gotten a small instalment for each of them to begin with, I called to ask how much I owed. "Nothing," was the reply of doctor *first*. "Nothing," said doctor *second*. "Nothing," said doctor *third*. It seemed as if all three had been consulting as to this "nothing." At all events each assured me, in almost identical words, that it was a pleasure to them, and payment enough, to see me restored.

Not only so, but the doctor who was first called went even farther than this in his goodness to me. He became acquainted with our circumstances, and knowing I could not be spared from home, invited me to his laboratory as frequently as possible, and at times when he himself could be present. And, during these visits, he taught me the A B C of medical botany and practical chemistry. I was an earnest as well as a grateful pupil. Soon the villagers who knew of this called me the doctor's boy. But this good man died suddenly in the prime of life. What would have happened had he lived longer, I cannot say, but, as you will see, the result of his kindness sprang up in due season.

A black look-out. This time of pleasant and plain sailing, comparative comfort, general progress, scholastic improvement, intellectual advancement, and spiritual joy, did not last long. All too soon, they were overshadowed by the darkest of all the clouds that had ever come down upon us. Not only upon us, as a family, but upon almost all around, especially the poor. The all but universal distress was appalling. Food was not only dear, but labour was almost at a stand-still, particularly the weaving department. Wages were not only reduced to the starvation point, but almost all work was withdrawn from the village, and what was found was reserved for the heads of families.

This change for the worse did not come suddenly. Wise men foretold it, and the poor felt it as it came creeping along, cold as death, weakening and chilling—in some cases killing. This overcast all my prospects of success, and at last they vanished as though they had been pictures of the imagination. This was sad enough, but sadder far was our increasing domestic sufferings. It was generally admitted that the idea of reserving what work there was for the heads of families, was a fair one. And so it was in some respects, but the rule bore heavily down upon us, in as much as my father was not able to apply for work. Of course, I asked for it in his name, but I was seldom successful in the village, and hence went often to Dundee, frequently in vain, to beg a brother of the earth to give me leave to toil.

CHAPTER VIII.—HARD WORK BUT NOTHING FOR IT.

No work to do becomes hard work.

AT certain seasons of the year, particularly when depression in trade is exceptionally severe on the poor, we hear the words, "We've got no work to do." It is said this statement is often made a pretext for begging, getting money for drink. This may or may not be the case. Sometime the accusation is a cruel lie. It would have been so in our case. In our sad experience, there was an awfully rousing truth in the words, "*No work to do.*" It would be wrong to say what men, however, independent in spirit, or honest in intention, would not do to avoid utter starvation; but I can say none who thus daily gathered in the hope of obtaining work would have asked for money without earning it, or would have spent it on drink that would have injured them. But men are not always the same under similar circumstances. A few rise above them, the many sink under them. Some retain the power of self-government and remain honest, many are controlled as an infant in the cradle and may be demoralised. But those with whom I met in search of work were, as a rule, those who respected themselves, men of thought and decision, men who would patiently endure as much as possible; but woe to the cruel oppressor, or the selfish tyrant when the consequent suffering becomes past enduring. Treated fairly, they would be as harmless as doves· treated unfairly, they, in time, would not only be wise as serpents, but fierce as lions. I could see all this in their faces, and feel it too, being one with them, plunged up to the neck in misery.

As for myself, all this became more and more intensified when I returned home disappointed, and found that home often without bread—all in it almost continuously hungry, and the most of them helpless.

As you may be sure, this roused the feelings of the sufferers, particularly those of strong sympathies, such as I had. "What is the cause?" and "What is the cure?" were two questions often put, but seldom answered. The successful rich seemed afraid to speak, and the unsuccessful poor were looked upon as incapable to form any opinion on the matter. As is too generally the case, the suffering poor are looked upon as very ignorant as well as very bad. But all the poor are not bad because they are poor, neither are they all ignorant because they are poor. At least for myself, I learned my first lessons in politics sometime before this—in my father's workshop when I was a *winder* there. Even then, I was interested in the debates on the various subjects under consideration. This, together with my own reading and reflection, gave my mind a political turn. I had learned something of the political union of past days, also about the Reform Bill which before this had become law. The latter became a central topic for discussion among the thoughtful Reformers, many of whom, like my father, looked upon its provisions as only "an instalment of what must come sooner or later." I have yet a vivid recollection of the "Old Tar" at work, with grave and thoughtful face, his finely formed head, and lofty brow, covered with a red cowl—a copy of some newspaper or some historical book side by side with a copy of the Bible, ready for reference should any discussion arise during the spare moments after meals. Often have I heard from him much that is now said by way of advanced thought in political matters by our Radical-Liberals, and even by our Liberal-Conservatives. At that time I did not fully understand the facts and sentiments expressed, yet I must have stored them up, for many of the *pros* and *cons* then put forth came fresh to mind when the hard times became harder when I became more radical than my father.

All things put together, added to the general suffering, and became as fuel to my inflammable soul.

No doubt, there were many among those who went in search of work who knew much more about such things than I did—for some were quite three times my age. But all of us were sorely distressed and sadly grieved. We were not angry because of our lowly condition in the social scale. Some of us hoped to see that improved by labour, thrift or any other means, kindred and possible. What roused our indignation was a conviction that we and ours were the victims of misgovernment and social wrongs, suggesting the questions, Does the wretchedness of the weak not arise from the wickedness of the strong? Have not those in authority become the stronghold of all that is base and degrading—a terror to the sufferers and a protection to the treacherous—an enemy to God and goodness and a friend of vice and villainy?

Keeping the white heat up.

In a measure, perhaps in a large measure, these suggestions were wrong. Poverty no less than riches, is sometimes blinding and uncharitable. Nevertheless our great suffering and dark prospect led to the supposition; and so convinced was I that these questions should be answered in the affirmative, that for sometime I felt as if I would, if only I could, unseat every Member of both Houses of Parliament. And yet, in justice to myself—perhaps, too, in justice to the majority of those who thought with me—I should also say, there was not in my heart anything that could be called malice toward any individual. Much of the anger, if not all of it, was caused by the gnawing hunger and tormenting misery.

But there were other things that kept up the *white heat*. Fortunately for me, the thoughts that filled my mind soon after my recovery from the all but fatal illness had a restraining influence. And these better thoughts were supported by the healthy advice and good reasoning of my father who was one of the moral force men. "Reform, certainly," he would say, "but keep within the constitution. Let us tell our grievances and urge our rights, but in constitutional methods." No doubt, this kept me all the longer from being carried away by the rising whirlwind of passion which swept across our land.

But the conflict continued to rage, and, in cases not a few, insult was added to injury, by some who were dressed in a little brief authority. When it became known that I had had my "first lessons in politics," those who, like me, went in search of work, came round about me as we stood waiting our turn to enter. Men twice, in some cases more than thrice my age, would ask all sorts of questions and so lead on to discussions, more or less heated. Perhaps I was not wise enough to know when to be silent. In other words, I was not cowardly enough to hear what I knew to be falsehood detailed without stating what I thought was the truth of the matter—the cause or causes of the general load of woe. This led some of the master class—or rather some of their subordinates—to raise discussions within doors.

One day, one of the latter asked me if I did not believe, "Whatever is, is right?" "Certainly not," was my reply, adding some reasons which he did not like. He felt very small, and must have his revenge.

That same day the master had promised me work, and I entered the warehouse in high hope; but this underling had the opportunity of denying me the work and he did so.

"Go home and live on the Charter," he said. From that day I was called the young Chartist, and began to learn what Chartism really meant.

When I went home that night I was not only disappointed, but very angry as well as very hungry. And when to this I saw the want at home, thoughts, not Christian thoughts, took possession of me. They became as fuel to the fire, the suppressed heat of which was about to burst into flame.

Nor was such horrid cruelty on the part of the uppish hypocrites the only cause of keeping up the white heat, intensifying the growing hostility between what were called the masses and the classes. As are found at all times and under all circumstances there were some who busied themselves in preaching contentment, even though they knew that with thousands the pangs of hunger were becoming all but unendurable. Some of these preachers to the sufferers, who would go to hear them, said that poverty was a blessing. This went down nicely with the well-to-do, who by this time were becoming afraid; but with the oppressed poor it made bad worse. Rightly or wrongly they looked upon such utterances as so much nonsense, and the speakers as their enemies, supporters of evil doers. Hence some of the greatest sufferers began to mutter terrible things.

"Despair meets us at every turn," said one of a group.

"No work, no bread, our families starving and all because of misgovernment," said another in an adjoining group.

"Better die in revolt than quietly starve in our homes," a third would add. And all such declarations were sustained by the words, "Hear, Hear!" from the assemblies around.

My first public Speech.

Thus matters went on day by day, to-day's experience being the same as yesterday's. And yet there was a change, but only for the worse. The poor, those in search of work, and those at home, manifested more and more of the signs of social wrecks, ragged and wretched, pale and pinched, hopelessly fighting with starvation, almost every face bespeaking the presence of unutterable woe. It seemed as if every source of consolation as well as comfort had disappeared, and some became hardened in despair.

In my case Christian restraints had ceased to keep me in bounds, Scotch caution left me and I became utterly fearless as I thought of the never-ceasing evils combining to crush the poor to death. Though without a single thought of ever embarking in secret conspiracy or open insurrection, I resolved to do my utmost in a constitutional way to help to bring about a change for the better. Most heartily and at last publicly, did I enter the strife against things as they were. But I never thought of becoming so prominent as I became. For a time, I refused to be put forward at the rate my associates desired. On one occasion, however, I reluctantly consented to ascend the platform. Only imagine, a mere boy (and a little one too) being put up to oppose an influential gentleman in the prime of life. Of course, my opponents said this was a case of daring presumption on my part, being only about sixteen years of age. I became the observed of all observers in the place of public meeting, the Lochee Weavers' Hall.

The meeting was a mixed one—some for me and some against me. I was first timid, then bold, and then so nervous that I could scarcely see the people before me, my applauding and hissing audience. But I was in earnest, feeling the truth of what I said. It is said that most speeches are the better for the reporters' corrections and polish, and no doubt mine was also indebted to the same source. At all events it read wonderfully well in the papers.

After a little practice I gained courage, and soon became ready to meet an antagonist any day. Indeed, the trying circumstances and the fierce life brought me so far down that, had hunger kept away, I would have enjoyed the fun of the stormy political meetings, then the order of the day. I fear my speaking out, as if I were "a born orator," arose from the fact that I had neither the time, the sense, nor the inclination to see my shortcomings. But those who agreed with me were pleased and that was some comfort in those comfortless times.

One thing leads to another. To this speechifying I also consented to add another equally unprofitable department of labour, to become "Our own correspondent," a "free lance" in my way.

Becoming "Our own correspondent."

At the same time—from necessity as well as from inclination—I was careful to be at my post waiting at one or other of the manufacturers where there was the least chance of obtaining work. But this almost continuous going hither and thither gave me an opportunity of gathering any floating news. My remarks and the intelligence I recorded were confined chiefly to what I heard or saw in my little field of observation. I set up my pen as the earnest friend of the poor and weak, in a humble way. Also as the sworn foe of oppression and deception. What first gained attention, even of my opponents, were the word pictures I gave of the miserable men, waiting in groups for the least possible chance of work. Perhaps they derived whatever of pith and pathos were in them from the fact that I felt, as well as saw, much of what I described in regard to the fearful sufferings of the poor during the terrible crisis. And whilst I upheld what I regarded as right, or kind, or helpful, from whomsoever it came, I wrote freely and fully, touching what I thought was wrong, or unkind, or injurious. Hence my weekly contribution was looked upon with something like dread by evil doers.

Thus between preparing speeches and writing my weekly budget, I had plenty of evening and sometimes of night work, but nothing substantial for it. That was the only drawback. To one given to fighting, and I thought in a good cause—there was something in the excitement, if only hunger had kept away. But the fearful want and the consequent woe nursed my rage to the sorrow of my parents and friends as well as the dread of my foes. The quiet plodding student was driven to become "the dreadful spit-fire," as some called me. I continued to give unfettered expression to what was then regarded as "the wildest of thoughts," but which are now regarded as the mildest of opinions.

It is said that nothing is lost. It is true that nothing *good* is lost, all good belongs to God and is stored up by Him. But I suppose the wisest and the best have said some things they would like to think are lost. This is how I feel in regard to these evil days. No doubt, some of my speaking and writing then was such that I would not care to preserve, even if that were possible. This I must say, if I was not always wise, I was ever sincere.

Chapter IX.—From Home and Back.

A CHANGE came, but not for the better certainly. For a long time it made an end of my public speaking and writing. The uncertainty of work increased. The poorest became even more destitute, more dilapidated, and more woe-begone looking. Hope had fled, and some had become sullen, even callous in suffering. And this was the case with the nation at large as well as in Lochee and Dundee. "Come weal, come woe, something must be done," was a sentence one heard wherever he went. The most of those who had any strength of endurance left became wilder in thought and more threatening in speech. Some were more bent on revolution than on reform, while a strange weight of care sat on every brow, the majority being painfully perplexed, asking each other what must be the end of this?

Joining a hungry mob.

My strength had gone with my hope, and an awful sickness fell upon me. I shivered inwardly. My father and all became alarmed. The doctor was sent for, the appearance being such as struck terror to the heart of all who came rushing in to see me. "I fear it is death," said the doctor after a careful examination. Every effort to restore animation was made. In the morning I revived so that I could see those around me, and hear what they said. About a week afterwards the doctor pronounced me "fairly convalescent." After a few more days' rest, I joined others in search for work; limbs trembling, at times the lip quivering as day by day I returned home to tell the same tale—"No work."

And, one day, not long after this illness, I joined what has been sneeringly called "The Pilgrimage of Folly;" but which may be more appropriately designated, "A Hungry Mob." Such it really was, and purely the result of prolonged hunger, studied insult, aggravated torture, and unbearable misery.

Under various leaders several assemblies gathered at stated points in Dundee. One of the detachments marched to Lochee to induce the unemployed to join them. I did so to the great sorrow of my father. We marched on to the Fairmuir, and there we found the other detachments waiting. From this we started for Forfar "to storm" that county town.

I was still weak, but in the excitement of the moment I continued the journey. On our way several addresses were delivered in the woods near to the roadside—where the branches of trees and the loudest of cheers were plentiful. The branches were shouldered to become our weapons of war; but not being a warrior, neither by profession nor disposition, I refused to shoulder a branch, and, besides, I had barely enough strength to carry my own emaciated frame.

I took notes of the addresses, but only retained a portion of the report of one. This is it:

"Dear Fellowmen—We are here, an' there maun be nae flinchin'. Hunger has brought us here, fellowmen, and we maun do our work. I hae lookit for the cause o' our poverty; I hae lookit at our ain hames, an' canna see it there. There is nae great livin' there. I hae lookit to the sky abune—to the sun an' the stars, an' the mune—an' I dinna see it there. Na, na, fellowmen, there is nae misery there. The sun has done its work, and there's the clear mune making the corn ripe afore ye. But I have also lookit up to the big Houses of Parliament in Lunnun, an' found the cause o' a' our misery there. Yes, fellowmen; yes, it is there, I assure ye. An' far waur than that, fellowmen, there is nane wrought an' starved like the folks o' Scotland; and why should we starve in a land o' plenty? Na, na, fellowmen, there maun be nae flinchin' noo. The Charter and no surrender."*

This address was followed by another of the same style. The last sentence of it—"Forfar must be captured and Scotland must be conquered"—was also loudly cheered. But instead of capturing Forfar, Forfar conquered us. Those in authority knew something of poor humanity in need of food. They were also kindly dis-

* I give this as it was delivered because any attempt to translate it into English would not improve it. Better ask the assistance of Jamison.

posed towards us, and knowing what we stood most in want of, they let us pass through the town to an adjoining field, called the muir. There they fed us.

I say "us," but that is not exactly correct. I was fed, too, but it was not there. A deputation went to Kirriemuir, and whilst waiting its return I fell asleep through sheer exhaustion. A poor fighter I would have been. One or two of the women who had turned out to see us observed me. In pity they took me to where I had some food and more sleep. This strengthened me for the return journey. After votes of thanks to the Provost and Town Council for their thoughtful kindness, we made for home, not in marching order, each one was left to make his way home as best he could—I understand one or two of the leaders never returned to Dundee.

Our homeward journey was more difficult, if not more dangerous, than the march on Forfar. By this time the whole country side was alarmed. During the day and night—for we had encamped in the woods for the night on our way—the most wonderful stories were heard and retailed, of course with additions. These served to rouse the county gentlemen and the Lord Lieutenant. He and his specials, mounted and on foot, were determined to "run the rebels in." The command, "Catch the little fellow," had gone forth, but I was not aware of this till after. The most of the so-called rebels were wise enough and strong enough to give the furious riders a wide berth. But, being weak —and innocent as a child of any revolutionary thoughts, and having done no harm—I put on a bold front. Having seen his Lordship and others pass on the way to Forfar in all haste I went straight up to two constables, who seemed to be looking hard at me. The cause of their suspicious thoughts were checked by my asking the nearest way to a place I knew to be near Dundee. They pointed out the way and advised me to get there before dark as these dangerous fellows, the Chartists, were about, and were reported to be on the road.

I thanked them and passed on in the direction advised. Not only did I wait till it was dark before I entered upon the outskirts of Dundee, I also preferred a round-about way to Lochee. I got home about night. Though I had thus far escaped, rumour had it that I might be called upon next day, perhaps that very night.

Becoming a tramp. Fortunately for my much needed rest, I was not called upon that night. Nor did I give my enemies much time, the next day, to arrange their plans. Though tired and worn out I left home early in the day, and became a tramp.

There were two chief reasons why I left home. One, because there was no work for me, and my prospect was as dark as ever. The other was, that my father, in the meantime, had so far recovered that he could apply for work should any be forthcoming in the village.

Before I left home that forenoon, I had written a short paper, for which I received a few shillings—the half of which I sent to my father through my sister, who parted from me on the Arbroath road at the well-known point called "Athole Brose." And thus it was with much sorrow but not much romance, I became a tramp.

"What next?" you may well ask. In the minds of many, the term "tramp" has in it much that bespeaks what is most offensive to ears polite. In your mind's eye, perhaps you see an able bodied fellow unwilling to work—lazy, cowardly, incorrigible and irreclaimable—a sauntering, ill-conditioned, utterly depraved savage, ready for any outrage, all the better instincts and nobler attributes of manhood having left him; his moral sense being so dead that he knows no gradation in crime, he being at war with mankind and with every social institution, neither fearing God nor regarding man. Be charitable. Certainly I was not better than I should have been, but, believe me, I was not so far reduced as that. From various causes I was much out of sorts, but more ways than one—a weak starving lad, growing weaker, without work, in search of it, of any kind of work, if honest and helpful.

It has been truly said that "a man willing to work, and unable to find it, is perhaps the saddest sight that fortune's inequalities exhibit under the sun." But thus begging a brother of the earth in vain for leave to toil, is sadder still when there is neither food nor shelter in the way. But surely the saddest sight of all, is when the poor wanderer is weak and not out of his teens, and yet has in him those strong emotions which bespeak an aspiring soul, all so sensitive. And this was my case when I was forced to become a tramp.

"A night out."

In these sad and disappointing wanderings, I met with one or two sympathisers, but they were almost as poor as myself; still their kind words and good wishes were of service to me. I passed on from place to place. Having gone through Arbroath without success, I next made for Montrose. There I was equally unsuccessful, so I made for Brechin. It was late in the afternoon when I left Montrose, I was then reduced to one penny. Being hungry, with it I purchased a small cake of gingerbread. Grief filled the stomach, but did not strengthen the body. Having eaten only the half of my cake, I was able to help a poor mother with some poor children to the other half, and my heart was all the lighter for a time at least. I plodded on, not very fast, for I was very weak, and every hour becoming weaker. The rich smile of fading day gilded my unbidden tears as they rolled down my pale thin cheeks. I had all along known something of the "heart for any fate," nor had the pleasures of hope quite gone. But now heart and hope failed—I felt as if dying; but, for several reasons, I did not wish to die. For a time I stood still and wept bitterly, and felt a little better for it. Hope, though only as a dim shadow, approached, and I continued my weary journey till the last rays of the setting sun had vanished, and the stars began in great numbers to take their place in the bright sky. Again I stopped and thought, and trembled. All was hushed. It was a thrilling hush, and the profound silence was only broken by the sharp beating within my aching heart. As the dreadful dreariness seemed to increase, I became faint and afraid.

At last a darting pang of hunger brought me to the ground—one of those pangs which can only be known by those who have felt them. But God did not leave me, I was really alone with Him. And to Him I could say, "Against Thee, and Thee only have I sinned." I was too far gone to tell Him my story, but He knew it all. He did not send me bread then, but He was kind nevertheless, and merciful. I was so far gone that I could not eat, so He sent sleep which I so much wanted. Lovely, kindly sleep, in sweet sympathy, threw her gentle arms around me so tenderly and wafted my weary soul to the land of dreams.

The poor helping the poor. Imagine, if you can, my surprise when I awoke and found myself, where I had fallen from sheer exhaustion, upon the hard bedewed wayside. At first, I felt bewildered, and again my spirit and heart almost failed me. But the good effects of the sleep—even though I had no pillow on which to lay my head—did me considerable service. Shortly after I regained a little strength and continued my journey, arriving at Brechin about 8 o'clock that morning. The weaver there, to whom I had a note of introduction, was almost as poor as myself. He did not mention breakfast—perhaps he had not any for himself. But our meeting was not in vain. There was no work for me in Brechin, but my going there was a link in the mysterious chain of a loving Providence. Armed with another note of introduction from this Brechin friend, I passed on, this time to Luthermuir—a village lying in a flat plain about seven miles east of Brechin, and nine miles north of Montrose. By the time I arrived my limbs could scarcely bear me up, but I found the home of the weaver to whom my note was addressed. Soon I became insensible. After a long quiet faint, I fell asleep and my new friends thought it was the sleep of death.

"Poor fellow! perhaps he has not had any food to-day."

"Possibly, not any yesterday."

"He is not a common tramp."

Such were some of the words I heard when becoming gradually

conscious. And in the matter of food, their supposition was too true. Save the mouthful of gingerbread, I had not eaten anything for at least thirty hours.

Here, too, the people all round were almost as poor as I was, but they had the will to help, and they tried to do so. Here, and as soon as possible, they gave me a share of what they had—a cup of tea and a little bread. And this was greatly enhanced by the kindly way in which this needed help was rendered.

When the neighbours had returned to their humble homes, and I was able to speak to those left, I was asked several questions, but they were not questions of doubt, nor did they indicate any want of charity in thought—their kind hospitality, hearty sympathy, and timely help bespoke that charity which thinketh no evil. My new friends simply wished to draw from me some idea of what I had undergone. It is said the *real* Scotchman would always be independant if possible, that he would almost sooner starve than beg, and I confess I was touched with this spirit; but on this occasion I endeavoured to strike out a middle course—that is, to reveal as little as possible of my past sufferings, and yet to give a reason for my sad condition. This reason was not necessary to lead to help. The help had been rendered. Without any questions, my new friends had proved themselves to be in possession of no small share of the milk of human kindness. They had the heart and the will, and that helped them to find the way. I could not but ask myself, what would the poor do were it not for the poor? Evidently the sorrow which marked every face I found looking upon me was not the sorrow of the moment. The careworn and anxious-looking appearance of all around me bespoke a long time passed in severe trial. The inhabitants in the village and round about were almost entirely weavers, and when I arrived all were without hope, at least what hope they had was what is called hoping against hope. Under this feeling, and the promptings of necessity, the men went that night to the agents to ask again what news. As if I had been the centre of attraction, many came rushing back to the home of my host in high glee, and addressing me, one exclaimed—" Guid news the nicht, man; cheer up! There's twa cart-load o' wabs come. All are supplied, an' there's twa for you. There hasna been the like o' this for six months afore. Ye hae brocht a blessin' wi' ye."

"There is nae fear o' us noo," sobbed his helpmeet.

I was delighted to see all so glad and grateful. The circle of softly brightened countenances, all tear-dewed, around me, reminded me of the heavenly rainbow in April. My own heart was so full, I could not say much, only two short sentences—"May God reward you for your kindness to me. I may be all the better for coming here."

"I hope so, and we too," responded a sensible middle-aged man, in the act of bidding me good-night. Seriously, yet smilingly, he added—

> "All places that the eye of Heaven visits
> Are to wise men ports and happy havens."

Some favourable results. To me it was no small reward for all the suffering to see a whole village rejoice that "twa cartfu' o' wabs" had arrived, and to hear one of the men thus made happy expressing his gratitude, and a grand truth, in fine poetry—all proving that being willing to work, and having enough of work, is a great source of happiness to every true workman.

As soon as a little strength came to me, I asked for work and obtained it, to the joy of all who heard of "the new tramp." But when I got my web, I did not know very well how to go to work—the fabric being so very fine compared with that to which I had been accustomed. Pressing necessity caused me to venture, but I was not long left in the dilemma. My shopmates were quick to see it, and as quickly did they come to the rescue. Having thus rendered all the necessary help to begin with, I was soon able to make as good work, and earn as much money as any in the village.

And then these wanderings were not without beneficial elements. One thing, I met with all sorts of people and saw life in its various forms. Some with whom I met were really better than they seemed to be, some were better to others than to themselves. There were also good meaning people with bad habits. All taught me something, I tried in my humble way to discourage the evil and encourage the good. This was more by example than precept. And this I found spoke louder than words—in this land of tramps, as Luthermuir was then designated.

By the religious people—those who went to Church on Sunday —we were regarded as heathens. But I do not remember anything that was done to draw us from heathendom, and win us to God. We were not all heathens though we did not go to any of the Churches. Many mis-applied the Sunday, but some worshipped God in their own way. Weather permitting, I went to the fields on that day, my lodgings being unfavourable for meditation. I went out to be alone with God, and there He taught me in His Lesson Books. "Against Thee and Thee only have I sinned," was my confession. The tears of repentance were many. That I had forsaken Him because of the wickedness of men bore heavily down against me. How foolish, how wicked. But my heavenly forgiving Father welcomed back His erring child.

And then there were favourable physical results, as well as spiritual. Of the former, the more immediate may be thus summed up: my visit to Luthermuir, together with the blessing of God on the kindness of friends there—enabled me, (1) to send home some help to my father still in Lochee; (2) to save as much as to purchase for myself a complete suit of new clothes; and (3) to return home with a little cash in hand.

CHAPTER X.—SOME STEPS NEARER THE MARK.

Becoming an Assistant Teacher.

SUCH being my condition—spiritually, physically, and financially—I was ready, spirit and soul and body, to resume my labours much on the same lines as before the fearful crisis. Not that I was without difficulties, but I had before found that difficulties were not impossibilities.

Before I left home, in our distress, I sold my books and all, but now I was able to purchase what was more immediately wanted; and soon my former desk (the old chest of drawers) had its attractions for me. There, and whilst weaving as before, I strove hard to bring myself up to, and beyond, the standard to which I had previously attained.

After attending the evening classes for a time, my savings enabled me to go once more to the day school—still continuing to weave late in the evening and early in the morning. My prospects of attaining my life-object were brighter than ever.

Thus I continued to learn and to weave until I consented to become an assistant teacher. At first I was timid in my new position, but the kindly ways of the Principal towards me imparted courage. At last I felt at home. Naturally, when some of the pupils were puzzled they went to him for help, but he would say, "Go to Mr. Hillocks, he will explain all to you." Only fancy a mere lad (the weaver *laddie*) to be called "*Mr.* Hillocks," and then this was followed by the pupils, "please, sir." I could scarcely believe my ears.

Of course, I went on with my own lessons, ever learning, having private help from my superior as was arranged.

In connection with the study of geography, in its enlarged sense, I added that of navigation.

Becoming a Tutor.

"In theory, you could be a captain of a ship," said my instructor, somewhat proud of his pupil.

"In practice, the sooner the better," said I to myself, for all at once the thought flashed across my mind that possibly I might have my mind thereby enlarged for greater usefulness by visiting foreign lands. And, besides, the suggestion recalled a similar desire which had been fostered by my father's detailed account of things abroad as seen by him.

I was sensible enough to know that before I could be an efficient captain I must first become a practical sailor, and before I could become a first class seaman I must be a sailor boy. So I got a ship and all things were settled. My last day as the assistant teacher came. It was arranged that I was to sail on the morrow, but this did not come to pass. On the supposed last evening of my life as the under teacher, an old fashioned *sneck* (latch) on an old fashioned door stopped the way. About 10 P.M. my face was brought violently against that latch which nearly forced out one of my eyes. The ship had to leave without me, and I did not become a captain.

Although the preventing cause was a source of regret, my friends were glad I did not go to sea. In time, I became resigned, and, as soon as possible, applied myself to the weaving until I saved as much as enabled me to place myself under a well-known tutor, Mr. George Hunter, then studying for the gospel ministry. He, too, had known something of obtaining knowledge under difficulties, as most of the ablest of Scotch students have done, and no disgrace to them. Doubtless, this, together with a fine, genial, cultivated nature, led him to take a special interest in me and to forward my advancement. A fellow feeling makes us wondrous kind, and then he was well versed in the various branches of learning.

By all this—together with his teaching abilities and my close application—my advances and the little I had of teaching experience were such that, by his advice, I, too, became a tutor in a small way; spending half-an-hour or so each morning and evening with three or four families, to help the young ones in their home lessons. Not long after, however, my services became more worthy of my new title. Some better-to-do parents who, during the early part of their married life, had not been able to give their sons and daughters all the schooling they desired, resolved to make up for this by having me to help for an hour each day. This was all in the right direction, but I could not help smiling when I heard my new title, especially when I thought of the vast distance between me and my own tutor.

But these preparatory steps gave pleasure, enlivened hope, and fostered ambition, leading me to look forward to the time when I might become the useful "Principal" of some academy.

Becoming a Public Teacher.

And at last I took one of the first of a series of difficult steps to attain this consummation, so devoutly wished by me. After persevering in learning and teaching and weaving, I sold my loom, rented premises, and opened a public day school—on the 25th of November, 1844, in the centre of a plot of houses a little north of the top of the Hilltown, Dundee.

The district was called Smithfield, and included the house in which I was born, not more than a hundred yards from that house. "Most wonderful," said some of those who had known of my battles to live and learn in time past.

I say "*difficult* steps" advisedly, for it would be wrong to imagine that my battles to live and learn were ended; but I was as willing as ever to fight the good fight, and as determined as ever, under God, to conquer.

In the small circular notice announcing my intention to open the school, I simply promised to teach "the three R's." But that arose from my hatred of quackery, and at that time what I most detested was the quackery so often manifested by young men when they became public teachers. This I resolved to avoid, and follow the advice—

> "Let all the foreign tongues alone,
> Till you can read and spell your own."

Hence I neither mentioned Latin nor Mathematics, because I was not sufficiently versed in them to teach them, especially if advanced pupils honoured me with their presence.

Then I did not open my school under distinguished patronage. I did not think of making the effort. Perhaps I would have failed. At all events, it was not so, and, no doubt, this in a measure accounted for the smallness of the number of the pupils who came.

Another cause for this, no doubt, arose from the fact that though I was not then *a member* of the United Presbyterian Church, I was looked upon as belonging to that communion. At that time that denomination thought it would not be consistent with their pronounced voluntaryism to take an active part in the day school education of the children. Therefore they left any of the teachers who adhered to them, to fight their way unaided. But the two other Presbyterian bodies—"Free" and the "Established" Churches—vied with each other in doing all they could for their respective schools and teachers. Some of the ministers, moved by a strong sectarian spirit, on Sunday, told their hearers to send their children to their "*own* schools."

Among the unfavourable influences brought to bear against me, I shall only mention one other. Some of the "great guns" of "the cloth" did not believe in free trade in teaching, so they also combined to put me out of the market as soon as possible. Their pretext had something reasonable about it. That is, it was more evident—they seized upon a fact, a fact over which I had no control. Seeing I was short in stature and young in years, (not quite 19 years, I am told), they called my humble seminary, "The Laddie's School," meaning a school taught by a boy.

These "high-souled" *teachers* easily persuaded some of the parents to suppose it would be useless to send any but very young children to my school. Then, even as now, there were parents who thought the ability and the will to exercise physical force the first quality of a teacher—being ready to give the children frequent "whackings."

Meeting pecuniary difficulties. Such selfish doings, together with other drawbacks, told against me and the number of my pupils. But I was not to be put down in that way. There was one important fact on my side, the ten boys and girls who came to me soon proved themselves to be dear children. They could not give me more than twopence each per week, but before long each one of them gave me a heart into the bargain.

But I must live. How? On one shilling and eightpence a week? Impossible. What then? Give way, give up? Never. Something *more* must be done, and I did it. I took a little more help out of the loom. What a blessing when one can work with hands as well as with the head!

By this time my father and the family had also removed from Lochee to Dundee, and not far from my school house. This afforded me the very opportunity I desired—of again weaving early in the morning and late at night. By this means I got over the first rent difficulty, and this was much.

Right so far, but this weaving by stealth began to be known. The prying gossips are everywhere. And if it became generally known that I was put to such shifts, I might close my school at once. And the news was all the more likely to spread because, having spent as much as possible on school furniture, I had only one suit of clothes; hence it was almost impossible completely to brush off the weaver's livery—the tow-dust. So I tried another plan by which I made both ends meet, as a few more pupils had dropped in one by one.

Before this I had been well trained in how to live on almost nothing a day—at least, on much less than the much talked-of "sixpence." For the strongest of all reasons I became a "vegetarian" without "the figs" and "the grapes." My school house also became my study, my cooking and dining room. As yet a servant was a long way out of the question, so I drew what consolation I could from the saying, "He is best served who serves himself."

My cooking utensils were few and simple, easily cleaned and put out of sight—a small kettle, a little jug, a tin spoon, served my purpose. The great guns with big schools would have called out, "*Infra dig*," if they had known, but I managed to keep the secret, and hurt no one.

This was the order of the day: I slept in my father's house; and, as a rule, I left for my school early in the morning to prosecute my studies. At 9 A.M. I had "a plain breakfast,"—a little toast and a cup of coffee. Then I joined my pupils in the playground where we had all sorts of fun and running about till 10 when we entered the school for work. My charge left from one to two, during which time I had my "luncheon,"—a little of my favourite gingerbread and water, and a little fresh air. The school was again cleared at five, when I had a cup of tea with a biscuit, after which I studied till seven, then went for my private instruction in Latin and Mathematics, from 7.30 to 8.30; returned at 9; studied till 11, and then left for the night.

The only variation from this course was when my interest in the subject made me forget the hour and remain later than usual. On Sunday there was a slight difference. When not "at church" I devoted my time to the consideration of religious subjects—collecting Bible facts and other scriptural information for my pupils as well as for my own enlightenment. From the beginning I considered it was my duty to teach Christian precepts as well as impart general knowledge.

Chapter XI.—Making the Best of my Position.

But I had scarcely overcome those trying difficulties when another very important problem presented itself—How best to train the truants?

Training the Truants.

Truants are generally boys who are against everybody and everybody is against them. They are either stupid or wicked, often both. Whoever is to blame they are to be pitied. They are always unwilling to be brought to any school, and unruly when there—a source of trouble and grief in all schools where they go, in all homes to which they belong—almost always enraged and ever determined to conquer first their parents and then the teachers. Always in boiling water, constantly at war.

At first, I was astonished that they were so numerous, but the amazement was not so great when I found that they were almost all brought to me; and the astonishment was still further lessened when I heard all the details connected with each case.

"Give him a good beating, sir," said an angry mother to me, pushing her boy into the school-room, and shutting the door to keep him there. After she regained her breath, she added, "He fears nothing so much as a thrashing. He is not only a grief to his parents, he is also a dread to his sisters. He had a temper even before he could creep; and since then he has been thrashed several times a day. You'll never keep him if you don't beat him."

I asked the boy to be seated, and told the scholars to go on with their work till I should return.

The mother accompanied me, and when we were out of the boy's hearing I said to her, "Have you tried kindness?"

"He is beyond kindness, sir," answered the mother, now weeping; "but try what you think best, only conquer him." She left still weeping.

The boy was well known to all of my pupils.

"Shall we try him?" I asked them.

"Yes, yes," was the unanimous response.

Turning to the boy I said, "Would you like these happy boys and girls to love you and help you to be good? All we ask is, Will you promise to do your best to become a good boy?"

He consented, and we soon found he was not beyond the power of love. True, he had a will stronger than that of "a strong minded woman," and my duty and efforts were to direct that will in the right way. By a pleasant simplicity of treatment, blended with firmness, the lad so changed that he was among the first and last at the school and none gave more attention than he did to his home lessons.

I have referred thus minutely to this case because it was not only the turning point with this, our first truant, but also the turning point with the school. The boy's parents told other parents and the talk was loud in the district, and all in my favour. A result was, when any urchin in the neighbouring schools had become the habit and repute truant, he was brought to our increasing school.

All this was trying, but I willingly endured all. I had a point to gain, and the gaining of that point was worth anything in the shape of self-denial. And then it brought joy to others as well as myself, to my pupils and to their parents also. *Realising my hopes.*

When I made up my mind to become a teacher, I resolved to *lead*, not to *drive*, and now I had found that leading was the best way to useful happiness for all, myself included. By this time my school was made up of three classes, but all were brought to run gently into one. These were my first ten scholars, those who were all my own so to speak, "fresh like young spring's first green;" those bright things shining in almost angel-childhood, ever obedient, cheerful and orderly; that would be a strange heart which had not in it an overflowing fount of love for a beautiful, noble boy, or a sweetly pretty girl, between five and ten years of age—in sympathy so tender, in joy so sparkling—uncomplaining, and gentle. After a time, this was the character of these pupils. I loved them, each one of them, and I would have been unworthy of my place if I had not loved them with all my heart.

The second portion was made up of those who came in afterwards. In their case it was not so easy to win and retain the hearts of even the best of them, while bringing them under school discipline. This was specially difficult in regard to those of them, the majority whose parents and teachers had previously imbibed and practised the ruinous notion that the mind of a child cannot be enlightened, that its soul cannot be purified, save by physical suffering. But even in the case of such, the pleasant and healthful fruit of a hopeful reliance on moral suasion, in the work of governing and teaching the young, began to manifest itself. But it is only fair to say that, in effecting this happy result, I was greatly assisted by the first portion who, in their pleasing enthusiasm, gave a practical proof that love and learning may go hand in hand. My precept and their example told well on each of the new-comers.

The third portion was made up of the truants, or rather those who *had been* truants. Till they came, matters were comparatively easy. It was by their coming that my patience as well as my plans were most severely tested. I found it had been easy to love the loveable, but to love those whose faces, words, habits, and outward appearance were repulsive, was not an easy matter. Naturally one is inclined to wish all such far enough away, but a true teacher has more to do than to study his inclinations. And then I had started with the idea that every seminary, however humble, should be sanctified by the presence and manifestation of love—a place for the discipline and direction of the affections as well as the training and filling the minds of *all the pupils*, including those who had previously been morally poisoned and all but ruined by bad example and bad treatment. For persevering in this thought I was at last amply rewarded in seeing a transformation that was useful as well as beautiful. The rough became refined, the rude became gentle, the ignorant intelligent.

And, in a remarkably short time, the three portions became as one in ready obedience, in willing work, and mutual affection. On this point, I may give the testimony of one of many who rejoiced to see the happy results. It found its way into the press at the time. "The young weaver," said the divine, referring to myself and the school, "now a youthful dominie, is already well known for his uncommon powers of winning children even the roughest of them. 'He that winneth souls is wise,' says a great authority. We venture to parody the expression, and say, He that winneth children must himself be a child, partaking of many of the many finer qualities which make childhood a thing so wonderful, so unique, and almost so divine. It is easy to terrify children, not difficult to cram them with knowledge, but to win them at once to yourself and to a love of learning is a rare and peculiar, though simple-seeming gift. It is always delightful to see him presiding in his school, a child among children, leading them, as Una led her milk-white lamb, by the unseen cords of love in the green pastures and still waters of knowledge, and by those ways of spiritual wisdom which are pleasantness and peace."

A picture by a poetic painter.

Before the close of our first session I was comparatively rich on less than "forty pounds a year." But there was much that was exhausting, not only in what had become "the delightful task" and in my own studies, but also in the absence of proper support for the body. Hence I was glad of the rest and change which the recess permitted.

First visit to Edinburgh.

At the parents' request a lunar month was the extent of the playtime, but this was long enough for my pocket. A week of this time was spent in Edinburgh. It was the first time I had visited that seat of learning. I only went as a sight-seer—as an inquiring stranger, anxious to become better posted up in some of the incidents connected with the history of Scotland. A few days filled my head and my note-book, but I need not stop here to give details. Sufficient to say that the lion-like Arthur Seat, and the time-defying Salisbury Crags were a source of amazement to me. Nor did the monuments to the mighty dead escape my notice. When visiting the various educational centres I felt most inclined to linger at the University, asking myself, "Is it possible that I may yet have the benefit of some of the instruction imparted there year after year?"

Chapter XII.—Pressing Forward and Breaking Down.

Our second opening betokened success. There was at once a decided increase of pupils, and the new ones soon fell into our ways. This stimulated my former desire to store up more necessary knowledge with the object of giving it out in the best possible way for the good of those under my care. Still I believed in following the beaten track in all that was good, but to go beyond it when necessary for the greatest good. But before the session was closed I made a mistake, to my sorrow. I mean in acting upon the usual plan in giving prizes to those adjudged "the best scholars."

Our Second Session.

I heard no complaints, nor did I begrudge those who were successful in obtaining "the rewards" offered. But inwardly I felt that those who were not successful deserved rewards also. Their conduct was equally favourable, their disadvantages at home were many, and their efforts were greater than the more successful. All were equally praiseworthy, hence I felt uncomfortable in my conscience, and thought out another course of action in regard to these things.

Whilst all were equally happy in their work, there were some brighter and some duller than others, some very timid and others the reverse. The bright and confident shone out immediately in any contest, particularly at public examinations. But the dull and timid fell far short of what was desired by those who judge entirely by *visible* results. I never did so. Justice said, think of all alike, help all alike, encourage all alike. Common sense said, create a love for school, cultivate a love of learning for its own sake, and that will do away with the need of special incentives. But there was one thing in which all could join in a friendly and beneficial contest—keeping up the good conduct marks, or rather doing away with the necessity of bad conduct marks. And this I encouraged while fostering the desire to advance.

But I began to find that my enthusiasm was leading my pupils as well as myself so fast, that we were likely soon to suffer from over work, and hence I formed two extra classes. This was not so Irish like as you may suppose. They were "The Reward Classes"—reward for good conduct in the widest sense, at home as well as in the school. They might also have been called "The Recreation Classes." They were open to all who really did their utmost to be the best possible behaved boys and girls.

A new form of Rewards.

The subjects were Anatomy and Botany. As members of these classes we met twice weekly, but not in ordinary school hours. From the beginning the girls preferred Botany, the boys Anatomy, but I urged the boys to strive also for Botany, because of the attendant recreation, and this they did. It was something to see us leaving school for the fields, like so many bees in search of fresh sweets from every open flower.

Here, again, the past and the present were linked. What, years before, I acquired in Lochee, under the careful teaching of the kind Doctor, proved to be very helpful to me and beneficial to my pupils—who knows the end of a kind act timely and kindly rendered?

Again, in the Botanical class, I was also greatly assisted by one of my literary associates—a fellow-member of one of the Dundee Literary Societies to which I belonged. I refer to George Lawson, who began life in Dundee as a lawyer's clerk. While a true servant of an indulgent master, he prepared himself for a situation more in harmony with his tastes, and became an assistant to Balfour, Professor of Botany, Edinburgh University; Mr. Lawson is now the able and highly esteemed Professor of Chemistry of Dalhousie College, Halifax, Nova Scotia. In his first letter to me on this subject is this paragraph:—"I highly approve of your proposal to treat your young charge to a knowledge of the rudiments of natural history. It has long been my conviction that, were the people more addicted to the study of such a pleasant subject, they would be all the happier for it. It would improve their moral feelings."

This we happily realised, and the benefit then obtained is telling in several homes to this day. But our rambles were also beneficial as a means of the much-needed recreation. They were delightful, particularly in spring and summer. No butterfly, with gay little wings, could be more lively, more sportive, than we were—along the banks, up the braes, down into the groves, through the wood, or over the fields.

And these rewards, and this mode of bestowing them, were profitable to all concerned, the parents included, they being invited to our short lectures on "The elements of Anatomy and Botany." The rudiments of these branches of natural history were all I professed to give, but this led to inquiry, recreation, refinement and joy, and without interfering with our other studies.

Some of the envious laughed at us; but we could laugh, too, being not only on the right side, but on the winning side also—our school increasing in numbers as well as happiness. *The unexpected comes to pass.*

"But this success must be stopped some way or other. At least, it must not go on unchallenged."

So said some of the teachers who thought they taught as well as any man, "and certainly better than the Laddie of Smithfield." The test was applied.

"Your school is in our *Ecclesiastical District*, and our Minister wishes to visit it," said the "Ruling Elder" of St. Andrew's Established Church, on a Saturday evening.

Most readily did I give a hearty assent to this request, but imagine my surprise when the elder told me that Monday morning at ten was the time fixed, if *convenient*.

The last two words, and the smile that accompanied them, bespoke the presence of a little dry humour in the mind of the speaker. Some of my readers may remember that, then even as now, it was the habit of parents at home and the teacher in the school to prepare the children for "the examination." At first this naturally came before my mind, particularly in relation to the parents, but I did not withdraw my consent, only asked the elder to urge the minister to explain to the parents why he had taken this out of the way course.

On the Sunday, the minister announced the proposed examination, and even this was a gain. Before, I had only a local habitation and a name, but now the latter became wide as the parish. The next day, that eventful Monday, came. As usual, 9. A.M. brought my pupils. I assembled them in the playground and told them what was to be in an hour, and asked them to go home with the news to their parents.

At 9.45 one of the pupils who had returned to the playground exclaimed, "They are coming."

"It is our Minister," said a little girl. "Mother likes him."

The boys seemed to be less concerned, and continued their play. Perhaps, they were less troubled about dress or more confident touching their lessons.

"The deputation," as the approaching visitors were afterwards designated, had ascended the Hilltown, no easy task. They were now making for Smithfield by the pathway which was so narrow that only one could walk after another. Foremost was the Rev. Mr Logan, who was lame. Then followed his "man," the church officer, who was also lame. Next was a fine faithful dog which was lame too. And next followed a very tall, and, at that time, a very spare man, the Rev. John Tulloch who became the famous Principal Tulloch. (He died lately, greatly lamented by many, including our good Queen.)

After our visitors were seated in the school, I summoned the scholars. The school was opened in the usual way, and Mr. Logan tendered the promised explanation. After giving him and Mr. Tulloch a syllabus of a week's school work, I told them that the school was in their hands. But both at once expressed a wish that they might be allowed merely to select the subject;

also that I should go on as if they were not present, they asking some questions at the close of each subject, which was in all cases suggested by them.

Finding the schoolroom overcrowded, I sent all the pupils to the playground save the class engaged. This gave us more room, but no child knew what was to be the next subject. This was continued for four hours, when the deputation not only expressed their "great satisfaction," followed by hearty expressions of approbation, but further explained to the parents present that their desire was *to see the school in its true, everyday, working order*. The same terms of special approval were kindly repeated in the Presbytery. So, to our joy, we gained in being taken by surprise.

The gains were pleasing to my friends as well as to myself. My pupils so increased that I became monarch of all I surveyed, so to speak—if that may be said of a school conducted on democratic principles—I reigned by the good-will of my loving young people. But I may be pardoned if I mention another of the gains.

There are teachers above envy. This was the case in Dundee. Two may be named as worthy examples—Mr. Macintosh and Mr. Hamilton. They not only called to compliment me on my success, but expressed a wish that I would consent to become a member of the Forfarshire, Perthshire, and Fifeshire Association of Teachers. I agreed, and so became a recognised Member of the Profession.

Our second vacation came, and again I was needing the rest. But this time I had not rest so much as change. Purposely "the time for play" was longer than the year before; but now I did not go so much as a sight-seer as to advance a few steps in scholastic learning—my motto being, "Higher and yet higher."

Our middle-class pupils.

When our third session was opened we found the school quite full, and more. Our new pupils were chiefly such as are found in our middle-class schools. This gave me no little concern, for I had been told that the human nature in this class was much more difficult to govern than their poorer fellow-creatures; that the former were given to caste-thoughts and inclined to be high-minded and overbearing. Happily my experience soon proved that this was not universally true. But I found this: that the most of them, at first, seemed to suffer from being pampered, as if everything had been done for them. There was not so much of the inclination to be idle as a deficiency in resolution, a lack of energy. This caused them to become more easily disheartened, in some cases discontented. But soon all this passed away from our midst. The girls came round to the right first; the boys after. In time the new-comers were one with the rest, and day after day contributed to the general progress and happiness, whilst I continued to be their friend and guide. To me it was truly joyous to see merry childhood and advancing youth all so beautiful and bright and playful, ready for work and ready for play. To them every department seemed replete with that interest which produced the earnestness of Milton, as seen in his tender years,

"Set to learn, and to know, and thence to do."

Breaking God's laws again. But I had been gradually becoming physically weaker. Whatever little triumphs had been gained over myself, whatever little good I had done my pupils, next to God enthusiasm had a leading part. Reigning in me it became contagious, and effected my young charge, helping us onward and upward, but it became too much for me. In regard to the good of others, I was earnest and careful enough; but I was not so careful of myself. From a health-point I forgot the laws of physical life, and hence I suffered, as I had often done before. This was particularly so during our third session. The results of overwork in an over-crowded school forced me to give the third vacation a week or two before the usual time.

After a short rest, in the country, I went again to Edinburgh; but finding I was unable to prosecute my studies as I did there the year before, I returned to Dundee, in the hope of being able to re-open my school at the understood time.

"Your nervous system has been overstrained, and is now so over strung, that at present it would be dangerous to enter upon your school duties. You must appoint a substitute for a time."

So said the doctor. I followed his advice, promising to my pupils to return as soon as my health would permit. However the illness continued, and he urged that I accept an offer made to me of a country school wherein no special efforts would be called for. Again I obeyed, most reluctantly, as you may well suppose.

Chapter XIII.—Some Important Side Incidents.

THESE three years at this delightful task are remembered by many *Literary pleasure with profit.* with joy, but none rejoice in the happiness they brought about more than I do. One who is proud to be called "An old scholar," just the other day, referring to those days, said, "they were our happiest—all love and learning." The last three words give the key to the great reluctance of teacher and scholars to part.

When that time came the scene in the school was such as to baffle description. Even the parents present wept as they heard the sobs of the elder scholars, and saw the younger ones clinging to me as if they thought of retaining me by force. I strove hard to restrain my emotion, but the effort only served the more to intensify my grief. The breaking up of this source of useful happiness nearly broke my heart.

Here, however, I must pause in regard to that point of the life wherein teaching was the chief feature. Being so absorbed in the things pertaining to what was latterly called Smithfield Academy, I neglected to mention other incidents, in one or two of which you are likely to be more or less interested—assuming that you are following me. These matters are not strictly scholastic, but their direction was onward and upward. The first I shall mention may be characterised as pleasure with profit.

Incidently I have referred to one of my "Literary Associates," and I may here add that there were a good few of us. Our weekly meetings were held in what we called The Halls of Lamb. In a volume very interesting at least to Dundonians—"Dundee Celebrities of the Nineteenth Century"—I find that "The Literary Emporium" is credited with assisting me in my mental progress. That is true, but it is only fair to state that "The Literary Insti tute" and "The Mutual Improvement Society" were also helpful in the same direction. Indeed, each of these Societies had its peculiar and beneficial characteristics. Whatever the programme was I enjoyed it, but relished the debates most. Whatever we were in our respective callings, we were mad-caps when we met at "The Halls of Lamb." Few, if any, were perfect. Almost every one had "a bee in his bonnet." Yet at times we could be as earnest and as grave as a judge, and almost every meeting became a source of profitable as well as pleasing recreation.

Of course, we sometimes asserted that each one had a will of his own, and that the will was not always the sweetest when it was the strongest. In time I, too, began to show in me there was a will. At first I adopted the policy of "grin and bear," and had enough to bear, for some would come down upon me like a sledge-hammer. I have found the training was useful. Then I regarded it as severe—occasionally unmerciful. In the end I took courage, returning to the charge, maintaining my ground. One of the most brilliant of our number gave an instance of this. As he records it much better than I can, I shall give it in his own words:—

"Mr. Hillocks belonged to some of the best literary societies for which Dundee at that time was renowned, and which have done much to brighten the intellectual, and form the finer tastes of that city. On one occasion Mr. Hillocks had incurred the displeasure of the chairman, who delivered a fierce philippic as a punishment. This the young lad regarded as unfair, and made several attempts to show that the statement to which he had listened was unfair, being *ex parte*. These efforts so roused the chairman that he lost both patience and temper, imperatively exclaiming: 'Sit down, sir; I say, sit down!' 'I'll sit down,' said Mr. Hillocks, suiting the action to the words, 'but I'll rise again.' He rose and conquered by sheer perseverance.

"The incident is slight in itself," adds the writer, "but it most aptly illustrates the character of the man—that indomitable perseverance which has ever been one of his leading characteristics, and which has not been weakened by misfortune, nor crushed down by opposition. His motto through his severe life struggles has been the very brief but most pregnant sentence, 'I'll rise again,' expressing in one terse phrase his energy as a man and his hope as a Christian."

I have given this in full, because I know the incident has been greatly blessed to many, particularly the phrase, "I'll rise again." But I should add that the writer was Bailie C. C. Maxwell, a successful merchant and a favourite in literary circles—and brimful of anecdote—the very one to store up such an incident.

It was seldom, however, that we rose to such a white heat as we did that night. As a rule, the intellectual gain was practical and otherwise beneficial. Our meetings, too, brought us in contact with all sorts of subjects urging us out into the great ocean of literature. And, besides, such fencings, in the form of essays, debates and criticisms, helped to open the mind and make it more and more receptive. I have since found they helped us to take a firmer grasp of themes or work, presenting itself for our consideration or effort. And, certainly a preparation of this kind, if not perverted, becomes fruitful in after life, whether the youth so trained becomes a merchant, lawyer, statesman, professor, or preacher. I found the exercise helpful then, I find it helpful now, and hence I am glad the opportunity was presented of taking part in these happy and profitable evenings.

Becoming an unpledged abstainer.

This was another source of joy going on while the school days were being filled with delight; but I am about to refer to incidents closer connected with the school life.

After my success became more marked, I had several invitations, some "to dine," some "to take tea," some "to spend the evening." Generally, but not exclusively, they came from the better-to-do parents. I looked upon the invitations as proofs of respect and kindness, but for several reasons they were not accepted. First, to have gone to the richer and not to the poorer would not have been according to my mind. Secondly, if I had accepted, my time for self-improvement would have been almost all absorbed, and then I had known some who had allowed themselves to be carried away under such circumstances, some losing their heads, and some losing their hearts. But though I could not comply with these well-meant requests, I announced in the school my intention to visit all the parents, reserving the privilege of dropping in sometime between the afternoon and evening classes. This proved to be a happy thought. One thing, I saw my young ones and their parents "at home."

"Na, na, Mester, ye must taste wi' us afor ye leave," said an earnest, sober, industrious mother of five children, on whom I had called.

When I had given some indication that I was about to leave she gave a speaking look to one of her girls, who, at once, understood what was meant. In a moment, the girl went to the cupboard, took something from it, put it under her pinafore, and went out. She returned soon and put something in the cupboard, and then began to prattle with the other children as before.

I saw this, and the mother suiting the action to the word, confirmed my fears—that she had sent for some spirits; I knew the customs but had never complied with them.

"Shall I refuse or accept this well-meaning token of friendship?" said I to myself. It was when I was debating the matter in my mind that she used the words quoted. Having more respect for the mother's feeling than for my own judgment, I suffered my lips to touch the whisky, but took care that none entered within, so the tongue did not taste it.

"Never, again," said I to myself, "shall I allow my lips even to touch strong drink by way of the drinking customs."

Being so deeply concerned in the advancement of my pupils during these years among them, I did not know much of the world outside. I did not know anything of Total Abstinence Societies nor of pledges, but I had up to this time persistently refused to have anything to do with intoxicating liquors. For one reason, as you know from the commencement of my struggles to rise, I required all the money I could earn for myself and others. When there was any money over, it went for books and toward my educational progress.

This was the mere money side of the question. But other reasons made me an abstainer. I had seen people, under the influence of strong drink, not only make fools of themselves but do harm to others, in a negative as well as a positive sense. The present was a case in point. I knew the father of this family was a hard working man, not very strong, and that his income was comparatively small. No doubt, this effort on the part of the mother to show her respect for me cost her a sixpence, and surely this would have been better spent in preparing a better supper for the worn-out husband. But, in addition to this, another wrong was evident to me. Even without any temperance training such as our "Bands of Hope" now happily impart—the girl evidently felt she had done wrong. She was trained to be crafty, if she had gone for a pennyworth of milk there would have been no need for the sly look of the mother, nor the artful way of her child. I could not help thinking that there was about the drinking habits something that was morally as well as physically unhealthy. Therefore I at once stood up against the habit of either taking or giving intoxicating liquors by way of the drinking customs. God has enabled me to keep my resolution. And, no doubt, He will do so to the end.

It was sometime after this before I became a member of a Total Abstinence Society. And this was done on the principle that what was good for me might be good for others, that I should do to others as I would wish them to do to me, and that, union being strength, I would in this become all the more helpful if co-operating with others of like mind and habit.

"Joining the Church." One of my special endeavours was to manifest a desire to avoid anything in the shape of respect of persons. But of the parents who took a special interest in me there was one, of the dear mothers in Israel, to whom I could speak more freely respecting myself, and who spoke her mind

freely to me. For instance, one day she kindly and earnestly took me to task because I had not become a communicant of some of the churches. I had excuses, if not reasons, ready; but she met them one by one and conquered.

But there was one reason I kept back from her, the strongest of all. I had carefully listened to most of the best of the ministers, and from almost all their discourses I gathered what I could not find in the Bible: That some were the objects of God's eternal love to the exclusion of others. At that time that doctrine was largely proclaimed and often angrily enforced. I never heard one dwell on the point who did not become angry and say hard things not only about man but also about God. I failed to see that this agreed with the Bible character of God, either with His Justice or His Love. The Bible told me that God made all, loves all, and yearns to save all. I was anxious to meet with a minister and a church that distinctly and freely declared this without any of the qualifications so often put in when these truths happen to be spoken.

But this good woman in a motherly way—and from no sectarian spirit, spoke of her own minister in glowing but becoming terms. He was not a stranger to me. I had heard him preach and lecture; and, besides, he was one of those who had visited my school at Smithfield, and was pleased to speak of it in a most kindly and genial way. I refer to the late Rev. Dr. J. R. M'Gavin, the able, devoted, and highly esteemed pastor of Tay Square United Presbyterian Church, one of the Ex-moderators of the synod of that prosperous and useful community. He was well known as a reformer of abuses whether in Church or State. It was in the pulpit, however, that he was most at home, a born preacher. His matter was instructive, his words were choice, his voice was musical, his delivery was effective.

I went to him. His first question was, why I had not thought of membership before? I told him the reason, that just given. But he said there was nothing in the views I held, as Bible truth, to prevent my joining the Church. I was received heartily by him, by the Elders, and by the Church. And to-day grateful thoughts follow that good mother for her fruitful advice.

In October, 1883, I was present at the celebration of Dr. M'Gavin's fifty years' ministry. Many kind words of admiration and affection were well said, but none admired and loved him more than I did. The gathering, the sight of the dear good man, and the addresses presented to him, brought to my mind much that makes me rejoice that I became a member of his church. This step, at the right time, greatly assisted me in the needed edification, happily advancing my spiritual life.

Meeting "Auntie Maggie."

I hasten to mention the last of the four very special incidents which transpired during my first three years of a teacher's life. It is a tender point, and I must go about it as delicately as I can. The truth is I would be altogether silent in regard to this matter were it not that to overlook it would cause a blank in these passages—it is to me, and to many more, one of the most important amongst the "All things" of which my life is composed.

I have heard the readers of the fashionable three-volume novels say, no story is complete and satisfactory which has not in it a little love and much murder. I protest against the murder, but admit we may be the better for a little love—at least, I have been the better for the love I am here to indicate, or rather to tell you how it came about.

Already I have taken you so far into my confidence as to tell you how I loved my young charge—the fine boys and gentle girls to whom my heart was bound. Save those of them who have been taken to be with Jesus, they are all men and women now; but wherever I meet them, they are still boys and girls to me —fairy things then, some of whom had scarcely passed their first decade—dear tiny beauties, tender in heart as well as in years. But holy and elevating as all this was to me, it was as nothing compared with what I have just hinted at.

Well, it happened in this way: I had made another of my

informal visits. And this time it was to see the parents of one of my first ten pupils. "Aggie" was the name of this lovely, lively child. Her father felt proud when he was called an educationalist, he looked forward with great expectation to the time when I would "drop in." Being aware of this, but without saying so, I selected what I called a free night—one in which I knew not of anything special to take me away early. But so far as educational matters went that night, the father was doomed to disappointment. This was why:

An unexpected stranger from Edinburgh was there. By Aggie, she was called "Auntie Maggie." I wished to retire at once; but Aggie clung to me so closely and winningly that, at the stranger's request, I consented to remain. Perhaps I could not help myself. A glance at Auntie Maggie's face and, well, to confess the weakness—I was done for. And coming down to plain prose, I must tell you I had no beard then to hide my blushes. I thought she blushed too. At all events, both of us were almost silent for the rest of the evening. But Aggie afforded some relief, for both of us seemed to take a quiet delight in listening to her childish chatter, and watching her varied movements. She would leap upon my knee so freely, and look bewitchingly into my face, and tell me so many nice things of this favourite auntie. At last the stranger ventured to express the fear that her niece was the pet. This I thought was an excellent opportunity. To my mind rushed a first-rate speech, but not a word would come from my lips, save the dry reply, "No favourites with me."

This led Aggie's father to express some of his pent-up notions on various philanthropic subjects. For that occasion, these seemed to me to be out of shape and out of harmony, and my replies must have been like unto those given by people who are very dull of hearing. All I saw, or wished to see, was the blooming blossom called "Auntie Maggie." On her all my thoughts were centred.

"There is something so sweet in that name, so charming in its owner," I said to myself, almost audibly. At this time I had just caught another peep into the loveliest face I had ever seen.

I was human, I tried to chide myself, but it was no use. I was *smitten*. That spark was kindled in my soul which poets, and even unpoetic people, call LOVE.

The result of that eventful night was not unfavourable to my scholars. Why should it have been so? I think it is Longfellow who truly said, "There is nothing holier in this life of ours than the first consciousness of love, the first fluttering of its silky wings, the first rising sound and breath of that wind which is soon to sweep through the soul to purify it."

Chapter XIV.—Round and Back to the same Point.

But to return, I mean, to the life of a teacher. I may say in passing that each of these incidents had an influence on my after career. Since then the schooling in the Halls of Lamb has been of great service to me in my efforts to be useful. Again, I have found that my avowed protest against strong drink, in all its forms, has not only been good for myself, but helpful to others. And again, having accepted the Divine invitation, "Come unto me," I found it well to be as closely connected as possible with those who had also done so. In this, emphatically in this, we realise that open confession, with happy association, is good for the soul. And as for the fourth incident it too proved to be more than the best of loving words can describe. Without all this I would have been a poor young man, but with them I have remained rich even without a shilling.

More play than work.

Well, I went to the country, and good for me I did so. My sinking life was revived. And though I was led into ways I could not have thought of, they were onward, among the "all things." The next scene of my labours was Roundy Hill School which had been purposely placed at the meeting-points of the parishes of Kirriemuir, Airlie, and Glamis. The school had been long established, but, from various causes, the pupils were reduced to a few young girls and little boys who could not go elsewhere. Financially this was a poor prospect, but otherwise it was all the more suitable to the doctor's orders—namely, "Read very little, study less, and ramble about as much as possible for the first six months at least."

The situation was also helpful in another direction. The various surroundings were well calculated to draw me out and about. Not far distant was Glamis Castle casting its shadow of a thousand years upon the grand old trees, and princely policy grounds. In another direction was the Linn, thundering in its solitude amidst crags and woods. And near—at least, near to the lover of the sublime and beautiful—was the Bonny House o' Airlie, in one of the most romantic regions of Scotland.

And here, too, I had the young tree to bend, but before long I found that child-nature was pretty much the same as it is everywhere—generally susceptible of kindly treatment, reluctant to be forced but willing to be led. My pupils were soon in love with my "new" ways—ways new to them. It would have been foolish, if not cruel, to have been unhappy with them. The parents also felt a pleasure in showing to me every possible kindness. Almost everywhere my company was sought. No party, in cottage or farmhouse, was regarded as complete without the presence of "THE NEW TEACHER."

Double work once more. Thus I passed the first six months in the country, faithfully attending to the doctor's orders, and daily becoming stronger. Most thankful was I to God, who in His kind providence over-ruled my having to leave my Dundee academy for a country school.

It was not long after this when my regained strength was called into action. I felt myself ready for full work, and kept more indoors, having resumed my studies. People had also begun to talk of my teaching "on new lines." Sons and daughters of the neighbouring and more distant farmers left other schools for mine. The school-room filled, but this did not test my health much. One reason was my being far ahead of the most advanced of those pupils who had come. This enabled me to be master of the situation. Even as before, to me teaching was an easy as well as a delightful task, and increasing success came with renewed health. And then my happiness was greatly sweetened because my means enabled me to have the pleasure of giving my dear father an extended holiday in the country.

About the last of the little parties I attended in the neighbourhood was one given by the late Robert Grant, then a prosperous chemist and druggist, Kirriemuir—an intelligent man, and thoroughly up to his business. Having heard of my interest in chemistry and botany he brought up that subject as one of the topics of conversation. On learning that I had attended some lectures in Edinburgh on these subjects, he asked how I first became interested in them, and I told him of the Lochee doctor's kindness and teaching, adding that I had a strong desire to become more acquainted with the healing art in the hope of increasing my usefulness wherever Providence might call me. And this led to new efforts on my part of which I had never dreamed. Mr. Grant was in want of assistance. He asked me to become his assistant.

On second thoughts I consented on the following conditions:— That I open the shop at 7 A.M., clean it and put everything in order, being otherwise useful till Mr. Grant came at 9; that I return to the shop at 5 P.M., and remain till 10 P.M., compounding and dispensing medicine. Thus in the morning I had between 9 and 10 o'clock to dress myself, take breakfast, and walk to my school, a distance of about two miles. In the afternoon I had from 4 to 5 o'clock to retrace my steps, take tea, and be ready for the duties of the evening. The only time for my three R's— reading, reflection, and recreation—was before 7 in the morning and after 10 at night.

This was severe enough on body and mind, but it enabled me to push through and so gain a special object without suddenly giving up my school, which I did not think would have been honourable. Besides the school had become "a paying concern," and I was saving up to get to the classes in Edinburgh as soon as convenient for all concerned. And again, the pleasing and invigorating nature of the rural life was so favourable to mental activity that I felt abler for double work than I had ever been. Still I felt I was doing too much, and that one or other of my two-fold occupations must be given up.

Mr. Grant brought me to the point, just as the time was expiring in which I had stated I would likely leave Roundy Hill.

He was pleased to appreciate my efforts to serve him in the way indicated, and asked if I could leave my school and learn more completely the trade of chemist and druggist, offering me a salary as a responsible assistant. To this I consented and entered upon my full duties as soon as another teacher could be had to take my place.

All things being thus accomplished, I continued the compounding of medicine and sale of the same till the time of my engagement came to a close.

Having thus obtained considerable knowledge and practice in this line—the healing art as far as medicine can go—Mr. Grant and I parted on the best of terms.

Trying to become "perfect." Having husbanded my savings, I thought of Edinburgh in the hope of becoming "perfect" as a teacher; I wished to reach the top of my profession. What young man, who really loves his calling, does not wish to be the foremost in it?

Of course, I had a parting as well as a meeting with my Roundy Hill school friends on the occasion of my proposed departure for our capital. Because of the many good and pleasant things that were said, because the school was again open, and because of the pleadings of the parents, together with the urging of my former pupils, I was almost persuaded to remain with them. But up came ambition with all its forces, and hence I kept to my resolve to go to Edinburgh. One thing, I had written giving my promise to be there on a certain day. Seeing this, one of the best of my country friends, with a little pawky humour twinkling in his eye, venturing to predict the result of my resolve, said:

"Well, if we are spared so long, we'll see you after you are perfect. I think you'll be very much as you are. But God go with you and in that case you'll get some good. *He* is the perfect one. My own private opinion is this: Your going to a Normal Institution to learn the art of teaching, reminds me of the saying about taking coals to Newcastle."

However, we parted, and before many days passed, I found myself a student at the Castle Hill Normal Institution for Teachers. I had been informed that whilst studying and practising the art of teaching, I would also be otherwise advanced in "the Classics." Another inducement pressed upon me was my chances of obtaining a high salaried school.

All this was tempting and I paid the money willingly; but it was not realised, save in the matter of the Classics—Latin, Greek, and Mathematics. As for the new light, in regard to the art of teaching, it never shone on me. The system—if there was any system—was very like what was too general. In my humble opinion it was wrong at the very foundation. Its essence was *force* not *love*.

The chances of being appointed to a school soon vanished when I was distinctly told I must first become a member of the Established Church. I do not say this was wrong, but I thought it would have been wrong *on my part* to leave the denomination to which I belonged merely for the sake of obtaining a more comfortable living in a high salaried school. All along I have been friendly with all the churches; but I had, and still have, my own mind to consult in this matter, while wishing every one to do the same.

However, I made the most of my mistake, by remaining the full time arranged for, and obtaining as much learning as the Institution could furnish—the L.G.M. were specially good.

At this time, too, I thought of a promise I made some time before. In the earliest time of my "Battles to Learn," I felt a great difficulty in understanding the "English Grammar without a teacher." Then I said, "If ever I am able to help others in this matter, I shall try." "The New Writer" was the result, and I have good reason to believe it proved to be useful. At all events it soon passed through several editions, and that is pleasing to an author, particularly in regard to first efforts.

Return to Smith-field.

Had my friend the village shoemaker seen me after I left the Institution, he would have given vent to a little of his dry and sly humour, at my expense, about becoming perfect in my calling and carrrying coals to Newcastle. The worst of it was, my savings had almost disappeared. And hence the important question, How may I add to my fast diminishing store? And strange to say, unknown to me, an answer was being prepared by others.

My Dundee friends, round the scene of the first three years of my life as a public teacher, had kept in mind my promise that I might return *if a favourable opportunity presented itself.* To the invitation to come back to my old locality, I said "Yes," and was soon surrounded by many of my former pupils, as much at home as before.

But, to our joy, before six months had passed, the premises which had been rented for me in which to hold my classes were too small. Larger premises were obtained, but before another six months were ended they were overcrowded. Once more my health failed by overwork, and again, I had to resign.

Now, however, I had two strings to my bow. Teaching, under these circumstances, had disabled me, so I thought of the drug business, and built a splendid castle—*in the air.* Of course, the absurdity of drugs yielding a profit of $11\frac{3}{4}$d. a shilling did not enter my mind; but I could look forward to the comparative leisure as likely to give a renewal of my former strength. I also hoped soon to save cash enough to give me the full advantage of a University training for the Ministry.

Two strings to my bow.

Having rented premises for house and shop, I handed over the responsibilities of housekeeping to my sister, and that was so much gain for her. Knowing that business does not grow in a night, I was content to wait, and while waiting, almost resting, I grew stronger. However, some of my friends seemed unwilling that I should have this comparative rest for any length of time. Two or three of the heads of families called to say their daughters were no longer inclined to go to a public school, but would be glad if I would, as a Tutor, spare an hour or so, on certain days of the week—an hour with one family, an hour with the next, and so on as my business would permit. To this I readily consented; and to help the arrangement to work all the better, I took my father from his loom to the shop. He liked to have something to do, and he had things much as he wished; but his chief duty was to tell any customer who might call, the time when I was likely to be present.

I succeeded beyond expectation, removed to more central premises, and again succeeded, but in the end various incidents combined to lead to new arrangements. My father became very ill and unable to take his wonted place, and an assistant had to be engaged. I had to attend more closely to the business, and give up the most of my private pupils. My sister got married, and I went into lodgings. Still prosperity attended my efforts.

There was no dwelling-house connected with the shop, but there was a back parlour, the upper part of the door of which was glass. When all the necessary work was done, and the customers all gone for the time, I entered the parlour and followed out my studies. These were more frequently interrupted than I desired by the passing calls of friends, not always on business. They were medical friends, political friends, literary friends, and friends of all kinds. Some came to have a "chat." One was Mr. Campbell, English teacher in the Seminary, and author of several popular school books. One day he found me looking over some MSS. in verse, which were very difficult to read, being badly written, on bad paper, with bad ink. He offered to help me. Several days passed before the task of deciphering and transcribing was accomplished. He selected forty pieces from the bundle as the best. "My Juvenile Wailings," was the title he suggested, assuring me they would bring me fame and fortune. He was quite in love with what he called "the sweet simplicity and child-heartedness." Some time after, my attention was called to an article entitled, "Another Scotch Poet." But the piece entitled

"My Mammy's awa'," was the only one which saw the light of day, and for this reason :

One day I was reading the MSS. of the forty pieces transcribed in a MS. book. A customer came in. I laid the book on the counter. Other customers came in. When all were served, I found my book had disappeared. I have never heard of it since. I confess the loss cost me several nights' sleep. Whether I was like the lover who would not court again, or whether the Muses refused to have my company, because of this act of seeming carelessness, I cannot tell, but I have disappointed my appreciative friends as to being the other " Scottish Poet."

CHAPTER XV.—ANOTHER ROUND OF EVENTS.

THE shop parlour became otherwise useful. When the assistant became better acquainted with the business, I had more time for retirement and study. Of course, I had frequent interruptions, but those of a business nature were always welcome. There were others not business in the strict sense, and some of them were made welcome because each one became more pleasant than another.

Auntie Maggie again.

Auntie Maggie's parents had retired to a quiet retreat in Lochee. She was with them, and there I occasionally spent an evening. Sometimes I also went in the morning before business hours *to get a bouquet* for this same back parlour. When I did not call she would kindly bring one in the course of the day. Naturally, she needed a rest. At least, I thought so, and my wish was kindly complied with. But I would have been reluctant to call this an interruption; it was an exhilaration which I longed for.

The flower was ever welcome for its own sake, but certainly not more so than the giver, who herself was so sweetly pretty, that she in my eyes, was "prettier than a picture." But *we* had unwelcome interruptions occasionally. Still *she* was wise enough to know I might be soon and often called to the counter. She did not seem to mind, only smiled. Time after time she became more and more freed from that kind of feeling which forces one not to move about. It seemed strange, that so sure as she called extra people flocked in for prescriptions and medicines of a kind requiring preparation. Nevertheless I was careful to make no mistakes, and that was something. And, to my comfort, when I returned to her I found that she too had been active. Everything in the little room was pointedly clean and neatly put in order.

My writings were carefully assorted and put at the proper end of the table. My books were also put upon the shelves. And yet there she was waiting for me as if nothing had been done—with this exception, her gloves were off, and I liked that all the better—a hand is better than a glove any day.

This suggested a new thought. One which many lovers forget till too late: It is pleasant to be near *one who has hands as well as a heart*. So I thought, and was almost saying what was in my mind. The heart spoke, but at this time I prevented the tongue from expressing my wish.

I liked the drug business very much. It gave me an insight into life which I could not have obtained otherwise. Still I looked on it as a means to an end—as a stepping stone to the Gospel Ministry in a financial sense. And all along the line this was in view. I had often said, to this end everything must give way. So I remained a philosopher, as I thought, for a day or two more—till I went for another flower. After that I would be all poetry. In my mind I would compose melting letters, but they were not written; and arrange eloquent speeches which were never delivered. And, again, settle down till another bouquet was brought. After this I found myself asking, "Lodgings, how much do they cost? Attention, how indifferent! Respect, how cold! Meals, who can eat them without some one to share them? What might love and inspiration not do?"

In a day or two more I came to the conclusion that whatever advantages there may be in a single life, they are merely negative. In married life, when all is right on both sides, all is positive—positive blessings—and these may help in regard to the attainment of my life-aim.

Thus love and philosophy, heart and mind, mind and heart, kept me thinking until I must have been thinking aloud in her presence. The end of it was that on the 24th of November, 1852, our destinies were united in holy wedlock. And a blessed day that was for me.

We set sail in fine weather, with all the prospects of a prosperous voyage. Our congratulations, from public and private sources, were many and hearty. Matters went on very much as we could have wished. Happy in each other, and thankful to God for each other, we were at peace with all around. We were also glad the desire to be as helpful as possible to others remained with us. But little did we know we were to specially experience the "suffering of service" so soon. *The suffering of service.*

After our marriage we went to Broughty Ferry, a prosperous watering place about four miles east of Dundee. There all things soon bespoke increasing success in the drug business. The friends of the poor as well as the poor themselves sought our help. Amongst the former of the good workers, was the late Dr. Dick, the well-known author of "The Christian Philosopher." The friendship of this good man was truly worth having, and this favour we enjoyed as long as he lived.

But the time came when we found that we had enemies as well as friends. As to details here they would do no good, and might injure those—or the offspring of those—who injured us. I may simply say, so successful was the intrigue, so suddenly was our prosperity checked, and so completely was our financial ruin wrought, that, with the poet, we might have said:

> " All were ours ;
> He counted them at break of day ;
> And, when the sun set, where were they ? "

Where are they who will not swerve from the rectitude which stamps the life of the upright?—who are true to the erring poor?—who refuse to co-operate in evil with the hypocrites?—where are such without enemies?—without experiencing, more or less, as we did, *the suffering of service?*

But our heavenly Father remained with us, our God and Guide. By means we could not have thought of, we soon found ourselves installed in Gaulswell School, *At Gaulswell School.*

under the kindly patronage of the late Sir James Ramsay, Bart., Banff House, near Alyth, Perthshire.

Being happy in God and in each other, we had no difficulty in setting about to make the best of our altered circumstances. Life in the school was new to "Maggie," but I was in my natural element. At first my new charge were strangers to my mode of teaching and training, but they soon felt at home and delighted. The income was small, but the work was light and our wants were few. The children took home such reports as induced their elder sisters and brothers to become pupils.

In due course, I also opened a Sunday School. It, too, was well encouraged. The people—adults as well as children—came long distances to it. The next step was the establishment of a "Mutual Loan Library," to the delight of all around. This was followed by the delivery of a course of popular lectures during the moonlight nights of every month. My subjects included those on which I spoke first at Smithfield Academy. In this, Sir James took a special interest, giving me the advantage of his ample library. This was helpful, for, would you believe it? at this time I had not a book left, all were gone, so complete had been the wreck. The late Professor Ramsay also called occasionally, congratulating all concerned, while Sir James would call special attention to what he called "Mrs. Hillocks' Little Palace," meaning the School-House—"A palace inside as well as outside," he would say, referring to the cleanliness as well as the tidiness seen in the arrangement. Nor did he forget the jug at the well, placed there by her that the wayfarer might drink of the cool pure spring, and be refreshed—as cool in the heat of summer as in the dead of winter.

Our first-born. Whatever we may remember in connection with our labours and our joys on Banff House estate, one event stands out above the rest, the birth of our first child and "only son," a sweet rose with all its sweetest leaves unfolded.

"It is well with the child," said the nurse, and we were glad.

"This is no ordinary child," she added impressively, but we had heard that every first-born was far from being a common child. We had heard and read much about first babies, but now we realised the inexpressible feeling. And then our boy was lovely in the eyes of others as well as his parents. Scholar after scholar pleaded to see "the young prince"—a name given to him because he was born in "the little palace." His soft-dimpled cheeks, when aglow with the holy smile of infancy, seemed too angelic for earth, and hence his other name, "the angel baby." As I looked and loved I found myself exclaiming,

> "My precious child!
> A joy thou bring'st, but, mixed with trembling,
>   Anxious joy and tender fears,
> Pleasing hopes and mingled sorrows,
>   Smiles of transport dashed with tears."

Like all those who become real mothers, this new mother always had a weakness for babies. I have known her stop mothers on the street to look at and admire their children. "How lovely! how heavenly!" she would say. But now in her own boy her joy was unbounded, as he tenderly touched her heart and silently spoke to her soul, with a wistful tenderness in his black eyes, beaming out from between the open eyelids and silken fringe. But the time came when she refused to look upon her baby boy. She had fevered, and became insensible for weeks. Grave doubts were entertained of her recovery. My fear increased lest our boy might become what I had been—a motherless child. But to the joy of all who knew us, it was not to be. She at last recovered, and life, in the school and at the hearth, went on much as before. Our joys increased because we felt this new domestic tie was binding us even closer than before.

The brave Tar goes aloft.

One cometh, another goeth. Life here, death there. So we found. Whilst we were rejoicing in our baby boy, our delight was greatly overshadowed by intelligence from Dundee, of the near approach of the death of my father. And in the message summoning us to the death-bed, there was the statement that the sailor-weaver had something specially to say to us, he was also anxious to see our boy.

"I am happy in Jesus," said the old Tar, anxious to console the weeping ones, for we were all gathered round his bed.

"That is right and joyous," I said, constrained to gently pat the cold cheek of my dying sire, aged by poverty more than years.

"Yes, yes," chimed the young mother, still weak but anxious to do her duty to one whom she loved.

"There now, father," she added, having smoothed the pillow and laid the aching head gently down.

"All right," he said a little after, "I'll soon be aloft, God bless you all."

After a little he continued, "God bless the dear boy, and both of you. May he be as great a blessing to you as you have been to me."

He died, and we were thankful to be able to do a son's part to a suffering father—suffering from honest poverty, for his was never self-inflicted.

I thought—and I confess there was a tinge of bitterness in the thought—how many such brave-hearted men are left to live without some acknowledgment of daring deeds on behalf of a great and wealthy nation. I could not help remembering that he had been foremost among those who had fought our nation's battles and won our national victories, yet left to starve, while others, who did no more, perhaps not so much, knew not how to waste the wealth thrust upon them. But then the gall in this strain of thought was partly extracted by the thought of the kind ways of God—how He had inspired and otherwise assisted the good man to give me my first few weeks' schooling. And how God in His providence so blessed that effort that I was again able to help to smooth the way to the grave.

Going whither we knew not.

Our efforts at Gaulswell school were regarded as special and popular, not only by almost all who were immediately concerned, but also by newspaper correspondents, particularly by the talented representative of the *Dundee Advertiser*. And, no doubt, this was how school committees and others interested in education came to know of me, and began to correspond with me, asking my services. One of my correspondents addressed his letter from " The Manse, Muirton, Laurencekirk." I knew the latter place was some way between us and Aberdeen, but " Muirton " I was at a loss to know. However, the offer he made seemed to be a good one. That is, better than the situation I held—more work and more income. The first I was able for, and the second I required. Hence I consented to go whither I did not know.

However, the Chairman of the School Committee was waiting at the place appointed. We had some distance to walk through a wood. Then we came to the foot of what was called " The Street," at the top of which stood a crowd, which had gathered to welcome us to our new sphere of labour. When we came in view, their shouts of welcome were hearty and joyous. Imagine my surprise when I found that this was no other than the same Luthermuir where I had been as a tramp.

This is the explanation. Laurencekirk was the post town for Luthermuir and surrounding places. Muirton was the name of a farm in Luthermuir. The church and the manse, the school and schoolhouse, were built upon a corner of that farm. Hence the address was quite correct. I knew what was, but I did not know what might have been. But if I may judge from my thoughts when I found where we were, I do not think I would have gone had Luthermuir been mentioned in the letter. Indeed, my first thoughts were to turn back. I felt it would be wrong to take a young wife and a dear baby to the Luthermuir I knew. But second thoughts came and I asked,

"Is not the providence of God in this?"

"Certainly," said Maggie. "We have been brought here for some good purpose, and God will help us."

At this time, in this place, there were some who were very bad, and more who were far from being good. The vast majority were non-church-goers, and these, at least, were admittedly in want of spiritual help—help for spirit and soul and body. The church-goers had "ministers," but the people had no "pastor," no guide. At once, it entered my mind that God had been training me for the work now to hand. I knew also that He had also given me the very helpmeet required.

Work in "the Muir." We settled down, and events proved we did well, from the point of helpfulness, a quality much required at the time, and pleasing to us.

The hearty welcome was immediately followed by the good offices of the farmers' wives and other ladies who soon put our house in order. On Sunday our arrival was duly announced from the pulpit, with many kind words of hearty appreciation. On the following Monday, the school was opened. The pupils were few, and the fees were small, but I was assured the number would soon increase, so we took heart and pressed on.

Of course, we missed Banff-House, and Sir James' splendid library. We also remembered the genial friendship of the parents and other friends we had just left. But this loss was, in a measure, made up by the hearty friendship of our new minister, and new friends; and besides, by hard labour out of the school, as well as in it, we were able, in various ways, to help the people, including those who, under God, saved my life by kindly help, when there years before in search of work. From the first, it was evident that nothing could be financially darker. The promised salary was small, and, worse still, the school was at a very low ebb. But it was also evident that no better field of usefulness could be presented to willing workers. And, to help all concerned, things soon began to look up. Before the end of the first year, the time for which I was engaged, the school increased in numbers and standing,

Because of this, I was all the more easily induced to enter upon another engagement, an addition to my salary was promised. Though my first aim was to keep up the school to the efficiency it had now attained, yet I continued in various ways to be otherwise helpful. For a time small-pox raged fearfully: and this was soon followed by cholera in all its terrible forms. As is always the case, the poor were the greatest victims, and this induced us to be all the more active. The neighbouring doctors not being able to overtake and check the suffering, my past experience and what knowledge, in the healing art, I had stored up in Kirriemuir, Dundee and Edinburgh, were put to the test.

As soon as a change for the better was brought about, I called the attention of the people to the fact that pre-vention was better than cure. This was done in a series of gratis lectures on health; another series on religion, and another on kindred topics. *The danger of becoming too popular.* But whilst all was now going on pleasantly, an evil spirit entered where least looked for. Whether in the form of envy or jealousy, I cannot say.

From the first, I was popular. Perhaps the touch of romance hovering round my twofold visit to "The Muir" led to this: but it was gradually increased by every effort I made for the good of *all* the people. But whatever the cause, evil not only entered but conquered to the regret of many, myself included. These popular lectures became as the last straw that broke the camel's back. They were regarded as "too much of a good thing;" and I was astonished when requested not to continue them.

Having pointedly put the question, if any fault was found with me as a teacher, and the answer being, "No, none whatever," I yielded the lecturing point as soon as the course on hand was finished, but continued my visits among the people. In time, however, I found that underhand efforts were being made to try to mar, if not to undermine, my usefulness. Being anxious to avoid contention, I resigned.

This surprised the sorrowing people, who pleaded that I should withdraw my resignation. But I felt my duty was to adhere to it. I was invited to a meeting, the object of which was to present me with a valedictory address as a token of gratitude. The following paragraph gives an indication of that address:—

"We need not particularise the various offices which you have filled since you came here. All who have witnessed the zealous manner in which you have performed your arduous and philanthropic duties know that your great efforts have been worthy of your generous heart. The manifest good which has been effected has been graciously blessed by our heavenly Father, and now stirs a deep sense of the gratitude and lasting affection in us towards you and yours."

The whole of the address was warmly endorsed by the press, particularly in Montrose, pointing out the good done during this stay in Luthermuir. To me, this was all naturally pleasant, and all the more so that gratitude to God for His help gladdened my heart. For I knew whatever of good came to pass, came because of the goodness of God. The obstacles to advancement were many, in some cases almost overwhelming; but, by the power of God, through human instrumentality, the drunkards became sober, the Christless were led to Christ.

Speaking for ourselves, I may say, though we did not succeed from a money point of view, yet we were cheered by the fact that not a day passed, from the time we went there, till our departure, without some immediate good to one or more. As for what followed, that is only fully known to God. But I may say that two of my Muirton-school scholars became ministers of the Gospel. One in the United Presbyterian Church, and one in the Free Church.

Chapter XVI.—More Turning Points.

SURELY I must have erred in some way or other. Those most in need of me rejoiced in my efforts on their behalf, but somehow or other there was always some one or more who did not like "this sort of thing." At all events, whoever was to blame—my opponents or myself—I suffered and so did those whom God had given to help in the good work of considering the poor. *The twofold string again.*

From Luthermuir to Dundee we were followed by many expressions of good will from the most of the well-to-do as well as the poor—from all who approved of helping the poor to help themselves. But pleasant as this was, it did not alter these two stern facts—that in Dundee I knew not of any opening for a school, and that there was no opening for a chemist. What was to be done? Stand still, we could not. An opening of some kind must be made, but how? Every day lessened our little store.

I found, to be let, a good shop in a good building at the West End, the Perth Road. The premises were handsome and capable of being made into a dwelling house as well as a public shop.

"In that case," said Maggie, "we could rough it without any one being aware of our circumstances, *if only we had a start.*"

This was a valuable clue. It meant that being private in our way, we could pinch ourselves, and so enhance the needed display in the shop, the better the appearance in the shop, we were the more likely to get on. Both of us were willing to begin life anew as it were. And after overcoming quite a round of difficulties, we opened business here, after a manner. She became a double partner—a partner in life, and an active partner in the shop. At the practical suggestion of a friend, we added stationery to the drugs, and in this department she became specially useful, and an apt pupil in other respects. She was first-rate at turning "the best side to London." Frequently, at night, after the shop was shut, we would clean and polish, turn and overturn, place and replace the articles in the window, on the counter and the shelves. Next morning the aspect of the shop would be so improved that it looked like a new opening, and as if more pleasantly inviting.

"With more money this business would soon become a paying concern," we would often say to one another, half encouraged and half desponding.

We encouraged each other. But I thought of a plan by which to save the steed while the grass was growing, by opening a school at the West Port. This was how we managed—taking a lesson from my efforts at Kirriemuir:—

In the morning—we had to start early in the morning—I put all things in order, and supplied my customers with medicine—those of them who came to know that the morning was the best time to call. I also assisted a little in the same during the midday interval. After the school closed in the afternoon, I gave my whole time to the business.

By means of what we could spare from the school-fees we added to the stock, and this, in turn, increased the number of our customers—some of the new ones could spend a shilling or two as readily as others could a few pence. I was also enabled to relieve Maggie by having a maid to care for the children and become otherwise helpful.

This success also enabled us to renew our efforts to help those *A stimulating incident.* in need of help, material and spiritual. Then, as now, to its credit, Dundee had much to do in Missionary and Temperance Work. And those who were trained for such were often urged to take a part in them. It was so with me. And whether taken up with my classes or with business, I tried to spare some time to be as helpful as possible. This was so even when time was short, and I felt fatigued.

One night I was asked to speak at a Mission Meeting not far

from our place of business. My heart being in such work, and having had considerable practice, I felt quite at home—in more senses than one. I stopped all of a sudden. Was this stop the want of preparation? It was not. From the beginning I held it to be my duty to God and man to prepare with care. The truth is, while speaking to the people my memory was speaking to me so forcibly that I had to pause and listen. Emotion choked my utterance. I had to explain. The fact was I found myself standing just where my *pirn*-wheel stood when winding for my father, years before. What had been my father's loom-shop was converted into a Mission room.

Applause followed my explanation. Evidently the incident was looked upon as a triumph of its kind. And let me confess I was moved by the same feeling. It filled me still more with bounding gratitude to God. As I was about to proceed with my discourse, I said to myself, "After this, what may not be?"

Something has been done in Dundee to remind the rising generation of the names and efforts of her good men and great events. And in the Perth Road such memorials have not been forgotten. Of such we have two worthy of note, "the Tree of Liberty, and the M'Cheyne Memorial Church." And this church had its rise in the Mission efforts just referred to. It was worth returning to Dundee to receive the stimulating influence which sprung from that pleasing incident.

In itself this incident was very simple but very effective, not only then but since. It really awakened new faith and enlivened our hope, giving fresh vigour to all we did. *Editing under difficulties.* Pleasant as all this was, the time came when we were reminded that we were not made of cast-iron. The country air at Banff House and Luthermuir had made me remarkably strong, and yet I began to feel the strain of this heavy work—physical as well as mental. But the test told more severely on the health of my helpmeet; and this led me to think about the best way of relieving her of some of her responsibilities.

About this time a proprietor of a Dundee weekly newspaper called and expressed his desire to secure my services as Editor.

We had been discussing whether the school or the shop should be given up. This visit put a new factor in the case, and led me to give up the school, to retain the business and get an assistant—the pay offered for the editorship being such as to warrant this arrangement. Indeed, the offer made to me by this gentleman, his general bearing and agreeable profession in regard to truth and right, were such that I consented to accept the chair—rather the right to sit in it.

According to the agreement, I had to be in the office not more than three days a week, from 10 a.m. to 4 p.m.; save on Friday, when I had to remain till Saturday morning, to revise the final proofs. As far as I could see, the change from the school to the editor's chair was an improvement. One thing, I had more time for the shop, and Maggie recovered in two or three weeks her wonted health.

"Very promising this," she said when she received the first month's salary.

And so it was. But soon after more time than was agreed for was required from me. An explanation being given, I did not object, for, up to this time, and a little after, the work was congenial and I was happy in it. However, before the end of the second month my eyes began to open a little. And at last I experienced some of the feelings which come with a sense of being unequally yoked. The proprietor—the "governor," as some of his fast companions called him—was not what I and most of the general public thought he was, far from being what he professed to me to be. A *promise* of payment was all I got for my second month's salary. But hoping almost against hope, I continued my increasing duties—increasing because of the proprietor's frequent and lengthening absence, and because he was also a jobbing printer, with which I had to become acquainted in order to be able to advise the foreman.

From the beginning, and on all occasions, my resolution was whatever came from my pen should be (what has been said of it) "distinguished by a pure and high tone of morality." But imagine my sorrow when, in spite of my repeated remonstrances, the paper occasionally assumed a scurrilous character—paragraphs, and even articles being inserted after the paper in its complete form had passed through my hands to the press, and a clean proof copy given to me before I left for home. Again and again I threatened to resign because of this; but appeals to remain, accompanied with promises that the like should not again happen, made me keep on too long. The arduous and trying nature of my labour did not lessen my enthusiasm. At last, finding it impossible to fight longer against the stream, I resigned.

As was expected by those who knew how matters stood, the firm went to the wall soon after I left the office. The trustee of estate paid me the second month's salary, but for all the rest due to me I had threepence in the pound. To us this was trying financially, but I was glad to get off in this way.

Still the sad effects of this loss were very depressing. I felt something like despair creeping over me; but when I was weak Maggie was strong, and both of us felt *Some sad effects.* that we were on the right side, though it might be the losing side, as it was. Getting to Edinburgh and advancing to the Gospel ministry seemed to be less likely than ever. We were once more thrown upon the shop profits, and had again to resort to roughing it in matters domestic; but this did not trouble us so much as the thought that some business debts had been contracted in the hope of meeting them by means of the expected salary. Threepence in the pound was as nothing. So I endeavoured to gather in some outstanding debts due to me. I got promises, accompanied with regrets, but no cash.

These distressing incidents, the desire to overcome the difficulties, brought to my mind the fact that I had been much sought after as a *gratis* speaker, and hence I set about preparing some special lectures in the hope of being paid for their delivery. The first three were on Mrs. Hemans: (1) as a daughter; (2) as a mother; and (3) as a poet. They were meant for Literary Societies. These were followed by other biographical lectures, such as, "Sir William Wallace—Lessons from his Life and Times," "Robert Burns as a Poet and a Teacher." Moral, social, and religious subjects next gained my attention. I had some engagements, but not so many as I expected, reasoning from the "loud applause," and hearty votes of thanks which I received for my *gratis* lectures. But the local and metropolitan press spoke very favourably of my lectures, and this brought back the hope of ultimately getting to Edinburgh, and perhaps to college.

I allowed such thoughts to cross my mind now and then because we had now come to the resolution to dispose of the business as soon as possible. Thus I built my castle (in the air). It was beautiful, but it was scattered to the winds.

Yes, " to the winds "—in this way: Notwithstanding our efforts and thrift and self-denial we found that by means of the business alone we could not get both ends to meet. Occasionally I went to lecture beyond Dundee. To the ill-disposed, and one or two whose wish was father to the thought—my absence gave a pretext for their circulating a rumour that I was to give up business at once. This was taken up and retailed by others, who knew of my losses. Little did they know the evils about to flow from their gossip.

This gossip came to my ears in Edinburgh, for I had been lecturing in Leith. As soon as my arrangements were completed, I returned home, and took the advice of those to whom I owed an account however small. I was able to show a balance in my favour after settling all, if I could get what was due to me. This I vainly tried to obtain. Hence I had no alternative but to return to my few creditors making two offers—either to take the business and make the most of it, or to accept my assurance that I would pay all as soon as possible. The latter course was preferred, but several years elapsed before I was able to fulfil my promise.

CHAPTER XVII.—ALMOST LOST IN EDINBURGH.

WE left Dundee for Edinburgh. There were five of us then. *Too little to be a policeman.* The mother, still far above rubies; three of the most precious children we ever saw—George and Aggie and Maggie. In one sense I was poor; in another I was rich. And, best of all, God was with us. Why should I give way now? We were crushed, there is no denying it; but we had learned to struggle, looking up. What had our Heavenly Father not done for us before now. He was the same in love and mercy, in pity and power. In the meantime we thought the Divine Hand pointed to the Scottish Capital, but were willing to go wherever Providence was pleased to direct, to will and do of His good pleasure.

What darkened our prospects very much was the fact that the Lecturing Season was drawing to a close, and every programme was complete. I had some promises for the next season, but that did not meet the present wants. O, dear no. However, I was willing to do anything in an honest way. Congenial, if possible. That at first I tried to obtain, but at first "unsuccessful" was stamped on every effort. Give up? No. What then? Persevere.

By advice, I betook myself to the columns of the *North British Advertiser*, exhibited in a large window at George IV. Bridge, and fixed my eyes on the column headed "Wanted"—being willing to be a *light porter*, even to carry *heavy burdens*. Morning after morning I scanned this newspaper.

At last, I down with an address, and up went my hopes. Next day, I saw the gentleman in want of the services specified. At once—and as I thought, abruptly—he manifested a desire not to listen to me, sharply saying there were too many applicants, and that he had not time to listen to the half of them. But the pressure at home urged me to call again. Believing that the office to be filled required a trustworthy person, I offered references as to character. They were, as he said, all he could wish; but he added, "You cannot perform the duties; *you* cannot answer *my* purpose."

Seeing he was so emphatic, I thought there must be some mistake, and said so, as I followed him determined to know what it was. Getting his ear, I told him I could write, showing him my note book.

"I know something of business, and have an unstained character, as to honesty and energy. What more is needed?"

This little speech, delivered with much energy, only brought from him these words; "I know all that, but *you* are not *the person* for *me*."

Again he left, and again I followed, saying, "Excuse me, sir, but tell me why."

"I'd rather not," was the reply.

"Perhaps you will," I urged.

"Well, if you must have it," he said, and then, pausing for a time, added, "*You are too little.*"

This shut me up. Under the pressure of want, I was willing to do anything possible, if honest and honourable, but to add to my stature was more than I could do. "Too little," said I to myself, "the man is crazy." But he was right. What he wanted was a man mighty in stature, to wear a long overcoat mounted with clear buttons, and able to wield a large cudgel—a man to stand at a bazaar door to frighten mischievous boys away. Truly I was not the person for him, being *too little to be a policeman.*

When I left him, I laughed right out. It must have been a wild laugh, seasoned with frenzy. The need at home and the disappointment made me nearly mad. It was one of my darkest hours before the dawn, for, after this, things began to brighten a bit.

A little run of success.
When I went to Edinburgh this time I was favoured with some notes of introduction to men moving in literary circles. But it is generally some time before such

well-meant notes become helpful. People must have time to think, and work of that kind is not always waiting a stranger.

Alexander Smith, the poet, was one of those to whom I was introduced, and I had reason to rejoice in his friendship long after, till he died.

The Brothers Gorie may also be named here. Through them I had some literary work in connection with the *Edinburgh News*, a popular newspaper.

This was a beginning though I had nothing steady till my services were required by the late Mr. Mathers, then an enterprising and prosperous newsagent at "The Box"—on the site where the Post Office now stands. He was also the proprietor and publisher of the "Scottish Time Table." It was for this publication I was engaged for three and sometimes four days a week. At first I found this to be "dry work"—perhaps drier than the woman found the reading of the dictionary to be when she lost the thread of the story. But it led to other things, such as writing the brief sketches of the leading places named in the time table. I also assisted in the preparation of the "Guide to Edinburgh," published by him.

Another help was Burns' Centenary. On every newspaper the staff of reporters was increased, and I was taken on. And besides reporting, I had to dress up the reports sent from the country. This was a nice thing for the newspapers, and it was good for us, especially for me. First there were the preparations making for the festival, and these had all to be duly described, and then the reporting, and generally the condensing of the speeches delivered at the various assemblies.

It so happened at that time that Mr. Mathers was able to spare me for an hour or two each day. Knowing what had been, he was willing that I should have the benefit of this windfall as fully as possible. We were glad and grateful.

A lecture making friends. This making hay while the sun shone not only enabled us to leave lodgings and get into a house of our own near to the College, by it we were also led to rejoice in the pleasures of hope once more. The goal appeared as if nearer.

And not long after this busy time I was occasionally asked to deliver a lecture—not that they were always paid lectures—indeed, I found in Edinburgh, as in Dundee, the demand for *gratis* lectures was greater than for those for which a fee was paid. But one of my lectures became useful to me at the time of delivery, and in several ways after—I refer to the lecture entitled, "Burns as a Poet and a Teacher." It was favourably noticed by the press, particularly by the Edinburgh *Witness* newspaper then conducted by Hugh Miller. This brought me in friendly contact with this able Editor and his partner, Mr. Fairley.

Notices of this lecture also called the attention of the Publishers, Messrs. Johnston and Hunter, to me—renewing the mutual kindly feeling manifested when I was the struggling student in this city. This meeting was timely for I was then discussing with myself the acceptance or rejection of a literary offer. The advice was readily and emphatically given. I acted accordingly, and events proved that in not accepting the offer I was wisely advised.

And sometime after the Editor of the *Christian Treasury* changed hands. To sustain that publication more help was required. An offer was made to me. I readily accepted it, and did my best. The work was congenial and the publishers were honourable.

Now I saw, or thought I saw, the possibility of attending to my studies, and finishing the prescribed classes. I also tried to spare a little time, especially during the evenings, for labours of love. One form of these efforts was the delivery of popular lectures, composed expressly to meet the capacities and wants of the poorer classes of Edinburgh and Leith. It was delightful to see how earnestly they seemed to take in what was laid before them. These lectures were also attended by the various committees and their friends, still my chief effort was to be simple and clear for the poor, rather than grand or eloquent for the more cultivated. This was specially so in regard to the last course I delivered at that time. The title was "Home, its Ties and Duties."

In such efforts to reach and raise the poor I became more and more enthusiastic. In this there would not have been any harm, had I not forgotten myself so much as to go too far beyond my strength. But this I did, and paid severely for it. Once more I was arrested, this time by a most dangerous attack of typhus fever which proved to be almost fatal. *Nigh unto death.*

Though this fever came of infection, caught when visiting, the doctor declared that the physical exhaustion caused by overwork, had greatly added to the danger.

Much of what came to pass, I knew not, being so long and completely unconscious But my heart and pen would fail to describe what I was told of the hardships and sufferings that followed. We were not only overthrown, but overwhelmed. This, however, may be said, that never were the affection and strength of my helpmeet more severely tested—all the past included—and never did she manifest more of the faith that soothes in sorrow, and fortifies for the battle of life. Dangerous as the fever was, she still entertained the hope that I would "come through," even when good Dr. Menzies had serious doubts. Long, long did she wait and watch night and day, for there were none to help her.

At last, one day the doctor's fine countenance brightened. He hoped, and he expressed the hope, that I had passed out of danger. This was good news to the nurse-mother. This precious gem was grateful even for the signs of recovery, a very slow recovery.

These signs had not long manifested themselves when my faithful nurse broke down, so much so that she could not walk from the bed to the door of the room without leaning with her hands against the table or a chair. Her illness increased until both of us became almost equally helpless. *My helpmeet almost helpless.*

As you know, we had suffered terribly before; and I may add our sufferings had been more than pen could describe, but the darkest shadows of grief had never been so fearfully sad. We had known all about the sinking, sickening, crushing, deadly forces of poverty, even the sting that comes with the sudden transition from comparative prosperity to the keenest of penury—but nothing like this. Till now one of us was, in a measure, able to help the other. Before this, intrigue, envy, and jealousy had each in turn brought calamity after calamity upon us; but not so this time. If fault there was anywhere, it lay at my door, in yielding to my desire to do as much good as possible, and to those most in want of it. True, I was urged on to this work of faith, and cheered by hearty applause, but past experience ought to have taught me to pause in time. True, almost all who knew me when well and working, failed now to think of me and mine, but then the fever was so dangerous that the doctor ordered none to come near unless to help. Perhaps a little real sympathy at this time would have been worth a thousand votes of thanks, but then I was no longer able to give the *gratis* lectures and other kindred assistance, which helped to brighten the reports. At all events, all—save our good physician and our kind minister—forgot we were still in the land of the living.

A convalescent home in the Grand City.

But the cup of our affliction was not yet quite filled to the brim. Here I would willingly let the curtain fall, were it not that I believe you are asking what more?

For long, all sources of income had been dried up for the reason just indicated. And our little savings—even that set apart for educational purposes—had gone, books and all. Because of this and our dark prospects, we sought a cheaper rented house, rather than go into debt. None of us were able to go for a house hunting, so we took one without seeing it, in the Potter Row. And this became our convalescent home for a time.

In Scotland there is much for all the nations to praise, much that is inspiring. She has her pure and simple, healthy ways.

Potter Row Ruins, Edinburgh.

Hence she is great in bodily strength and mental power, together with the capability of enduring hardships. But those who know life there, are aware that there is also much to make quite another picture. Proud Caledonia has her social wrongs—her drinking habits, and poisonous cesspools—much that is not only unhealthy, not only depressing, but also degrading. And the natural tendency, the almost certain tendency of all this, is to make some of the men and women unworthy of her name. The Scotch, like other people, are not beyond human frailties. And all round, particularly in her large cities, the causes of degradation are many and deep. Districts not a few are overrun with corruption, physical and moral. Even Edinburgh is not free from such. This city, like most of great cities, had two aspects—one grand and beautiful, the other quite the reverse, where distress is generally followed by degradation.

Yes, the Modern Athens has her Cowgate as well as her Princes Street, the Potter Row, as well as Heriot Row. I may be told, as we sometimes read, that Potter-Row has been "an ancient aristocratic locality;" that so late as 1716, it could boast of being the residence of a live lord; and that the poets Burns and Gray, had been there. This I do not deny, but " for a' that" it was a dirty wretched place when we were under the necessity of making our home there.

That new home was one room, and that a garret, but we were glad of shelter anywhere. Of course, the space was small, but our furniture had to be sold for bread. The walls presented a mass of corruption, but we had plenty of ventilation. Sometimes we saw the hailstones dancing on the rotten floor, and at times the wind would sweep from hole to hole, as if trying to blow out the candle; in this it occasionally succeeded. When we could muster as much as would buy a little coal, our eyes were almost smoked out of our heads. This was our convalescent home in philanthropic Edinburgh; but then there were those in the city who would not have permitted this if they had known of it, and we thought there was a commendable independence in neither saying where we were, nor how we were suffering. So here, again, we were also much to blame; all this told me that one might be lost in Edinburgh even as in London.

Forgetting myself. As you are now aware, before this illness I was well known, and made heartily welcome as a visitor, as well as a speaker. But such is the peculiar constitution of some of the leaders of even good work, that after the heavy and trying and dangerous *gratis* work has ceased, the worker is soon forgotten. Out of sight out of mind. But I fear this is the case, or often the case, with other leaders of good work in other places beside Edinburgh. When good people read the reports of good work, they seldom think of the sacrifice of the real workers—those but for whom the names prefacing the reports would be mere ornaments, as they too often are, but God knows all about it, and the real workers too. To some this thought is a source of consolation. It was so to me, and yet I was so foolish as to forget myself for a time—even to go so far as to find fault with God, as to rebel against what proved to be His kindly leading.

As soon as I was able to get about a little, I tried to get something more to do. One day I had searched as long as my strength permitted. One thing was evidently against me, I was so visibly weak that those on whom I called must have thought the hospital was my best place. Very few spoke to me. Only one or two asked the cause of my weakness. Scarcely able to continue walking, I stood for a time near to the edge of the pavement on the north side of Princes Street. At that time the rich and the gay were about. The grand carriages, splendid horses, with high-headed attendants were dashing along in all their prancing pride.

"Why is this contrast? They so rich, I so poor?" I mentally asked. After a pause, came another question—"Is this just?"

Still the rich throng passed on, and the carriages rolled by in splendour, and my spirit grew more and more rebellious. One carriage stopped close to where I was standing. It was a large one, with tall and richly-attired attendants. One alighted, spoke to the lady; then he left for the shop, but the lady did not follow. There in the carriage she lay, stretched on her back, her head slightly raised, but move she could not.

This led me to think of another contrast this time in my favour, so I thought. True, the lady was rich and I was poor, but I could walk though but feebly. I had just been raised up after an illness all but fatal, but the lady could not rise. Then came the heartfelt sorrow and deep repentance because I had in mind, in effect, allowed myself to charge God with my sufferings, and the suffering of my dear ones. I had forgotten what God had proved, that He is ever near to all His creatures, including the poorest of them; that He is ever waiting to be gracious, being goodness itself.

The lesson was not without good fruit. Our trust in God remained. God-like, He renders good for evil.

Chapter XVIII.—Sowing some Seed.

Found out at last.

Though we suffered much after this, yet the tide seemed to turn from that day. At all events, the flowing mercy of God had freer course. At least so we thought and felt.

One morning we had only three halfpence—no food, no fire. The pangs of hunger had come and gone, and save for our four dear ones, we were willing to die, and should have done so but for a remarkable answer to what we thought was our last cry to our Father in heaven. We spent the night in this state; but next morning we received a letter by post, which had been going a long round, having been sent to the former address. In that letter was a post office order for one pound. We could not understand how the sender had come to know of us, but seeing the money was for us, we looked on it as a God-send, and so it was. We learned all afterwards.

And not long after this we had our first visitor. I mean the first friend who had been successful in his endeavour to find us. I was surprised when, once more, I heard his well-known voice. Though our poverty could not be properly classed with such as is called self-inflicted, we were ashamed of it.

"Good God! is such a man reduced to this?" he asked, as he entered our abode.

The scene was one to be long remembered: The abashed wife and timid children enveloped in smoke. Beside the tall, healthy energetic gentleman, I stood—the pale, thin, trembling invalid. But evident as was the striking difference between our physical condition and social position, in both of us there was the same object, at least so far as the nobler features of humanity were known to us, and felt by us. Both of us desired the glory of God in the elevation of man, and had laboured to this end.

This was our first meeting since we parted on the platform in a public assembly where we were heartily cheered for our speeches.

We had other visitors before, but not of the sympathetic kind, rather the opposite—the "I-must-be-faithful" kind, without heart, if not without head. They called themselves Tract Distributors, and called chiefly on Sundays. With rare exceptions, their one aim—those of them who had an aim—seemed to prove to their own satisfaction that we poor mortals were doubly damned—by God and by them. When I think of this I am tempted to speak strongly. In the meantime, however, I shall only say I pity such visitors. There are many such in our day. They appear to be sincere; and no doubt they think they are serving God by cursing man. But more of this some other time.

Purging Shakespeare. But happily all our visitors were not of this stamp. Not long after we were "found out," a lady called on a week-day. Her presence in our district must have made the Potter Row think of the return of the days of Lord Norton. The carriage rolled up to the narrow, dirty passage which led to our abode. The young lady alighted, and with no ordinary courage entered the passage, passed through the court, and ascended the dark crumbling stairs to our attic. I am not so much concerned because she was a carriage lady as because of what her visit led up to. Much as a lady will do for a bonnet, she will do much more if there is "a bee in her bonnet." Perhaps this partly accounted for her adventure. But if she came for the honey she did not get it. There was none to extract. What she wanted was not to be found. Her mission was "to try to do good to the reading world," and her object in calling was to secure my help in that direction. She was intelligent and she knew what she meant. In her words she was kindly. She said:

"I have read your book which a friend sent to me—I mean your 'Thoughts in Rhyme'—and having had this conversation with you, I see two things—first, that you love poetry; and, secondly, that you prefer work to money-help. I love poetry, too, *when it is pure*. I have brought some work for you, and this is ten shillings as a first instalment of the payment."

We all listened attentively, if not gratefully. You should have seen the glow of satisfaction as it danced on the faces of our young ones. When poverty is so ruled as not to blunt the wit of the young it generally sharpens it. I could also see the tears of gratitude start in the eyes of the yet helpless mother, as the young lady handed me the ten shillings with the parcel of well-written MS.

"To purge the poets, beginning with Shakespeare; to delete the objectionable, and fill up the blank with something better. That is what I wish you to do for me," added the lady, and then pointed out some of her own efforts in that direction by way of example. She then left promising to call.

I promised to think the matter over, and to do my best, if it were possible to do anything. If I smiled there must have been something of the comic in it.

With headache, and soon with heartache, I plodded on, but made no satisfactory progress, finding that every attempt to disjoin the original sentences weakened the force of expression, rendering the whole passage all but unintelligible. I felt convinced that the result of any such effort would be as worthless and as fruitless as the play of "Hamlet" would be were Hamlet's part omitted. And then all the circumstances were against me. They were dead against "the poetic vein." One could scarcely see to read—far less to go on with the work of excising—Shakespeare. So I gave up the herculean task in despair, regretting I had accepted the ten shillings.

The lady called, and I told her all. She seemed surprised, but I ventured to point out, from her own MS., that, in regard to the alterations she had made, in no case had she sustained the poetic flow. I ventured also to suggest other ways by which she might be useful, and in which I might help her—by gathering together and publishing the *beauties* of the poets. But this did not seem to please her. She looked as if greatly disappointed—almost angry. But she gave me another ten shillings. We parted, and I have not seen her since. So far as I know, this pound's worth of work—quite a fortnight's hard work—was misspent. At all events, I have never seen a "purged Shakespeare," though I have seen several copies of the beauties of the great poet.

The poetic lady visitor meant well, but a practical lady called and did better. The latter had no pretention to "LETTERS," but at the close of one of our short conversations on literary matters she said, "Have you any MSS. by you that may be turned to good account at this time?"

A practical lady visitor.

This proved to be a happy thought, for I had several MSS. by me, but my mind ran to one which before that time had been highly spoken of. Besides, it had a little history of its own, and ladies, as well as gentlemen, like little histories, touching stories.

When yet in Dundee, and not long before we left that town for Edinburgh, a friend incidentally informed me of a notice he had seen months previously. It was an offer of prizes for the best "Lives of Working Men," written by themselves. At first I thought there was little use of my competing, and besides I thought I had not for years been a bonafide "Working Man"—not since I was a boy of nineteen when I left the loom for the school. However, this gentleman induced me to write to headquarters to ask if one such as myself was eligible to enter the list of competition. "It is the lives of such men we desire," was the reply, with the emphasised information that all copies must be to hand for the adjudicators within ten days from the date of that letter.

I wrote the "Story of my life" as briefly as I could, avoiding the more public incidents lest it might be known who the writer was. The title I gave was "The Weaver's Son," and my motto was "Onward and Upward." I was surprised and glad when the announcement reached me that I had taken a "first prize." But notwithstanding this little but pleasant triumph, I did not see in "the narrative" all that was said in praise of it.

However, the gentlemen who were anxious to see what was in

"those who had risen," did not wish to make money by other people's brains; so they gave me the copy with the right to publish it when I thought well.

The lady listened breathlessly, and then said, "I am going to London, and I have a friend in court"—meaning in the literary circles.

She took the MS. with her, yet I could not see what could come out of such a hastily-written story of one so poor, scarcely up before he is knocked down again. But on her return, the lady said, "Through my friends, your MS. has been read by Charles Dickens. Though he did not think it was suitable for his publication, yet his kind note predicts for it a large sale and much usefulness if published in book form."

This was something gained, and we were thankful to the good lady and to the great author, as well as to God. I lost no time in forwarding the MS. to the Rev. George Gilfillan, together with Charles Dickens' note, asking the author of the "Bards of the Bible" what he thought of the story. The opinion of the two literary men was one.

"Something at last," said I to myself; "but how is this approved narrative to see the light of day?"

"I must not sink *now*, something must be done," I added, and this was done: With the two notes, Dickens' and Gilfillan's, I applied for conditional orders, in advance, to the most likely booksellers; first in Edinburgh, then in Glasgow, and so on. Having thus obtained orders sufficient to cover the expenses of publication, the little book appeared entitled, "Life-Story: a First Prize Autobiography."

At Dr. Thomas Guthrie's Breakfast Party. At the suggestion of the same lady, I had added one or two of the incidents which had transpired from the time I first closed the Autobiography till the time of its publication. Not the least of these incidents—I mean in the light of Providence—was my acceptance of a kind invitation from the late Rev. Dr. Thomas Guthrie to one of his breakfast-parties.

At first this invitation led us into confusion. How could I appear in the midst of so many, and all so well to do, generally from other lands as well as our own? By this time, my "best clothes" were reduced to one suit, and that had become very shabby, bare and shiny. My boots were comparatively good, though down in the heels; but oh, my poor hat! Yet I consented hopefully though reluctantly. I say hopefully, for I believed in the doctor's good heart, and knew of his wide influence. And our hearts beat in unison.

Everything underwent a process of renovation, and I had "a clean shave"—there were no beards in those days, in my case at least. The little whiskers I had were also trimmed. My lately grown "coal-black hair" was duly parted, and to finish off, Maggie, by her own hands, adjusted the little curl on the top centre of my already bare forehead, *à la Beaconsfield*. "There now," she said, after I had undergone this ordeal with the greatest amount of possible patience, "you are almost yourself again. Never let me hear you say after this that you have been forgotten."

With a kiss and "God bless you," I left for the doctor's quite in time—none are late when Maggie commands. I was taken to the drawing-room—what a contrast from the "room" I had left! It was with difficulty I kept from the requirements of the tenth commandment, "Thou shalt not covet thy neighbour's house." Bell after bell rang, every one after the first two or three making my timid heart leap. At last the doctor came, radiant with smiles. We were all introduced to God and each other in prayer, family worship was held before we left for breakfast. The assembly was very large. Afterwards I was led to understand that this was the meal at which our happy host was in the habit of meeting his friends.

This breakfast party, for such it was, was lively as well as large. Some of the guests were from abroad, but all were at home. The doctor's fund of telling humorous anecdotes was as exhaustless as his knowledge of men and manners was great. Almost every sentence he uttered indicated a deep insight into human nature, incidentally, but clearly showing that his large heart, like his great work, was in the vineyard of humanity. The subjects of conversation were various, but the doctor was ready for whatever turned up; still he was evidently more at home in his own special field of usefulness—Christian philanthropy as developed on behalf of the suffering, especially the young. For instance, one of the subjects of conversation, which had not a little of attention that morning, was the propriety of exposing evil. Some held whilst it might be proper to expose evil, the doing so was dangerous to those who undertook the duty, the danger of contamination. The doctor held that true men and women were in no such danger, that the atmosphere in which they were called upon to live, or work, or write, did not harden nor stain the heart. As a case in point he referred to an incident in the life of Thackeray.

"One Sabbath afternoon," said the Doctor, "this fearless fellow, during one of his visits to Edinburgh, was going down the Canongate, when his attention was drawn to three almost naked children *at the end of a close.* It was very cold, and their bare feet were red as *collops*, and yet they were singing, 'There is a happy land, far, far away.'"

"This scene," added the Doctor, "was too much for Thackeray, It opened the floodgates of the large heart of the great Author. He wept like a child."

After breakfast, our host asked me to a private interview with him. He said, "My attention has been called to a book of poetry of yours. I have also been told of your long illness, and some of its results. Are you yet able for work? Have you any thoughts ready for publication? Can I be of service to you? Give me your address."

It was clear the Doctor did not have the least idea of what I had endured, nor what we were enduring. I felt that the time he was giving to me was so much taken from his other guests, and that was one reason why I did not tell him all, but I promised to write to him. This I did, but not till I was able to send him a copy of the Prize Autobiography *revised and enlarged.*

But what of the "Story," you naturally ask? First of all, according to arrangements, the booksellers' ordered copies were supplied. These copies were sent to the press, every member, save one, dealt kindly towards the little book. There is always an exception as if needed to prove the rule. Next I sent copies to my private subscribers, and this brought us help almost immediately—the booksellers' orders having paid all expenses. Having got shelter under a better roof, and some furniture, we felt at home again.

Life "Story" becoming helpful.

Our young ones were much taken up with our change of view and fresher air. Even Jeannie the baby seemed to enjoy the relief—her sweet, lovely face looking all the lovelier.

We put a dozen copies apart to be sent (1) To those who had previously manifested a willingness to help me to genial work. (2) To those for whom I entertained a high respect because of their noble worth. (3) To those whom I thought might likely be able to help me to my desire.

Eleven of the dozen were posted, and amongst those who most promptly answered were Professors Blackie, Miller, and Aytoun. In the course of a conversation with the latter, on the past and what might yet be, he said, "Why not send a copy of your Autobiography to the Queen?" assuring me that it was such a book as Her Majesty would read with interest. I smiled as if doubting, thinking that such a book was not likely to be honoured with Her Majesty's attention. He told me he was in earnest, and I believed him; but I kept the thought to myself for several days. However, one day, my counsellor in chief called my attention to the copy yet left, and I asked, "To whom shall I send it?"

"To the Queen," was the prompt reply, smiling the while. I smiled too, and told *my* queen of Professor Aytoun's advice. This was enough. She felt there was "something in it," and the copy was soon addressed—simply, "To Her Majesty the Queen, Windsor Castle."

Chapter XIX.—Stepping Stones to London.

Professor Blackie was among the first to write. He also called, saying "he wished to see auntie Maggie and the bairnies." But events proved that he also had another object in view—to assist me to the ministry by giving me an honorary ticket to attend his Greek classes.

In the Professor's chair.

"This," he said, "is my mark of respect to you for your persevering endeavours to rise to usefulness."

Gladly did I avail myself of this privilege as often and as long as circumstances permitted. On leaving, he invited me to his residence to receive some books and have an extended conversation. The hours I spent with him and his lady were pleasant and profitable. According to appointment, the Professor and I arrived at the college together. For a moment he left me alone in one of the apartments adjoining his class-room. He then returned, ready for work—the delivery of his opening address.

"Come this way," he said, and I obeyed.

We ascended a few steps, and in a second we were on the rostrum facing a large number of students. "You must either deliver the lecture or occupy the chair," said the Professor to me in a voice sufficiently loud to be heard. I felt bewildered, but in the midst of a prolonged shout of applause—such as only students can give—the Professor whispered to me that, as chairman, my task would be an easy one. He introduced me as the author of a piece of real life, called "Life Story," following up this remark by an eloquent panegyric, amplifying the ideas expressed by him in a letter to me in relation to this little book. Though I felt very strange in this rather elevated position, I had this consolation, that I could say—what many of our A.M.s, LL.D.'s D.D.'s, and other college dons, could not say—I had been unexpectedly and unanimously called to occupy the Professor's chair in one of the proudest and best universities in the world. But there was little time to spare for such thoughts. My mind, like that of the other students, was soon trying to follow the Professor in his lecture. For the time all else was forgotten.

After this the postman was no stranger to us. Letters came from near and afar; not only from those to whom we sent the special copies, but from many whom I had not known. *Expectation running high.* They contained such notes of encouragement as these: "Go on in the strength of God," "I commend you and yours to God," "Excelsior is your motto, stick to it," "God will make way for you, and provide for your good wife and dear children."

Among the writers in the upper walks of life were, His Grace the Duke of Argyll, the late Lord Kinnaird, the late Sir George Ramsay, Sir John Ogilvy, Dr. Robert Chambers, Duncan M'Laren, late M.P., and Thomas Cooper. One of the letters promised well to relieve us from the trouble which comes of a very insufficient income. It was written by the late Lord Brougham, expressing his hope of being able to further my desire to get congenial work when he saw Mr. Hastings, the secretary of the Social Science Association. Another letter contained the offer of an engagement on a London newspaper, but Dr. Menzies would not hear of this, until I had more completely recovered.

Another letter may be mentioned here, that from the Rev. Dr. Thomas Guthrie, containing a second invitation to his house. He, too, had read "Life Story," and wished to make more inquiries. (He did not *then* say why.) Before this, the editorship of the Edinburgh *Witness* newspaper had changed hands more than once since Hugh Miller ceased to conduct it. Dr. Peter Bayne had lately left that post for another of a like nature n London. He was succeeded by the late Mr. Troup, the able, plodding journalist. To him Dr. Guthrie introduced me at once, referring to the little book in appreciative terms. It had been previously and favourably reviewed by the stated reviewer, but the editor now read it himself, and then sent his copy to a friend in London. That friend was the Rev. Dr. Wilson, then the secretary of the Congregational Home Missionary Society. And, after reading the book, Dr. Wilson wrote Mr. Troup, saying, "The author is not altogether unknown to me. I see he is still aspiring to the Ministry, and I shall be glad to use what influence I have to help him."

This letter Mr. Troup kindly forwarded to me with some encouraging words of advice, and soon after Dr. Wilson wrote to me conveying the same offer, but added, "Whatever influence I have is centred in those known as 'The Congregationalists.'"

I knew what that meant, but I wrote at once and stated these facts: (1) I had, before this, carefully considered the principles and polity of that denomination; (2) that though I had no fault to find with the United Presbyterian Church—in which I had been trained from infancy—yet my reading and reflection in regard to the whole matter had led to some correspondence between myself and the Rev. Dr. W. L. Alexander; (3) that only a week previously I had had a long conversation, on the same subject, with my esteemed minister and dear friend, the Rev. Dr. W. Reid; and (4) that after a second conversation with him he suggested such a reply to Dr. Wilson as would encourage him to carry out his suggestion of help in regard to the Congregational Ministry. This advice I followed, and soon received an assuring reply. This strengthened my hopes more than ever.

Becoming a "Mission Teacher." Still I kept myself open for whatever good work might come my way; because I did not know when I might be called, and because the present was still pressing—though the little book brought in a few shillings now and then.

About this time a few kindly disposed ladies asked me to undertake the duties of what they called a Mission Teacher.

They significantly added the *saving* clause—till something more remunerative might turn up. The truth is, the good ladies had more heartfelt benevolence in their hearts than spare cash in their purses. For this reason the salary was very small, but the work was very trying to my feelings as well as my frame.

My labours were among the poor, and I was almost as poor as any in regard to physical comforts; but the work opened before me a new field of observation and thought, and this was a gain. My pupils, if I may use that word, were not assembled in a special class-room, but in any of the most suitable apartments available in any of the socially lowest places in the city, and among the most wretched of the people. One day I might be in a back kitchen, the next, perhaps, in a rickety attic.

My charge, or charges, were divided into little groups; sometimes of four or five; sometimes of ten or twelve. They were understood to be made up of children, but others of maturer years frequently came to listen. Half-an-hour was the time appointed for each class in one place, and that only once a day. This enabled me to overtake a large number of stations each week.

In one sense, my task was unpleasant. The homes of the people were so bad, and I had to go to the worst of them. Instruction to the young and advice to the old were what I was expected to impart. Food and clothing were also much wanted. But I had to be content with the words of the apostle—"Silver and gold have I none, but such as I have, give I thee"—sympathetic compassion and kind words. Feeling this compassion I loved the work, and because I saw the blessing of God accompanying it. And, besides, I was thus learning much that has not been forgotten by me.

In time, however, some of my friends, who knew something of my past as well as the present, would say to me, "Take it easy." But the very remembrance of the past, the wounds of which were yet green, urged me on to greater activity on behalf of those who were suffering much as we had suffered. Hence I considered it was my duty to do as much as possible before and after college hours.

Employing the pen again.

This kind of labour opened up before me scenes romantic and terrible. Each horrid aspect kept so staring me in the face and impressing itself on my mind that, to the student mission teacher, I added that of a word-painter, to the annoyance of some in authority. These pictures appeared in one of the city newspapers, but the authorship was not known. My past experience and field of observation combined to make each contribution tell—sorely vexing those who were unwilling that the plague spots should be exposed to the public gaze. Some of the more responsible of those in authority went to see the places described, but they did much more by way of abusing the writer than by way of improvement. This only led to my speaking out all the stronger. Without pretending to be a prophet, I predicted that some of the houses would fall, mentioning one as an example. Later on this very house fell, to the horror not only of Edinburgh, but of the nation. The last words of one of the many murdered victims—a former pupil of mine—are still remembered, "*Heave awa', lads, I'm no deid yet.*"

As murder will out, so will the authorship of disagreeable exposures. But, in this case—not often so in my experience—I gained a little more than abuse for daring to defend the poor from a kind of murder. The stir roused told me I had regained a little mental vigour. But that was not all. I was soon asked to contribute an article on the same subject to *Tait's Magazine*. There the title was, "What the Homes of the Poor ought to be." All this added a little more to my small income, and my hopes continued to rise as my labours increased.

Her Majesty's Letter.

After I had almost forgotten what was done with the last of the dozen copies of "Life Story," and the first edition was nearly sold out, we were happily surprised by a letter all the way from Windsor Castle. In some respects this was the most important of all the letters, not only because our Queen is the highest in social position, but because of what Her Majesty was pleased to say.

It is possible you know something of poor human nature devoid of divine charity. It is so ready to associate wrong-doing with poverty, and that without evidence. It conceives evil thoughts, then utters them; which thoughts are caught up and developed until the poor one is not only neglected, but shunned. With an affected amazement it asks, "Who would have thought it?" leaving all who hear to ask, "Thought what?" Mr. or Mrs. Hearsay comes up with answers in abundance, while respectable Mr. or Mrs. Well-Meaning takes up the refrain, assuring all round that "there must be something wrong, for God never permits His *true* servants to come down so far and suffer so much."

We were not without our full share of this experience of the poor. Naturally, and of necessity, I had been very weak, very pale, and very broken-down, having but lately recovered from the effects of the fever. Perhaps I should not have expected the healthy, and strong, and prosperous, and sprightly, to acknowledge me in the street, even though they knew me well, and I had been a popular favourite. The exercise of Christian principles, such as self-denial, was necessary for such people before they could venture to run the risk of speaking to one so weak and shabby. This, in the mind of some, would never do, where, in a caste-land, every eye is so keen. But this letter changed all that as if by magic. The Press took note of it. In some cases, they published the words in full. And from that day there was no more passing by on the other side, but a gushing approach, with a pouring out of congratulations by many who were careful to tell me they had "read the book."

But there were other reasons why I placed considerable value on this letter. To the mind of the careful reader there were several defects in the little book, but they were such as I could not mend—defects which I have not mended even in this edition. This has been well put by one eminent in literature and upright in heart. Writing to me sometime after this, he pointed out that "the story was too briefly told." He said, what was also true, that it was evident I had "told the truth, nothing but the truth, but not the whole truth." Then he went on to say, "You have therefore laid yourself open to the charge of being imprudent. On one page we find you on the heights of usefulness; on the next, perhaps, you are down, socially at least. Why is this?" The reason I gave—and the only reason that can be given still—was this: "Those who, intentionally or unintentionally, had injured me, might, in turn, be injured, and their usefulness lessened to the extent of the influence of the little book." Hence I preferred to be silent. God had helped me to overcome, and in some cases to render good for evil. Still the circumstances were such as to suggest inquiry. And this Her Majesty had done, and stated that the inquiries were "perfectly satisfactory." This was a valuable and pleasing testimony, and proved helpful.

Perhaps it is well here to mention yet another reason why I valued this letter—from all I learned it was a source of delight to others. To write to one so far down, socially, said something pleasing not only for Her Majesty but also for the Prince Consort, for His Royal Highness was still a living counsellor at the throne.

I have always thought—and in the little book there was no attempt to hide my thoughts, and I think still—that it is an evident sign of moral weakness on the part of any one to speak in the highest terms of any personage *merely* because he possesses a title, however high. I have ever detested such pratings. On the other hand, none admire more than I do the valuable manifestations of personal goodness in *any* one. History has shown that high station may become a great power for mischief. It always is so when true moral principles are absent. But it has been a source of delight to all concerned, when grace and power are blended, when those in high places prove that, by God's help, the august and the good may be united; when true moral greatness gives that dignity which befits one in authority, and fills the people with confidence, leading on and up, as in our case, to that general and sincere admiration which our Queen enjoys, because of her personal virtues, and because she is a true woman, as well as a watchful sovereign. Hence a confiding people delight to see notice taken of the smaller things of common life as well as the greater things of state. And hence I still like to think of the Queen's letter to me in 1860.

More letters came. One from Lord Brougham. Amongst others was one from London which led me again to seek the advice of Drs. Reid and Alexander. *The pain of parting.* At last I replied thus: "I see no sacrifice of principle in accepting an invitation from the Congregational body, should Providence think it well to open the way to a vacant church in or near London. As I see it, the leading difference between Congregationalism and Presbyterianism lies in the matter of Church government—a matter which is very important in its way, but I look at the good I see in both systems. And my past experience has proved that I have been able to work with all earnest, liberal-minded Christians."

This cleared the way, and the invitation to London soon followed.

"Go, certainly," said another good and wise friend whom I had consulted. "It will be the making of you in ways you think not. God is there as well as here; and as to finishing your education, London is the best place for that. Your attachment to your native land is all very well as a sentiment. Your place is where you are likely to be most useful. And, besides, South Britain is one with North Britain."

To this I offered no objection, not even to his reference to the necessity of having to leave my "present charge"—the poor children and their parents. Still, when it came to the point of parting, I felt as if I would rather not go. I not only pitied the poor, but I had learned how to help them in various ways to help themselves. And I knew what had been done in this out-of-the-way mode of working, in thus helping them to make the most and best of a hard life, amid strong temptations to evil. Even among the adults I had seen growing improvement; also evident signs of striving after the good—some had been enabled to look to Jesus as *their* Saviour.

There were also the ties of friendship which have always been strong in me. All my farewells have been more or less passionate and for several reasons this one had become even more thrilling. In spite of much that I have but slightly indicated, I had found that "friendship improves happiness and abates misery by doubling our joys and dividing our griefs." I may here only mention one name, as representing those whose deep sympathy, wise words and loving deeds proved their sincerity—Alexander Smith, the author of Life's Drama, so genial and cordial and hearty. The pleasant and elevating co-mingling of our souls was real and ardent.

And yet another cord, the strongest of all the ties must be stretched for a time at least—about 400 miles. Because of the absence of sufficient means, I must leave our young ones and their mother in Edinburgh. Though it was understood that they were to follow me as soon as possible, yet leaving them added greatly to the pain of parting.

Night thoughts. The day of my departure for London came. I left Edinburgh by what was called the night train. The night was dark and cold, but I was too much troubled to think of either. And yet I had an inward conviction that my usefulness was likely to be greatly increased. After I was a short time on the "Up-way," my mind ascended higher and yet higher, until, in faith, I could say,

> "God will sustain my weakest powers
>   With His Almighty arm,
> And watch my most unguarded hours
>   Against surprising harm."

Almost all my fellow passengers in our compartment had fallen asleep, but I continued turning over in my mind much that I had thought of, and not a little I had learned, in brave old Caledonia. I had known her to be stern as well as wild, but I loved her still —perhaps never more intensely than now. I thought of her rugged history, and my struggles for life and usefulness, but I could see how God, even by means of her trials, had stirred in her that daring which led on to the enterprise and effort which have resulted in the attainment of her useful position in our United Kingdom, in the world. For this, her trials became one of the means of her preparation. There she was, grand and beautiful as ever, and ready for more work. Why not her struggling child?

Various other themes claimed consideration. One was the mercy of God. In that mercy He had shown to me some encouraging facts. I could look at results and praise God for His kindness. My preparation for the work was trying and severe enough, but it was a preparation, and that was something. And all this might, in the end, help some poor ones to realise the truth of the words—"A fellow feeling makes us wondrous kind."

Such thoughts greatly soothed me, and I gradually settled down to something like a dream, "a vision of the night." *A vision of the great metropolis.*

Sometime after, I described this vision to the Author of the "Bards of the Bible;" and later on he gave my simple narrative of the incident in his own way. This was done in "Life Struggles." The picture painted by the noble-hearted prose poet was so true to life, as I afterwards saw it, that I shall here quote a few sentences from his graphic pen:

"When the mind has leisure or inclination to turn from its own concerns to a general review of London, what thoughts arise. Doubtless they are elevating and inspiring. Particularly when the mind thinks of the many majestic movements of which London is the centre—the commerce, the literature, the art, the benevolent enterprise, the political action, the moral and spiritual influence, the whole nations of important and able men it contains within its limits, the noble buildings and institutions and churches it folds within its ample arms, and the ever playing pulse of active life which beats within its veins. But, alas, close to these glorious thoughts, there lurk the giant shadows of poverty, guilt, vice, fraud, folly, misery, madness, soundless abysses of sin and woe—the murder alleys, theft corners, lust lanes, and broad blasphemy squares of this city of destruction—the gin-palaces, brothels, gambling houses, the whole streets of starvation, the thousand and one under ground railways to hell, and rivers of loud sounding or lazy perdition. One is first struck with the over-awing image of immensity which the great city presents. And then there is the bustle in the streets, the eager haste and hurrying in from all quarters towards that stupendous pile of gloom through which no eye can penetrate. The increasing sound like enginery of an earthquake at work. Sometimes a faint yellow beam of the sun strikes here and there on the vast expanse of edifices; and (in the fine thought of Burke when *he* entered the city) churches and holy asylums are dimly seen lifting up their countless steeples and spires, like so many lightning rods, to avert the power of evil."

A little further on the same writer adds, "And this is the city into which Mr. Hillocks entered eager to join the noble army there manfully fighting against the myriad-armed demon." Such was my vision slightly but truthfully amplified.

From this dream I was roused by the request, "Tickets for London." We arrived safely. It was on Saturday morning, December 14, 1860.

I found London enveloped in one of her darkest fogs; but, by means of a cab, I found my way to Bloomfield Street, City, wherein were then the Offices of the Congregation Union of England and Wales.

INDEX TO PART FIRST.

The Paternal Side, 9; The Maternal, 10; A Life Given and a Life Lost, 12; The Loss of a Mother, 13.

Dundee about Sixty Years Ago, 14; The Mitherless Bairns, 17; Another Mother, 17; The New Nursery, 18; Doing Three Things almost at Once, 19.

Pressed into Service, 21; Craving for Mental Food, 22; Three Months at School, 23; Improving the Little, 25.

About to Sink in the Deep, 27; Whirling in the Air, 28; Hanging over a Precipice, 29.

The Minister's Visit, 33; At the Sunday School, 34; Rising in the Labour Scale, 36.

Our New Abode, 39; My Study, 41; Seeking Relief in Rhyme, 42; My "Mammie's Awa'," 42; Up in Mind, 45; Down Bodily, 47.

Re-reading the Bible, 49; Other Books, 50; First Lessons in the Laboratory, 51; A Black Look-out, 52.

No Work to do becomes Hard Work, 54; Keeping the White Heat Up, 56; My First Public Speech, 58; Becoming "our own Correspondent," 59.

Joining a Hungry Mob, 61; Becoming a Tramp, 64; "A Night Out," 65; The Poor helping the Poor, 66; Some Favourable Results, 68.

Becoming an Assistant Teacher, 70; Becoming a Tutor, 71; Becoming a Public Teacher, 72; Meeting Pecuniary Difficulties, 74.

Training the Truants, 76; Realising my Hopes, 77; A Picture by a Poetic Painter, 79; First Visit to Edinburgh, 79.

Our Second Session, 81; A New Form of Reward, 82; The Unexpected comes to Pass, 83; Our Middle Class Pupils, 85; Breaking God's Law Again, 86.

Literary Pleasure with Profit, 88; Becoming an Unpledged Abstainer, 90; Joining the Church, 92; Meeting "Auntie Maggie," 94.

More Play than Work, 97; Double Work once More, 98; Trying to become Perfect, 100; Return to Smithfield, 102; Two Strings to my Bow, 102.

Auntie Maggie Again, 105; The Suffering of Service, 107; At Gaulswell School, 107; Our First-born, 108; The Brave Tar goes Aloft, 109; Going Whither we Knew Not, 110; Work in "the Muir," 112; The Danger of becoming too Popular, 113.

The Twofold String Again, 115; A Stimulating Incident, 116; Editing under Difficulties, 117; Some Sad Effects, 119.

Too Little to be a Policeman, 121; A Little Run of Success, 122; A Lecture making Friends, 123; Nigh unto Death, 125; My Helpmeet almost Helpless, 125; A "Convalescent Home" in the Grand City, 126; Forgetting Myself, 130.

Found Out at Last, 132; Purging Shakespeare, 133; A Practical Lady Visitor, 135; At Dr. Thomas Guthrie's Breakfast Party, 136; Life Story becoming Helpful, 139.

In the Professor's Chair, 140; Expectations Running High, 141; Becoming a "Mission Teacher," 142; Employing the Pen Again, 144; Her Majesty's Letter, 144; The Pain of Parting, 147; Night Thoughts, 148; A Vision of the Great Metropolis, 149.

END OF PART FIRST.

Christ Preaching on the Sea-shore. (See Chap. VII.)

PART SECOND

OF

HARD BATTLES:

BATTLES FOR USEFULNESS.

"Not being untutored in suffering,
I had learned to pity those in affliction."

PART SECOND.

BATTLES FOR USEFULNESS.

Dedication.

The Right Hon. W. E. GLADSTONE, M.P.

Respected Sir,

Accept of my sincere thanks for your kind permission to dedicate to you these BATTLES FOR USEFULNESS. I expressed that desire because, on more occasions than one, you were, in the providence of God, the means of helping me in these efforts. You may forget what I refer to, but gratitude is the best of mnemonics.

Besides, your high and hearty service in the welfare of the people, particularly the toiling and the suffering, draws my heart closer to you, and leads me to believe that you are all the readier to appreciate the efforts of others, however humble. Appreciation is encouraging.

And, in addition to my thankfulness for past kindness, there still remains with me a profound admiration of your rare gifts, impressive earnestness, lofty purposes, all of which have been long manifested in your wide field of Christian usefulness.

Believe me, respected sir, Yours faithfully,

J. I. HILLOCKS.

CONTENTS.

Chap.		Page
I.	Between the Cup and the Lip	11
II.	Some Helpful Incidents	21
III.	Still nearer the Mark	29
IV.	Indoor Efforts	33
V.	Battles in the Open Air	40
VI.	Three "Doms" against the Poor	54
VII.	Pastor or Evangelist	62
VIII.	A Two Years' Ministry in the Country	68
IX.	Some Unlooked-for Events	75
X.	Renewing the Work in London	82
XI.	Something about the Work	89
XII.	Seeking Health and facing Figures	97
XIII.	The Sphere still widening	103
XIV.	Closing the Autobiographic Narrative	110

SEE INDEX, END OF THIS PART.

THE CONNECTING LINK.

DEAR READER, I shall assume that you have read PART FIRST of Hard Battles for Life and Usefulness, namely, *Battles to Live and Learn*. If so, you will all the better understand this SECOND PART, *Battles for Usefulness*—to help the poor to help themselves. If so, you will see that though each part of itself is complete, as far as it goes, yet the one is closely connected with the other. In *the first*, I have endeavoured to give some idea of *the preparation* for the work; in this, *the second*, you may learn something of *the work*.

Another link between the two is seen by what, to me, appears evident; that save for the first, the *preparation*, it is not likely there would have been the second, the *work*, and but for the work the preparation would have been almost lost.

This seems to be the opinion of others. In *Sword and Trowel*, Rev. C. H. Spurgeon says, "Some live for others more than themselves, and are designed for the permanent illustration of certain principles of Divine Government. This accounts for Mr. Hillocks' life struggles."

The *British and Foreign Evangelical Review* says, "Mr. Hillocks' aim has not been merely personal advancement, but the elevation of the whole platform on which he stood."

The *Contemporary Review* says, "His battles differ from most others in that they have been struggles for usefulness, as well as for life."

The *British Quarterly Review* says, "He gave himself to the service of the poor first in Scotland, and then in London."

I quote these sentences because they present the point better than I can. There is in this part a difference of scene, but the aim is the same. I was as anxious to be helpful in Scotland as I could be in England. Nevertheless, in the former country, my efforts, particularly my earlier efforts, were more *personal* than relative. In this part of the narrative, the efforts have been more *relative* than *personal*. My "Battles to Live and Learn" have not ceased, I am always learning, but now the battles are more for others.

This desire was not engendered by my crossing the Tweed, it came with my earliest aspirations, but a wider field of labour fostered under God, and enlarged the thought—of trying to become more and more useful, in helping the helpless.

As in the first part, so in this, I have endeavoured to bear in mind that this is not a *treatise* but a *narrative*. But though I have purposely refrained from discussing the merits of questions relating to Christian helpfulness, I shall all the more freely consider their *pros* and *cons* in the promised Sequel, which I mean to follow as early as convenient.

J. I. H.

EDEN HOUSE, 127 STOKE NEWINGTON ROAD,
    LONDON, N., *December*, 1888.

"Modern Athens is truly grand."

BATTLES FOR USEFULNESS.

CHAPTER I.—BETWEEN THE CUP AND THE LIP.

PERMIT me to anticipate so far as to say the visionary glimpse of London—with which I closed PART FIRST of these Hard Battles—proved to be a sad reality, a veritable vision. *Sunday in London.*

When, on that 14th day of December, 1860, on my way from King's Cross Station—to the offices of the Congregational Union of England and Wales—I found myself silently asking, How many come to London to sink? How few to rise? How many to leave the paths of righteousness? How few to walk with God? How many yield to temptation and give way to despair, dying in obscurity, unlamented and unknown? How few to manifest the necessary courage, to wait the proper time, to take the proper place, in this great whirlpool of life? What is the cause of all this? As men and things are, disappointments must come, but what is in London life, or in those who come to live in London, that stands in the way of rising above circumstances?

As it happened I had no preaching appointment, neither for the first nor for the second Sunday after my arrival. This gave me an opportunity of seeing the Metropolis, but I could not see in it any likeness to the city I had just left. In the vast extent, London is GREAT; in picturesque beauty, Edinburgh is magnificent. Viewed apart from her wretched homes of the poor, Modern Athens is truly grand.

But what, at this time, was more impressive and thrilling to me was London on Sunday—a sight never to be forgotten by one brought up to reverence the Lord's Day. What I saw on these two Sundays convinced me that in these scenes lay deep down one of the answers to the questions I had just asked myself.

Like the most of sight-seeing strangers the Sunday Morning Markets had my first attention. These scenes I have elsewhere described, what I saw then and after, and I may do so again, but here I cannot do much more than say the whole combined to force upon me the impression that something was very wrong at the very centre of the social system of London. The New Cut, Whitecross Street, Bird Fair, Petticoat Lane, were the chief of such places as gained my attention.

The presence of detectives told that thieves were not absent. In addition to these there were many idlers, who had come to while away the time; but the greater bulk of those present were those called working men, skilled and unskilled, with their wives and daughters. Those who had goods to sell—suiting all tastes and all pockets—were in earnest, and so were those who came to buy or barter. None seemed to think they were doing what they should not do. Some had formed a habit of frequenting such places and would have been disappointed if they had not been present.

But Sunday traffic was not confined to such localities. I soon found there was much truth in the old ballad. Here is one verse:

> "Go where you will, up and down every street,
> Some sort of cry you are sure for to meet;
> In winter or summer, as the time of year flies,
> You will find in London a melody of cries."

And with all this there were the open shops of which it was said, if placed side by side of each other, would extend beyond sixty miles. However there were two things I had not then learned. The first was that many, if not the most, of the poor had been drawn into this Sunday traffic from necessity, because of unfavourable circumstances. The other point of which I was then ignorant was the sad fact that many of the rich, without any excuse, were far from observing the Sabbath day to keep it holy. Among those who, like myself, believed it would be better if all kept the Sabbath in a truly religious, the pious, sense, many spoke harshly of the poor, but had not a word to say to the offending rich.

But though I afterwards learned to make some allowance in the case of the poor in purchasing what they called the necessaries of life on the Lord's Day, there was one thing which I have never been able to look upon as necessary, namely, the Sunday drinking. I have ever looked upon it as bad as week-day drinking. Nor was this Sunday drinking of strong drink confined to the poor. True, so far as could be seen, this was so during the early part of the day. From early morning there were evidences that strong drink was among the things that could be purchased, and that in defiance of the law which held that the legal time for opening the drink places was one p.m. But it was after six p.m. that these places were in full swing, doing mischief, not only to the poor but to many who would scorn to be regarded as such. It was then and later on that the signs of social and moral debasement became more general and evident. True, the most degraded of the drinkers frequented the inferior drunkeries, inferior in outward appearance but not in destructive power. And what was too evident was the fact that these dens were more thickly planted in the squalid localities, making the more repulsive of our fellow creatures more and more hideous. True, at the beginning of Sunday evenings some of the throng passed the doors of the blazing public house, temptingly planted at the corner of almost every street. But, later on, many of the apparently well-to-do of the pleasure seekers joined with those whose highest aim seemed to be to drink and appear to be merry. Later still the throng as they had left the public house, or the "Tea Gardens," gave proof of how low they were in their tastes, how strong in their appetites, how fierce in their passions. I pitied the children. Some were asleep, some had been made drunk by gin or beer administered by their parents, some screamed. With few exceptions the mothers were as much under drink as the fathers.

These observations were sadly verified as my knowledge of life in London extended. But from the first, I looked upon each blazing gin palace as portion of a blasting traffic, on Sunday as on week-days. True, "the house"—looked at apart from the ruination going on within—has a brilliant aspect in the eyes of those who have not seen the like before. With putty and paint, pewter and crystal, ivory and glass, brass and mahogany, all burnished and polished, with the glare of artistically arranged gas gleaming upon them, house decorators had tried to convert a fearful demon into an angel of light, but only to prove that a grave bedecked with roses is a grave still. These things gave me one answer to the question, why so many fall so very far in London as elsewhere?

Greatly disappointed. But whilst I thought of others and their temptations to evil, in the great metropolis, I had but little idea of what, in my own case, was to pass between the cup and the lip.

From the nature of the correspondence and the invitation referred to at the close of PART FIRST this was the idea I had entertained: That I was to settle down at first and at once in a quiet suburban pastorate. But I was greatly disappointed. Events took quite another turn. I was surprised, and almost compelled to suppose I was not nearer the mark than before I consented to leave Edinburgh. And yet it seemed as if no one was to blame. As was to be expected, Dr. Wilson received me kindly at the offices of the Congregation Union.

"You require a few days' rest after such a long, cold journey," he said, and then added, "I have provided a preacher for to-morrow (Sunday) to supply the pulpit in the church to which you were going."

After a little conversation, he asked me to meet him on the following Friday. Anxious to suppose the best, I looked upon this arrangement as an act of kindness, for I was in need of a few days' rest. But when I called, instead of being sent to the appointed place, I was asked to take another week's rest. I did so, but this time found Dr. Wilson much troubled.

"I am perplexed," he said; "the minister I sent as supply has been asked, and he has consented to become the pastor of the church. But another door may soon open for you."

I trembled, but remained silent, unwilling to allow myself to express my feelings in regard to the disappointment. But they must have been seen on my face, for an explanation was tendered; and it is only fair to all concerned to give it here:

Our mutual friend, as soon as he saw something of "the express" connected with the invitation, and being aware of our circumstances, wrote to Dr. Wilson to say I might find a difficulty in starting at once. Not knowing this, I also wrote as soon as I saw I could start as desired. But his letter was a post earlier than mine, and that caused the appointment of the minister for the Sunday. The rest followed. But what a change, and so sudden.

Here I was, in great distress of mind, and with very little in pocket even to meet my own wants, far less the wants of those dear to me, yet in Edinburgh.

"Yet things might have been worse," said I to myself. "Had I, as a probationer, preached even once to the people, and been unexceptable to them, I would have blamed myself, and been more troubled." In this there was something consoling, still I felt as if almost buried in the depth of disappointment—almost alone in London.

I had letters of introduction, but felt unwilling to call because of the turn things had taken. My faith, usually firm, seemed as if about to be extinguished; and my hope, generally buoyant, was as if fast disappearing. A feeling of sinking sadness took a firm hold of me. For the moment, I forgot that others were as bad, if not worse, than I was; that others, also under trying circumstances, had entered the great city, and, under God— coupled with industry, frugality, perseverance, and sagacity—had become useful and honourable. But this wayward wavering had an end. Now that I knew the extent of my present disappointment, I mustered as much courage as to tell all to my help-meet, confident in her proved womanly wisdom and courage. And, once more, she was equal to the occasion. Her advice was short, but to the point—one verse,

> "Trust in the Lord, for ever trust,
> And banish all your fears;
> Strength in the Lord Jehovah dwells
> Eternal as his years."

Another door opened. In the meantime I had been asked to meet a committee of ministers at Bloomfield Street. The details of what had come to pass, in regard to myself, were fairly given, and all present expressed the hope that a suitable church might soon be open for me, now that my name was on the preacher's list for appointments. It is only fair to Dr. Wilson to add here that in his remarks touching the turn events had taken, he pointed out that they had not arisen from any fault of mine. None spoke more highly of me than he did. Even the remarks of the Rev. Thomas Binney, on that occasion, were not more appreciative. This was somewhat consoling. But what was I to do whilst waiting for an occasional preaching appointment. In my bewildering distress I had been as foolish as to think more about erring man than of the loving God. I have often had to regret such errors on my part; but here Maggie's note brought me to my senses. These precious lines reminded me that God was an ever present help in every time of need, the One to lead to ultimate triumph. I also remembered the encouraging sentence, "If thou hast courage to banish, by persevering trust, the putrid waters, the swamps will change into fertile and beautiful fields, and the deadly fever will depart, and thou wilt rejoice as a strong man in health." That courage, which means "trust and try" became mine once more; and our united prayer was that God might, in His boundless love and wise ways, lead us through the hidden path, that He might turn and overturn all things for good—not only to us, but also to others.

Having found the truth of the saying, "there is much between the cup and the lip," and believing that all honest work was honourable, I felt ready for whatever my returning strength could accomplish. But where? Anywhere. What? Anything.

Sooner than I could have expected, a door opened. I accepted an invitation from Mr. W. Tweedie, the Publisher, to spend a day with him at Brompton. He was the publisher of "Life Story." Naturally he asked all about matters, and I told him what I have just recorded. Giving vent to some feeling, he asked, "What's to be till *the something* turns up?" Anxious not to enlarge on what he called "this unfortunate affair," I simply answered, "As a probationer, I hope to have some preaching appointments, and perhaps a call from some church soon."

"Yes," he said, "but the steed may starve while the grass is growing."

"Let us hope better things," I rejoined by way of taking off the keen edge of the matter which was yet cutting me severely.

"I am in want of a handy-man to do everything required of him. Will you come, if only for a short time?" said Mr. Tweedie, smiling at his extra demand.

After expressing a fear that I might not be able to do *everything*, I consented, and a few days more found me a business man once more. And as it turned out, my duty really was to do almost *everything*.

For instance, you might have seen me at the desk registering orders; now at the parcel table supplying the world with Temperance Literature: now arranging books; now taking a hasty glance of some reviews of the new edition of Life Story (about this time, the notices from all parts were pouring in); now extending my neck and putting my ears on edge when someone had something to say about its author—not knowing he was so close at hand: now assisting in putting to rights the figures of the A B C Railway Guide, and then writing paragraphs, and doing a host of things, too numerous to mention.

One thing this taught me that nothing is lost. My salary, rather my weekly wage, was not large, but I was thankful. Perhaps Mr. Tweedie thought I was an appren-

The past becoming useful.

tice to this kind of work, but it was not so. Book-keeping was not new to me, neither was the writing of paragraphs, and every druggist should be able to make up a neat packet; nor was the work of assisting on the Railway Guide altogether new to me. My Edinburgh experience was useful. On I went, becoming almost in love with this new departure, the evening part of the work especially. For this—after the daily round was over—I washed and brushed up, made myself as fresh and tidy as possible for temperance and other meetings. If not the speaker, I was there in the capacity of reporter—the only thing I objected to, was to report my own speeches. If any such reports were wanted, as was sometimes the case, another member of "the staff" had to be sent.

No doubt, so much speaking rose from the fact that I had become known as an earnest temperance reformer. As such, I went as an honorary deputation from the National Temperance League, of which Mr. Tweedie was the honorary secretary. Of course, this meant *gratis* speaking, which did not help to fill the mouths depending on me. But if I did not get cash for speaking, I was made much of, and became "a little star" in my way. And, no doubt, this arose partly from the paragraph notices, and sometimes editorial leaders which appeared in some of the newspapers. The nature of such may be gathered from the following extract:—" One of the features of the evening was a speech from James Inches Hillocks, late of Edinburgh, author of " Life Story," a first prize autobiography. J. C. Campbell, Esq., Treasurer of the National Temperance League, introduced Mr. Hillocks by reading the letter addressed to him by Her Majesty the Queen, after Her Majesty had read his autobiography, and made some inquiries about the author."

My family brought to London.

If popularity and success in unpaid oratory could make a man happy, I might have leaped with joy, but I did not. How could I? If my heart was not in the Highlands, it was in Edinburgh. My dear ones were there, and I thought of them even in the midst of London hearty applause. But happily, to the joy of all concerned, our re-union came to pass earlier than we could have thought of.

As the thoughtful kindness of the Queen enabled me to bear the expenses of getting to London, so the thoughtful kindness of the Right Hon. W. E. Gladstone assisted in bringing my family to London. Like many more in high position, he read "Life Story," as he said, "with deep interest." He wrote to me characterising the little book in a manner that was pleasing to me. And this was all the more gratifying, the opinion coming from one so eminent in literature, and so upright in heart. His letter also proved that he was an impartial judge. He spoke after he had read: what he said showed he knew every page of it. He pointed out some defects. He said that the "story" was too briefly told. "Doubtless, you have," he said, "told the truth, nothing but the truth, but not the whole truth. Hence you have laid yourself open to the charge of being imprudent. On one page we find you on the height of usefulness, on the next, perhaps, you are down, socially at least."

Having given instances, he asked, "Why is this?" In my reply I gave a full explanation, names and details; but asked that my letter might be regarded as private, because those who, intentionally or unintentionally, had injured me might, in turn, be injured, and their usefulness lessened, to the extent of the influence of the little book. Like the Queen, he was pleased to make inquiry, and like Her Majesty, he afterwards kindly expressed his impression, and asked me to accept the value of the cheque he enclosed as a mark of his "appreciation of extraordinary self-denial."

Like myself, my family arrived on the morning of a foggy day. It will be long before I forget the tone and expression of the mother after being seated in the cab at the station.

"Mercy on my bairnies!" she exclaimed. "How can they live in such an awful place?"

On went the cab, leaving the fog behind, and when we arrived at the little home I had ready for them, the sunshine was pleasant if not inviting. But it did not bring back Maggie's usual brightness. There was a smile occasionally, but there was about it a peculiar sadness. Though the careful wife, as well as the loving mother, even as before, she was depressed. After the young ones were asleep in bed she gave vent to her feelings.

She said: "You are so jaded, killing yourself as before."

She was right, I *was* jaded, but I tried to be as sprightly as possible. Her words of warning were not an hour too early. My former error, overwork, during my first months in London, was fast working its way, and all the faster that I had no one to restrain me.

Of course I promised to do better, and I meant it. This promise brought forth the sweetest smile that true love can produce, but it shone as the bright sun shines through the soft rain when the rainbow spans the sky, for she was still—

> "Beautiful, and excellent, and fair,
> Fairest when seen in darkest days."

The little "lecture" over, the load from her heart was lifted, and we resolved to become Londoners. We settled down and I continued my manifold work in the office, on the platform, and occasionally supplying vacant pulpits.

Chapter II.—Some Helpful Incidents.

But whether it was that my home soon became much more inviting, or that the kindly pampering there, had a tendency to make me a little lazy, or that I was actually much exhausted, I cannot say, but I felt as if becoming less and less able for work, and had to admit it. At this time, however—as I thought at the proper time—I was favoured with a hearty invitation to the country for a fortnight, not for rest but for change of air, at the same time to do all the good I could.

A fortnight in the country.

"What we want is a Christian worker who sees and feels the necessity of evangelistic and temperance efforts going together."

Such was the chief sentence in the letter. The town was Hitchin, a lively market-town in Herts, and the writer was J. H. Tuke, Esq., who was a "friend" in more ways than one. He not only belonged to the religious denomination called the Society of Friends, he was also a friend of good repute to his neighbours, particularly to the poor ones. He was also one of the few friends of good work who do not forget the workers.

"The very thing needful, and come when most wanted," said my partner in life, her countenance beaming with gladness. "It may be the first of the turning points," she added after a little reflection.

It was so, and a good beginning it was. It is a great help to a worker, and hence to the work, when he knows that his dear ones are comfortable at home. Alas! some well-meaning people, with a very good name, forget this. The remembrance of these happy days bring such pleasant feelings, that I yet rejoice when I have an opportunity of seeing that good man.

And then it was the time of bud and blossom. There was the fragrant hawthorn, stretching its white arms, inviting the passer-by to pause, to look, to inhale. There was a sweet smile on the lovely face of the wild flowers, scattered in picturesque disorder. There were lights and shadows coming and going all along the sunny bank and shady lane. All so fascinating, so delicious, so reviving, so strengthening!

But this was the poetic side, the beautiful. There was another side, even in this market town. And I went thither to see both sides and help all. Though, as you know, I had been in the country in England before, I only arrived on the Saturday evening, preached on the Sunday, and then left on Monday morning. Now I had time to breathe the pure air in the lovely lanes, rejoicing in the surrounding scenery; now it was that my lungs as well as my eyes had their daily feast. But my main object was to see the country people as I had not before seen them; to meet them in the fields, in the market-places; to visit them at the fireside, and to address them at meetings.

From the first night to the last I was in good trim, and meeting after meeting became more enthusiastic. My first subject was "Workmen and their difficulties." It went home to the audience, especially the male portion. Seeing this, the chairman announced that my next subject would be, "Workwomen and their difficulties." This announcement was received with hearty applause by the female portion of the audience. I admired the tact, and consented.

"It is only fair, sir," said one of the women to me, as we were leaving the place of meeting. "You've given it to us to-night. Give it to them to-morrow night. They'll all be 'ere and us, in course."

They did come. The crowd was great. The interest was intense. This was well. I was made welcome as a friend at their homes. This gave me an opportunity of knowing their virtues and their failings, their ignorance and their sufferings.

Meeting after meeting increased on week-days and Sundays. Our last meeting—on a Monday evening, I think it was—was held in the Town Hall, and even that could not contain all who wished to come. A schoolroom near by had also to be opened. I spoke first in the one place and then in the other.

I returned to London in due time, quite a new man physically feeling as if I had obtained a new lease of life, and was ready for any amount of effort. I was happy because I had learned so much more of life, the life I wished, under God, to elevate; and because I could be more useful in that way than I had thought of. Indeed, had my income been a little more, I would have been willing to continue in this school.

Stealing a march on the bishop.

By this time, I was well known to London audiences, having been asked to speak at all sorts of assemblies having the good of the people as a leading object. But a test of this readiness to meet the wishes of good people in all sorts of good objects was at hand.

Among the lady-workers were Mrs. Ranyard, author of "The Missing Link," and Mrs. Bailie, author of "Ragged Homes and How to mend Them." At this time the latter was, with her husband, the Captain, making some special efforts at the West End, in a district called "The Potteries." I was asked to take a part at a public meeting of the Gypsies there, in what was called the Workman's Hall. To this I consented all the readier, because I wished to see life among all classes of the poor, and because I had never seen English Gypsies.

Dr. Tait was then the Bishop of London, afterwards Archbishop of Canterbury. He was to be one of the speakers, and I the other, both Scotchmen; but his lordship was high up, and about to rise to the highest point in his church, while I was beginning life anew, and on lines not thought of before. As was arranged he was to be the first speaker. That was as it should have been. "Honour to whom honour is due." "How can I follow a Bishop?" I asked myself, and this anxious question was followed by another, "How can I speak to an English Gypsy audience, composed of fathers, mothers, and children?"

At last a happy thought came to my mind as a relief. The speakers, workers, and other friends had their tea on tables placed on the platform. As soon as I had taken a cup of tea at the platform table I went down amongst the people, talked to as many of them as possible, one after another, learning how they lived, and what they did during the various seasons, particularly in the cold winter time in the Potteries. And with this information I caught a few of their phrases.

In time the public meeting was duly opened, and the Bishop rose to speak amid great applause. His speech was quiet, neat, and solemn, and might have done for a portion of a good sermon. But it fell flat even from a bishop, and this made me think of giving up the address I had prepared, knowing I could not expect the reverent attention which a good bishop might look for. So I rose without knowing what to say; but fortunately for me, my rising was also followed by applause, and my newly acquired knowledge of Gypsy life enabled me to say something which called forth another round of applause, and which was repeated at every point I made, I hope, for good.

"Is he a missionary to the Gypsies?" I overheard the bishop ask some one near. He was evidently astonished. This favourable reception did not arise from any special ability on my part, especially when by way of smooth, beautiful sermons I could not hold the candle to his lordship. It was this little fact—I had been amongst the people. I got to the end of my speech evidently before the audience wished it. Even in the more directly religious part—that toward the close—there was nothing of the sermonising. I simply told my earnest listeners the precious story of Jesus and His love. The well-meaning poor like to hear of the love of God.

With a full-robed clergyman.

Again the unexpected transpired. Not long after this effort, in company with the bishop, to entertain and cheer the poor West End Gypsies, a clergyman in connection with his lordship asked to have an interview with me on "the secret of success in Mission work." When parting, he obtained from me a promise to attend with him one of his Sunday morning open-air services, held at the corner of Brand Street, Hornsey Road, Holloway. I consented on the condition that I came merely as a listener, because my training as a speaker was not in that way. I told him also that that kind of work was not in my way and possibly I might break down if I tried.

Being ready to co-operate with Christian workers of all denominations, I went and arrived in time to see the clergyman robed in an adjoining school-room. While I looked on, I could not help smiling. The time was when I would have laughed right out. I looked upon the display as ridiculous. But I thought the clergyman and his friends might have an idea that this was the best way to reach and raise the people.

There was something to look at. Though thin he was tall. The gown was long and stiff. He walked along to the corner of an adjoining street with firm step and slow—majestically, his friends thought. We lesser creatures followed meekly. A group of people were waiting round the corner at which we took our stand.

The clergyman mounted the chair. His first words were awfully solemn. His tone was also very unnatural. Whether or not this, together with the clerical garb, was meant to awe the people, I cannot say; but the result proved to be the reverse of this. Almost from the first, it became evident the people, or, at least, the most of them there, were anxious that we should get out of their way as soon as possible. From being, or seeming to be, merely indifferent, they manifested positive opposition. Their clamour was first deep, then loud, followed by several rounds of random wit, enough to put even a Wesley or Whitfield down.

The speaker found he was beating against the wind—not only making no impression, but losing headway. At last he also lost the thread of his discourse. And seeing all respect and attention gone, he suddenly bethought himself, changing his tone, and assuming the semi-comic, he said, "We have with us to-day a little Scotchman, perhaps you will hear *him*."

Because of this breach of contract I was taken aback. For the moment I did not know how to act. I could not think of a word to say, yet I felt bound to ascend the chair-pulpit, thinking though the clergyman did wrong that was no reason why I should do wrong. Inwardly I asked for help from above, and help came. First, the sight of my audience quickened me, and made me forget my supposed inability to speak in the open air, even under more favourable circumstances. And this help came in a very natural way—recalling past incidents to my mind and giving me ready utterance. The word "Scotchman" brought to my mind a Scotch story which I had read as a mere boy. I told the story. The audience, now greatly increased, listened attentively. It suggested two points of observation, namely, (1) What we are, (2) What God is.

I was enabled to speak freely for more than half an hour. At the close many came round about me anxious to shake hands with me. One was a strong navvy. His heart was evidently filled with emotion, deep and grateful, as he asked, "Can you come again, guv'ner?"

A sojourn in Islington.

These three incidents run into each other. They also had an influence on my mind. I was convinced that without divine help I could not have been able thus to gain the favour of the English country people, or win the hearts of the English Gypsies, or obtain the confidence of those who at all times attended such open air gatherings. But the results also convinced me that God had prepared me for other forms of Christian work than I had thought of, such as that called the work of an Evangelist. And it was my belief in this that led me all the more readily to consent to undertake the duties connected with my going to this reputed orthodox parish.

"A gentleman has offered a donation of £40 to help towards the salary of the author of 'Life Story,' could he be induced to labour here."

So wrote the same Clergyman who asked my presence at the Sunday morning service referred to. At first, I could not overlook the fact that the writer of this—and the other letters in regard to the invitation—belonged to the Church of England, and

I was a Non-conformist Probationer. But against this stood the question, which came up before me, "What has Christian work to do with Sectarianism?" In stating my terms I was careful to state that my duties were not to go beyond leading souls to the Saviour, *not* to any of the Churches in particular.

This being agreed to by all concerned, I entered on my labours in hope. My designation was "The Missionary Lecturer," but I was the Evangelist all the same—the Preacher as well as the Lecturer, the Social Reformer as well as the Christian Visitor—my influence with the people steadily increasing.

In this I was cheered and sustained by a small band of earnest co-workers. In aim, we were one. The leading spirits were the late T. B. Smithies, then editor of the British Workman, and the late Sir Hugh Owen, then of the Local Government Board—two of the earliest of my London friends. They, with others, attended our Monthly Conferences in the drawing-room of another dear Christian Worker—a wise, earnest, gentle lady. These little gatherings were helpful in many ways. To me they were suggestive and encouraging. One reason why they proved so useful was the fact that they were without any denominational bearing.

The work and results went beyond all expectation, and those whose chief desire was the glory of God in the good of man were glad. But this proved too much for the envious Sectarian. In spite of this desire for union in all good work, the never failing source of disunion became more and more manifest. The best friends of our work were one with me in my resolve to resist the pressure to work for any one denomination. I was called there in the interest of the people, at least I was told so. My motto was Christ for the Christless. No words but His—"Bring him to Me," bring her to Me, had my attention and obedience. But Sectarianism in some of its most inconsistent forms became too strong for my usefulness increasing. Indeed, some of the good done was being thereby damaged; and at last I resolved to resign as soon as Providence was pleased to open another field.

Soon after this resolve became known, the desire to retain me in the district became stronger than I could have thought of.

With the view of gathering up and sustaining the happy fruits of God's blessing on past efforts, those who had been rescued, and other Christians who had been co-operating with me, proposed the formation of a "Christian Church," if I would consent to become the Pastor. I was able to appreciate the motive, but I could not consent, believing the time for my taking such a step had not yet come.

I kept to my resolution to leave Islington, the following is an extract from the valedictory address presented to me on that occasion:—

"We take this opportunity of expressing our sincere gratitude to you for the invaluable services rendered to us and to the public generally, since you were providentially placed amongst us as Missionary and Lecturer. We were glad to hear of your character and ability as a Christian Teacher, and we now rejoice to know that your energetic and unwearied perseverance has far exceeded our expectations. The various ways by which you have gained the affections of the people are well known. Be assured of this, that you carry with you the warm affections of every heart."

Chapter III.—Still Nearer the Mark.

St. Pancras was my new sphere. The centre of operations was the junction of Hampstead, Tottenham and Euston Roads. The circumference was left to my own judgment, and in this my conscience became very large. But though, at times, I went beyond St. Pancras, I kept true to it.

My new sphere.

This invitation came from the London Congregational Union then in the course of formation. It was formed for the purpose of doing for London what the Congregational Home Missionary Society was doing for the country.

"Do what you can in the best way you can."

Such was the sum of the directions given to me. I thought this was in harmony with the Divine commission so beautifully illustrated by the Redeemer, "Who went about doing good." From the first, my prayer was that I might be able not only to cling to Him as the only Saviour, but also to follow Him as the best example.

Here, at my express desire, I was known as "The Evangelist." As far as the work was concerned, the designation meant much of the Missionary and not a little of the Pastor, not of any stated Church, but of the people of all ages, of those who had no spiritual home.

Some said I went beyond this, perhaps they were correct from their idea of what a Christian worker should be and do. But of this you shall judge when you read the Second Series of these Battles for Life and Usefulness. One thing I may say here, I never would be fettered. Red tape and I never did agree.

Near the centre just named is Tolmer's Square Congregational

Church, then newly erected. Here I worshipped on Sunday, when not preaching elsewhere. From amongst the members of this church I gathered the most of my co-workers—ladies as well as gentlemen. In these, as in other fellow workers, I was fortunate.

And, besides, the minister of this church was one of the best of men, learned and helpful. I mean the late Rev. Dr. John Guthrie. Before this time, and since, I have been well-favoured with some dear and precious friends in good work, but none more hearty, genial, liberal, and loving than this friend was. Young needed no nobler example to enable him to say with truth, "A Christian is the highest style of man." We attended to our own special work, each one helping the other.

My aim was a large one, to "study universal good," to promote the best interests of London, particularly the welfare of the poor and more particularly the poor next to me, wherever I found them.

A friendly glance at the work.

At St. Pancras, as at Islington, I met with only a very few who considered that religious people should take any part in solving social problems. Hence only one here and another there went all the way with me in the work. Indeed, the general impression was that I was going beyond the work of an Evangelist. But my Bible told me that I was bound to look at things as they were, particularly such things as brought about the misery of the poor. My Saviour's example, as the Healer of Men, was enough for me, so I went on with my work.

But it is only fair to those who were able to co-operate with me to say that but for the help of such we could not have made the progress in which so many of the poor rejoiced. And to none was this more evident and welcome than to our genial and hearty friend the Rev. Dr. John Guthrie. Nor was he slow in expressing himself in regard to what he knew. His ready cordiality was manifest from time to time in his accounts of the work written for the Annual Report of the London Congregational Association. I may be pardoned for giving a brief extract or two from his ready pen:

"The work under Mr. Hillocks, in the North-Western district, has been abundantly blessed. He has opened for himself and the gospel message a door into many hearts. We find he is doing much, under God, to link the poor to the sanctuary, and we feel it would be a calamity to lose his services."

When this was written, there was a rumour that I was about to accept of a pastorate. But I decided to hold on, my whole heart and hope being in this work. Hence in the following years' reports references were made to my continued labours, to their nature and extent, and from the same appreciative pen. A sentence may serve here as an example.

"In addition to visiting the people at their homes; to his indoor and outdoor services; to popular lectures—speaking as often as sixteen times a week to large audiences; in addition to all this, with many kindred efforts, he is often found in the police courts pleading for those in trouble. Also attending the sick at the hospital, and helping the poor at the workhouses."

The want of sufficient space prevents me from attempting fully to describe the varied forms of which this friendly glance but faintly indicates. But much of what is therefore excluded I hope to give together with fuller details—in the Sequel. Here I cannot do much more than refer to some of the leading lines of labour. *Organising the forces.*

While thus plodding on endeavouring to find my way, amidst many difficulties and adverse criticism, I tried to show, by precept and example, the good that is likely to come of individual action. But I was not slow in availing myself of the possible assistance of organization. Though at first my followers were not numerous, and some of them were somewhat afraid to advance with me, yet I sought the co-operation of all who would go as far as they could, suggesting for them the work nearest their heart. This encouraged kindred spirits whose sympathy and help I had from the beginning.

This effort had its fruit in the formation of the North-West London Evangelistic Association, the generous merchant prince, the late Samuel Morley, M.P., being the President. Like every effort we made, the object of this Association was to promote the social, but, above all, the religious well-being of the people. It consisted of a pleasant combination of several societies, each one of which was distinct, yet tending to advance the common object. There was the Christian Instruction Society which sought to gain an entrance into the benighted homes and hearts, by domestic visitation, religious services and open air preaching. There was a Total Abstinence Society, and a Band of Hope, seeking to promote Temperance among old and young. The Mending Home Society seeking to improve home and home-life, the membership being open to all wives and daughters. The Mutual Benefit Society was also useful in taking care of the savings of the poor, and assisting them in the purchase of coal, articles of clothing, and other necessaries, on advantageous terms.

This Association had its juvenile department in what became widely known as the Bud of Promise, with its various Bands. The aim was not only to improve the members spiritually and morally, mentally and physically, but also so to train them that the happiness they enjoyed might be enhanced by their becoming helpful to others.

Thus it was that I got every willing hand employed, each in the line he or she preferred. And, thanks to my co-workers, this machinery went so well, that others outside began to speak favourably of it. One of such was my friend the late Sir Hugh Owen. He spoke of what he was pleased to call "the manifestation of organizing powers." He, and others who agreed with him, thought and said it would be for the greater good if I had a central office in the city, where I might, by advice and effort, assist the churches and other societies of the Metropolis in organising and carrying on work like unto that I was doing in St. Pancras. The Rev. Drs. Guthrie and Fleming also thought well of the idea, but suggested that things should remain as they were for a time. This was my opinion also, so the subject dropped, and the work went on.

Chapter IV.—Indoor Efforts.

I WAS sorry to find that much of the so-called "visiting the poor" was saturated with cant, gossip and absurdity. There was no such thing as "*house to house* visiting." What there was of visiting was, as a rule, confined to certain localities wherein the physically poor were striving to live. And, with rare exceptions, the visitors went not on sufferance but as a right. Generally the poor looked upon their presence as a tax upon poverty.

Visiting the poor.

The larger portion of the visitors were very offensive. One portion of them merely went for fashion's sake, and their own amusement. I have known of such designated the salt of the earth, and they liked that immensely. They looked upon themselves, and affected to be up in the social scale; and they looked upon the poor as the dirt among their feet, and expected that what they said would be accepted as gospel, though it was often the reverse in word and spirit. They were full of caste and eaten up with second-rate-boarding-school ladyism. They liked to be accompanied in their rounds with "gentlemen" to match. Whatever else they obtained in passing they picked up subject matter for parlour gossip about "the awful poor." This matter, in some cases, was relished at such "assemblies" as are now known by the name, "At home at five." It served as a much beloved relish to their "*chit chat*," and called forth frequent attempts at sardonic wit which would have been laughable but for the interest involved.

There was another class of visitors, mostly gentlemen. They had less of the giggle about them. They too had a purpose, and they carried it out with a vengeance. Their wish was to get vent to some dearly beloved notions, made up of some little patches of truth, or something like truth. Each tried hard to push his patch down the throat of all who would listen. This and only this was the passport to heaven. All who did not agree with them were doubly damned.

Neither of these two classes made headway with the people, and no wonder. The visitors and the visited looked upon each other as enemies, neither believed nor trusted the other. Those of the visited who were pauperised pretended to receive the visits and to listen, and told all manner of falsehoods, but this was only for certain expectations. But for these expectations many of the poor would shut their doors against such visitors as "awful bores."

But I met with a few visitors, men and women, who were intelligent and sympathetic, who forced not themselves upon the people, but went to them by silent permission, finding the door opened for them. In all humility and love and pity, their only desire was to be useful; particularly to pour out the balm of consolation by speaking of Jesus as the Friend of the poor. Such visitors were made welcome. The pity was they were so few in number.

But however far the thoughtless, and selfish, and uppish, may pervert fundamental principle, yet I found that visiting the people at their homes is of the first importance in all the work of reformation, whether spiritual or physical, social or domestic. By means of proper and regular visiting the people at their homes we find the hope of evangelization—face to face, heart to heart, in loving kindness, and the Holy Spirit presiding. Here, in this way, I learned the virtues and the failings, the wants and wishes, the spiritual and physical condition of the individual, of the home, and much that was outside of it, and yet greatly effecting it, often adversity. A power for good, of imparting help, is lost where visiting the poor is neglected.

Our adult meetings.

This visiting at the homes of the people was followed up by all sorts of indoor gatherings. In this department of work, as in visiting, I had much to contend with, at least till the people knew me. Many of them—as was too generally the case all over London—were pauperised by those who had been labouring more for sectarian purposes than for the good of those whose presence they coveted. Those in this condition generally run to a new place, expecting more of the creature comforts than they had been receiving. But against this mode of getting an audience I at once set my face, even though I was told that our meeting place would soon be empty. On this matter I was emphatic; and, true enough, those who would not be advised to self-help and self-respect withdrew, but in most cases only for a time. And, ultimately, there was this marked difference in our services, we had nearly as many men as women—men of brain, and, as some have since proved to be, men of heart.

Perhaps I should add here, " the winning of the people's attention and affection," did not arise from any special novelty, nor from pandering to unsustainable prejudices. The people were heartily invited, and lovingly treated as fellow-creatures. When they came, they heard no new doctrine. My theme was " the old, old story of Jesus and His love." My words were the words of the Bible warnings as well as Bible promises. I strove to impart the whole truth as it is in Jesus—that whilst the unsaved had no peace, no hope, no excuse, no escape, the saved in Christ had in Him not only the Saviour, but also an Upholder, a Mediator, an Advocate, a Brother. I was also careful to point out that there must be communion with God before there can be testimony for God; that right doing is a proof of right believing; and that both put together simply mean walking with God, in the sense of being *for* Christ and *against* sin.

This was all, and many rejoiced in it after they clearly understood what was really meant by right believing and right doing.

Perhaps I should state here that I thought well to introduce *what some designated* " a novel way of going to work." This was it: On a given Sunday evening in each month I carried out a plan which drew to our gatherings some of the more intelligent of the skilled artizans, particularly those of them who were confused doubters, or earnest inquirers. A London newspaper whose special correspondent honoured us with a visit referred to our assemblies in these words:—

"Much is being said in connection with the Working Classes and Religious Institutions: and we rejoice to think that some of those who are best acquainted with the sons and daughters of toil are advancing so as to meet their wants aud wishes, temporal and spiritual. Amongst this class of earnest hard workers is Mr. Hillocks. We have with pleasure noticed his week-day work in connection with the souls and bodies of those who look to him for help and consolation, and now we rejoice to see the manner in which he meets such on Sunday at his religious services.

"These services are of the simplest kind, and they seem to be enjoyed by all present; the devotional part is truly impressive. The attention to the discourse—whether a sermon, a lecture, or an exhortation—is earnest and thoughtful. But that to which we call special attention, is the turn which the service of last Sunday evening took. It was the first of his 'monthly *conversations* with the people.' The subject—Rom. xii., 1—was given out by him on the previous Sunday. After the worship element of the service was over, Mr. Hillocks spoke on the text named for about fifteen minutes, and then threw the meeting open for forty-five minutes, during which any one in the meeting was at liberty to speak. The only rule he prescribed was, that they speak in the spirit and in the name of Christ. This is another of his steps in the right direction; and the result, even of the first night's work, was such as delighted the preacher's heart, and his people felt at home."

Though, on these occasions, doctrine and duty were taken up alternately, there was no special pleading for any creed nor for any church polity. Our desire was to "prove all things and hold fast what is good." My aim was to strengthen the desire generally felt by man, to be free to think, and I was glad to see this freedom of thought exercised in a manner at once commendable and profitable. I studied to make my short papers more suggestive than exhaustive, and more readily do I admit that in the short speeches that followed, there were remarks which were suggestive to me.

This was an hour of mutual improvement. And some who only came on these monthly occasions were afterwards seen at our other Sunday services and week-day meetings.

Finding this to be successful, I occasionally did the same on week-night meetings in connection with my lectures on subjects likely to instruct and interest and entertain the audience—lectures on Health, History, Biography, and so on.

Caring for the young. Nor were the advancement of the children forgotten for a single day. This was natural in me. The love of children, and a desire for their welfare have been developing at least since 1844, when I became a public teacher. And I had carried this with me to London, wherever I went. The very word, *children*, has ever had a charm for me. When all is right that word bespeaks beauty and simplicity, a sweet innocence and rich instinct, a graceful as well as a lively being endowed with a happy energy and a telling reality, a teacher as well as a pupil, divine as well as human. "Of such is the Kingdom of Heaven."

But all is not right, and hence all children are not as we would like them to be. Human folly, evil habits and affected artificialism do much to bring about a life of suffering in which the children suffer most. This is so with the children of all classes, but more particularly with the young of the poor. And even some parents seem to forget that children were given for our care as well as our delight. Convinced of all this I have given free course to the feelings of love and pity, which feelings have led to corresponding action on my part whether labouring as a teacher, a missionary, an evangelist, or a pastor. But none have had from me more care and attention than the London children, because nowhere is the work of caring for the young more necessary than in this great metropolis. Nothing touched me more deeply than to see the sad condition of the poor waifs from the courts and alleys.

It was so then, even as now. Then I found by far the larger

portion of them had been born, and were still living, in the direst poverty, surrounded by all forms of degradation, many sick unto death, having passed through all sorts of diseases. With all this before me, I asked myself, what can I do to help to save the children from pending destruction? An answer to this came as if inspired—Gather the young together and lead them to Jesus, and hence the formation of the Bud of Promise with its various Bands.

Each Band had a night for itself, and these meetings were happy and useful. For instance, one night we had a very large gathering under the auspices of the young Samaritan Band. It was a delight to meet with this loving Band as with each of the rest. But 1 had just come to this meeting from visiting some cases of sore distress among the young, sick and starving. After bringing some of the cases before my young friends, I asked, "Is it possible to provide wholesome dinners during the winter as well as on Christmas day?"

"Yes," was the unanimous response, and they meant it. The well-to-do in this noble Band were led by my own dear son and his winning sisters, but all the poorest among them, rendered some assistance. And what these young Samaritans could not do themselves, they got others to help.

This became known through the kindness of the press, and the work extended beyond our first conception. During this and the following winter 3,207 hearty and healthy dinners were given at our own house, besides what were sent to those too weakly to come for them. Thus were started what is now so widely and happily known as "Dinners for poor children."

And it is pleasant to have to add that almost all who were thus cared for, fed and clothed, proved themselves worthy of the efforts made on their behalf. No doubt this was happily due, not to preaching at the poor during the meals, but to the teaching and training at our various Bud of Promise meetings. I take it as another proof that among the young, as well as those more advanced in years, the fine traits of humanity and the holy element of divinity are likely to appear under good influences. In the midst of these my young Buds, even in the larger assemblies of many hundreds of them—I have felt as at the very gates of heaven.

But many and happy as the results were in regard to the members of the Bud of Promise, the good to others extended beyond. It made my heart glad to see "Our young ones at work." And this good was felt in many of the homes of which they formed a part.

I have referred to the Samaritan Band, but that was only one in seven. A pleasing spirit pervaded the whole, but particularly in the Christian Band. Words cannot tell the joy I felt when, after calling attention to the words and ways of our Saviour, the earnest request was made, "Please, sir, let us sing, 'I want to be like Jesus.'"

Chapter V.—Battles in the Open Air.

Open-air preaching.

But in addition to this, experience taught me that visiting the people at their homes was not enough. Neither were such indoor efforts as meetings, services, sermons, lectures, enough. So certain was I on this point that I felt convinced that no evangelist—be he missionary or pastor—can give *full* proof of his ministry unless to these he adds open-air preaching; unless he, to the utmost of his strength and abilities, goes quickly to proclaim the gospel in the streets and lanes, in the highways and byeways.

I readily admit the fact that had any one previous to the delivery of my first open-air address told me that open-air preaching was to become one of my leading lines of labour, I would have been unwilling to believe him, but he would have been right. So much has this been the case that a leading journal thought it well to devote considerable space to my work in this direction. The writer favoured the motive but not that mode of doing good. He wrote as if this form of effort was my *only* work. This mistake—arising from not knowing the whole facts of the case—was of no consequence. One good thing the notice did. It seemed as if it added to my audiences such as those who were given to reading and therefore generally intelligent, and for this I was thankful.

For years after 1860, as for years before, the task to preach in the open air was not an easy one, not so inviting as now. It was as pleasant to be "Beneath the blue sky," but there appeared to be more darkness on the ground. The heathen seemed more enraged. But the need was as great if not greater. A knowledge that people were perishing while salvation was nigh, urged the warm heart to go forth with a clear head and clean hands to tell of the Bread of life, in dependence on the Holy Spirit.

Let not the last six words be misunderstood. They mean what they say, but no more. In this respect the Holy Spirit does two things. He teaches by means of the Word, and He brings what He has taught us to our remembrance. These things I realised on the memorable Sunday morning referred to. Before then, in Scotland, He had taught me, then He brought much of the result of the teaching before my mind and gave me courage to tell it, as far as was necessary to meet the case. He does not encourage idleness by pouring something into us that we, without thought, may pour it out on some special occasion. I always went to preach—whether indoors or outdoors—in dependence on the Holy Spirit. Sometimes I did not know when I was to speak, nor what was best to say; but I was careful to keep myself well prepared. Generally I carried about in my mind the outlines of several carefully thought out discourses, giving the one I felt most suitable for the people, the place or the occasion. Without doubt this readiness was helpful. Clearly it was approved of by Him who sent the Comforter. Even as at first, I realise the presence and support of Him who spoke on the sea shore.

Speaking roundly, the opposition to this mode of Christian work came from three classes. *Three opposing classes.*

The first I found in unexpected quarters—from the churches or rather from many who were in the churches. The formalists, though they went to the churches occasionally and held themselves up as religious, were dead against this work. In this they were backed by some who wished to be regarded as very devout. To their severe criticisms of the preachers they added such statements as this: "It is dreadful thus to cast pearls before swine." Neither of these critics came to see for themselves, far less to advise those whom they knew to be fighting against great odds. They preferred to remain afar off and blindly criticise. This was chilling, and none like the cold shoulder of friends. But, when in the battlefield, we had little time to bemoan our isolation from those who were so ready to help in indoor work.

Another class who opposed my efforts in this line were some of the leaders of those known by the indefinite, but general, name of Infidels. This may be said in their favour, they were sober, so far as strong drink was concerned; but the most of them were very intemperate in words, while others were so hardened in sin that they sneered at God and all good. Judging from what they said, they assumed that they were the intellectual giants of the day, looking down upon Christian believers as "trifling nonentities." Each of this class of opposers seemed to be ready with his "Bible objection," to which he had paid special attention. And this he endeavoured in every possible way to bring round, so that it might appear to have some connection with what I had said. But what knowledge they had was one-sided and shallow. What they called their logic was hollow. So long as they kept to words they were easily settled, and it was seldom they resorted to blows.

A third class of opposers were those who called themselves "Romanists." Among them were some who were generally well-meaning in the things pertaining to this life, but in things pertaining to what they called religious life they were fierce and fiery. For the most part they were exceedingly ignorant, but there were some of the well-disposed who were well read—at least in some of the subjects they thought well to speak upon in opposition to those whom they called "heretics"—another word for Protestants. Another portion of this same class was utterly ungodly though, as they said, they "adhered to Rome." They were drunken and ready for any mischief. Strong drink fired their demoniac passions. To call them brutal would be to stain the brute creation. They were not only possessed by the devil, each one was himself a devil.

My first open air audience. In these times, even as now, the audience is often made up of all sorts, as was the case in regard to my first open air audience, at the corner of Brand Street, Hornsey Road, Holloway. It will be a long time before I forget that sight.

The majority were thirsty miserable creatures, the most of whom had come to that spot in the hope of having a drink on the sly at the public-house adjoining. Some of the men as well as some of the women, were bare-headed, but this was not in honour of the service. Those of the former were also without coats or jackets, some without vests. In most cases the shirt was unbuttoned, the neck being bare and red, as if sunburnt. Their trousers were fastened up by a strong belt round the loins. Their feet were encased in strong, lacing, earth-covered boots, not laced. They seemed angry and ready for any fray. But there were other men, evidently as thirsty for strong drink, and even more wretched to all appearance. The shoemaker, for instance, who had been working late the night before, or perhaps that morning, had also come. His hands were black with rosin, his face as dirty, a cap sufficiently set on the side of his head to reveal his bushy, uncombed hair. His eye and face sharp, with something of the appearance of a proud, stern intellect, ready for debate or any other form of opposition to such services. The coster, too, was there with his large handkerchief round his neck and the latest Billingsgate slang and oaths pouring out from his foul mouth. There, too, was the London rough, ready to lead in anything that would give him the opportunity of taking what was not his own. The young cockney was up to all sorts of annoying larks. And there also was the subdued old man, laden with the sorrows of sin, the burden of iniquity bearing heavily down upon him. He has come either to get beer or is in search of peace. The female portion of the audience was as varied, perhaps not quite so wicked looking; many were sad and evidently suffering much. And staring vacantly was a little girl with a large jug in her hand. Her feet and head were bare, and the rag of worn-out, tattered dress scarcely covered her thin frame. She looked wistfully at the door of the beer-shop and then at the window. But seeing no chance at present to get her jug filled, she forced her way to the front, next to the chair upon which I was standing.

When I thought of the gracious help then so readily rendered, and the precious blessing so freely bestowed, I felt encouraged, even when the opposition was more determined. But I found that all audiences were not the same, in appearances at least. For instance, there is the above, and here is another at Chelsea.

Nor was the opposition always of the same nature, sometimes it was very mild, mixed with affected humour. *My life threatened.* This was after the most of my hearers knew me, and believed I meant their good. At other times—especially when I was attempting to hold a long lost fort—there was an evident bitterness, sometimes a maliciousness in the opposition. In the former case, my triumph was comparatively easy, in the latter case, at times, my life was threatened.

The danger was greatest in the "courts" and "places" most noted for dirt and drink—such dark spots as had an inlet at one end, but no outlet at the other—the free passage, as well as free air, being prevented by means of some dead wall.

PREACHING IN A LONDON COURT.

Let us pause a little in one of the "places." This *cul-de-sac* has, in days past, been a neat double row of small houses, each having a back yard and a patch of garden ground in front. The pathway between the two rows had been paved,

Preaching at Whitestiles, Chelsea.

and no doubt all looked neatly then. Now, however, all is slummy and of the worst kind. The pavement is broken up, and not a little has disappeared. The holes are filled with all sorts of moist mud, black as pitch.

There is—as a matter of course there must be at the corner of all such places—a public-house ready to supply what those interested in the drink traffic call "a felt want." As far from this drunkery as possible I took my stand.

Here I thought the worst of my open-air battles were over, but I was mistaken. Partly because of the good I had endeavoured to do the people in regard to the sanitary derangement all around, I had considerable hold of the most of them. At least, no speaker could be on better terms with his audience than I had been for some time past. But evidently this success was too much for two classes of the enemies of the people. Those whose wish was that the people remain in heathen darkness, and those whose interest was to stand in the way of those who urged the people to abstain from strong drink. And both classes, with their equally wicked tools, conspired to prevent my presence in the place, as they had previously turned out other preachers and visitors.

One evening, as I was preaching and many were earnestly listening, a band of men emerged from this same public-house, and made straight for the place where I was speaking. They were a dozen in number, the age of each was some way about twenty, more or less; they were led to their work by a man about thrice their age. In a moment they dashed me against the wall and smashed the chair.

This the women, who had been listening, vigorously resented, and when I came to my senses I found a furious battle still raging between the "*brave* thirteen," and the women. As to the latter, their only weapon of war was the blinding pitchy stuff that surrounded them on every hand; but they conquered, the men had to beat a retreat. dirty enough.

But though I was at that time much injured I was improved so far that I returned to the same place on the following Sunday morning as usual.

"Don't go, sir. You have a wife and family. These fellows are plotting to kill you," said some of the women who met me at the entrance. "They've got more money and more drink to do what they failed to do the other night."

To this kind entreaty I listened respectfully, but told them my duty was to go forward, not only because the ground already gained would be lost, but evil would triumph, and they would again be without a preacher. So I passed on. When nearing the spot where I usually stood to speak, one of the men came out from the ring into which they had proposed to drag me. At this moment the women screamed.

On the Saturday night before, a wretched street-girl had suddenly met with her death, and had been taken home to her parents that morning, at one of the hovels near to this spot. I had heard of this, and meant to call.

"Do you know of that awful death last night?" asked the man who had stepped out from the group.

"Yes," I replied, adding I must go to visit her parents. And for that purpose I passed on, meaning to return to preach if permitted. I returned to find a change had come over the mind of the conspirators. The ring had broken up and all but one of the links had disappeared and that was the man who spoke to me as I had passed them. Another chair was provided, and the service was held. The occasion was a solemn one, and God blessed it. I did not preach the sermon I meant, but God once more brought all that was needed to my mind, and the utterance was as free as if nothing special had happened.

Their next effort to drive me from preaching there, was much worse for me. It was on a week evening, and I was alone, as in both of the other cases. The same big burly drunken Irishman with his young companions in wickedness came from the same public-house. They did not assail me at once, but rushed upon me when I was on my way to the street. I was so injured that I was laid aside for some weeks. The doctor's expectation of my being able again to preach was very small.

In the meantime, however, the leader of this gang repented, and felt anxious to see me, but the doctor would not hear of the meeting. On a Saturday he went to work as a bricklayer's labourer, missed his footing at the top of a large house and fell to the ground. He was killed.

Among the first visits after my recovery was to his widow. She was glad when I assured her I had forgiven him as soon as I heard of his repentance. That assurance on my part and other helpful efforts, added to such as I had previously made, gained for me the former confidence of the most in the district, Romanists and Protestants.

The difficulty over, I was as ready as ever. Some times by means of helpers in this work, I would open ten or a dozen open-air stations in a summer evening. I generally spoke longest at the latest opened. Here the opposers met in force, endeavouring to find a pretext for interruption. This was the case with the more intelligent objectors, called "infidels," a few of the ablest of them being told off to meet me, some following from station to station. I observed that when they saw the audience drinking in the truth they became more and more restless until they could not contain themselves. *An easy victory.*

For instance, one evening our meeting was such as an enthusiastic preacher would rejoice in. The night was quiet, the assembly was large and attentive, and clearly power from on high moving the throng. This proved to be too much for those who had purposely come to resist God and oppose His truth. Several attempts were made to interrupt, but I held on, till at last one of the band became enraged, calling out, "Tell us of some one we all know."

Stopping short, I quietly said, "Perhaps our friend may be able to tell us who that one is."

"Garibaldi!" was the triumphant reply, and some in the audience shouted, "Hear, hear."

At that time this "Liberator" was the subject of much deserved praise, and his generous deeds of daring flashed across my mind.

These I depicted to the amazement of the infidels. Then from Garibaldi I turned to Jesus, from the great liberator to the Greatest Liberator, and showed what He had done, what He was doing, and all He had promised to do for man, "to seek and to save the lost."

"That will do," said the leading unbeliever, at the same time marching off with his followers.

My audience looked upon this as another triumph, and I was glad it was one in which no feelings were hurt. In that case good results were more likely to follow. I resumed my discourse, the subject being the certain misery of sinners away from God, and the certain happiness of believers in Christ.

In itself, this incident was a small one and soon over. But it was often the subject of conversation. So far as this class of opposers were concerned, I was henceforth left alone, but the number of intelligent doubters increased. They came to listen, and some went away rejoicing.

To say that much good has been done by able and wise open air preaching is to repeat what is well known to all who have any knowledge of the facts. And I thank God that my humble efforts in that line of good work have been blessed by Him. My own experience in regard to happy results would fill quite a volume, and I must remember I have other important matters of which to speak.

It is truly said that preaching in the open air is much easier now. The preachers have also greatly improved in matter and manner, and under God, much of this is due to the work and influence of the Open Air Mission which has just issued a valuable volume entitled, "Beneath the Blue Sky." The book is stimulating as well as informing.

Immediately connected with this line of labour, there were *Kindred fields of labour.* others of a kindred nature. The scenes were at such places as "the Music Halls," the "Tea Gardens," the Race Courses.

Willingly would I stop to give details of fearful life as seen in such places, but I must at present pass on with only a word or two. I do so all the readier because I have elsewhere written on these abominations, and because I mean, in the promised sequel, to refer to their ruinous influence on the nation, as well as the individual.

The two first were generally combined. In my case, they were the most dangerous to life and limb. My object was twofold, to see and to do good. This I took no pains to hide. Though I was in Rome I refused to do as Rome did. I also refused to have anything to do with strong drink and tobacco in any of their forms, but freely purchased milk or coffee, or tea, when they could be had. After going the round of the most noted of these dens of iniquity, in some cases more than once, I wrote six papers on them. Though threatened with "criminal prosecution" the threatening parties thought it well to let the matter drop. But happily that was not the end. As some of them found, the license to continue was refused, and some of the more abominable of such places were closed.

What led me, in the first instance, to take such steps was the urgent request of a dying mother who recounted to me how her once promising daughter had come to ruin by frequenting such places. Hence I also strove hard to prevent others being added to the diminished list. In this, too, I was successful, to the peace and comfort of those who lived in the neighbourhood in which the attempt was made.

I suppose that "the Derby" is considered the chief of races, and some say it is the chief in wickedness and evil results. This I know, it presents the greatest variety of the utterly detestable which one's eyes can look upon. As you may gather from what I have just said, I have seen various forms of vicious amusement wildly indulged in by men and women of all kinds of social grades, the fast and the base, the profane and the obscene, as if they lived in and had come from the lower region; but I never saw all the forms of iniquity massed together as I saw on Epsom Downs. And then chief in this reign of rascality, was the spreading of the spirit of getting money by chance, that spirit of gambling which is one of the greatest curses of our day.

On the occasion of my first visit, I found myself asking the questions, Where do the many of the miserable sleep on the night before the Derby? Is it possible to do them good, whilst disengaged late on the eve or early on the morning? Accordingly next year found me doing my best among the poverty-stricken who were trying to rest on the green sward. From "town and country," there were men, old and young, old women and even children. Also many girls, almost children in years, but already old in vice. Some of the men were hilarious, being uproariously drunk and ready for any shindy. Generally these were the young and the strong. But there were also the grizzly-grey ruffians, and women to match in appearance and disposition—drunken, soddened, blear-eyed, brutal-looking creatures; and included among the squalid and miserable—some of them having bruised and battered faces—were what is known as broken-down gentlemen, lingering out the wretched remnant of existence, anxious to remain unknown, and in constant dread of being recognised. As to the cause of all this miserable degradation, there was the one answer, " Drink and gambling, gambling and drink."

As "the Derby" is said to be a West-End holiday, so Fairlop Friday is an East End one. In both, the devil and his drink hold carnival. It was in response to an appeal, "Come East to help," that first led me to "Fairlop Festival." I went, and with many others, tried to help, but the good was as the drop in the bucket, as compared with the ocean of evil. There seemed to be a few who felt as if they must *endure* the vice of the time; some also *pitied* the vicious, but clearly the vast majority *embraced* the vice.

True, many efforts were being made by earnest good friends to bring about a change for the better on other evenings as well as on the night of the so-called festival. There were many preachers, and Whitechapel boasted of the only known open air pulpit, but the preachers of iniquity, within the public-houses, and on their balconies, overshadowed every effort for good. The sights and sounds seen and heard from Aldgate to Stratford, particularly from betwixt 9 p.m. and midnight, were

> "Abominable, unutterable and worse
> Than fables yet have feigned or fear conceived."

What a night! What scenes! "The waves of fiery darkness against the rocks of dark damnation break." Midnight finds no improvement. The short hour sees the people still besmeared with drink and dirt and degradation, riotous drunkenness and open debauchery standing out in their naked hideousness all along the terrible line of the concentrated essence of sensuality.

OPEN-AIR PULPIT, ST. MARY'S, WHITECHAPEL.

Chapter VI.—Three "Doms" Against the Poor.

The field as I found it.
Thus I continued the work. (1) In the homes of the people. (2) In all sorts of meeting places. (3) In the open air. And, in each department of labour, endeavouring to follow the Master, who taught the people wherever He was, on the mountain side or by the sea-shore.

But, as was needful in London, these efforts run concurrently with others. Alas, we had, as we still have, two leading and terrible curses to contend against—the slum and the drink. And by legal pretence, aided by use and wont, Slumdom and Drinkdom were intermixed with Bumbledom. Each of these three "Doms" was doing its utmost to damn the poor, and with great success. Hence I openly declared war against each and all of these terrible curses.

As in Islington, so in St. Pancras—indeed, at that time, all over London—this kind of warfare was regarded as beyond the province of a minister of religion. It was to be expected that the ill-disposed enemies of the poor should say so. From wicked motives they desired things to remain as they were. But how the well-meaning people could coldly stand by and see the poor destroyed by these combined curses I felt at a loss to understand. The manifest inhumanity was beyond conception. The robbery of the poor on the one hand, and the neglect of the poor on the other, were alike fearful. Looking upon all this in the terrible light of the fearful facts which my labours among the poor brought daily before, I was roused to indignation.

True enough there were Christian hearts, and some kind of Christian efforts, but little or none of Christian heroism; and hence the varied forms of grinding evil rose above the good aimed at by the well-disposed, so much so, that it seemed as if all

House in High Street, Edinburgh, with Memorial Window.

Christian heart and thought had vanished. With rare exceptions, those whose thoughts were better than their actions, rather inaction, were too timid to defend the poor against the wicked ways of those whose interest it was to foster every form of evil which brought ill-gotten grist to their cursed mills. The evils in bumbledom were scarcely known, and what came to light only received a passing notice. The corruption was going deeper and deeper. While the slum-curse and the drink-curse were nourished, if not cherished, not only by the State, but also by almost all the churches.

Nor was this state of things at that time confined to London. I found it on the north as well as on the south of the Tweed. Its evil effects were telling against all concerned throughout our United Kingdom. As you know, Edinburgh was far from being an exception to this. On the High Street there is a memorial of neglect in regard to the poor in the slums. Even after the plague spots of that naturally grand city were exposed, those whose duty it was to see to the homes of the poor did little or nothing by way of improvement till what was predicted came to pass—till the human remains had to be extracted from beneath the fallen pile of rotten ruins.

And what in my mind made bad worse was the thought that in Scotland, as well as in England, in Edinburgh as well as in London, to the most of the leaders in the religious world nothing was more annoying than to insist that the word Christian implies that those who claim it as their title are for Christ and against sin in every form. Because of this winking at evil instead of opposing it, iniquity had free course. At least the opposition of the churches to evil, personal and relative, even the most glaring forms of iniquity, was faint and almost fruitless.

Seeing all this, and feeling for the poor, the suffering victims of these three *doms*, I refused to go with the dead-sea stream, and took my stand against all evil, national and parochial; at the same time doing my utmost for the promotion of all good.

Workhouse horrors.

Here, however, I am unable to do more than refer to one of the special battles on behalf of the poor—that is against the wicked ways of Bumbledom. One reason why I refer to it in particular is the fact that, because of its cruel constitution and shameless administration, it has within it the fostering, if not the engendering elements of all the curses. I pleaded for its reformation, but it continued to prove itself to be past redemption.

Still I must add that even in St. Pancras there were some in parochial authority who were not so very bad as compared with the worst. With those who would listen, I pleaded for the poor. At times they promised well, and, no doubt, they meant what they said, but their influence was overpowered by those who were the reverse of being friendly to the poor. I fought for long almost single handed, till at last a few outsiders began to open their eyes to the state of things. Some ventured to remonstrate, for instance, one lady, the Baroness Burdett Coutts—whose undoubted sympathy for the poor is well known—ventured to send a letter to the St. Pancras "Guardians," protesting against "their system of administration," of actually exposing paupers to the danger of being buried alive. She was womanly enough, and daring enough, to suggest that paupers should not find a living grave within the walls of the workhouse.

An ecclesiastical dignitary also ventured in vain to advise in the sad matter, refusing to countenance such horrid cruelty. However, I maintained my ground against all comers—the jests of some, the gibes of others, the unsympathetic looks of others. I put them all together, with the reviling malignity of those who persisted in their horrid cruelty to the poor.

About to be buried alive.

The generous Baroness, and the Archbishop, referred to the same case of work-house horror, which I had just exposed: namely, that of "Wee Bessie Green," a child whom I found there laid out alive, prepared to be taken to the dead house while yet living. But these great ones of the earth were doomed to have showered upon them a share of such abuse from Messrs. Bumble as was being heaped upon me. They were bullied to silence. However "The Fourth Estate" was not to be put about. The press was ready to give sight to my exposures of these fearful instances of horrid inhumanity. The comments were various, still arriving at the same conclusion. This was it: "Of all the workhouse horrors there is none more harrowing than that narrated by the Rev. J. I. Hillocks. No words of ours can add to the force of his simple narrative. It must rouse the indignation of every mother, and of every human being."

The sad facts brought to light were confirmed not only at the Coroner's Inquest, but also by the Local Government Board of Inquiry. The verdict was that "the death of the child was greatly accelerated by being laid out for dead while alive, swaddled like a corpse." Three special resolutions were by the Jury appended to the verdict. The third related to myself; namely, "The Jury beg to express their approval of the course taken by Mr. Hillocks in bringing the matter before the public."

The medical journals, and the press generally carefully watched the case throughout. After declaring that "the evidence on oath, even of the workhouse officials, added horror to horror," the editor's opinion was that "the verdict gave unqualified satisfaction." But the combat deepened, Bumbledom would have pocketed the censure with the shame, had it not been for the Jury's third resolution. That was the sting which made those in authority kick; but their kicking made matters worse for them, and better for the poor. Their attempt at denials led to more revelations. At last, however, they thought they found a mare's nest. They searched far and near in search of a flaw in my moral character. At last they found one, and forthwith proclaimed the undeniable fact that I had been a weaver. My friends were proud of this fact, but the emphatic declaration, on the part of those sitting in judgment upon me, only made them more ridiculous. Nevertheless, trying to make the best of a bad job, their mouthpiece tried to bring home his indictment against me by pompously asking his audience, "Is this vast parish, wielding so much money annually, to be governed by a Dundee weaver?"

Aids to triumph.

I have referred to the press as helpful, and that was so in a very special manner. About this time there was considerable writing on parochial conduct, particularly that manifested in St. Pancras. The most of that writing was earnest and sensible. As a rule, it was in favour of the poor. Some of the papers were severely cutting, but no more than the heartless conduct of Messrs. Bumble and company called for. Even before I was generally regarded as on the winning side, one of the Dailies, in the course of a leader wrote:—

"The attendants on whom this little waif of babyhood fell, decided that she ought to be dead, whether she would or not, and treated her accordingly; but even after a gentle admonition, the infant reprobate declined to depart. Even in the hour of death she was resolved to trouble her benefactors and guardians, and in that wicked design she was abetted by a Minister of the Gospel, who happened to be present in the workhouse. That gentleman in his zeal for suffering humanity observed while visiting the Union, the child 'laid out' for dead was still alive. He ordered a doctor to be sent for. He was informed that no medical assistance could be obtained without the sanction of the superintendant, yet Mr. Hillocks persisted in his wilful endeavour to interfere with the established order of St. Pancras Union. Even the believers in the sanctity of St. Pancras will find it hard, however, to point out the individuals whom they consider responsible for an act that looks so like an outrage on humanity. Of course, if everybody were like Mr. Hillocks, things might be different, but then it is the fashion now-a-days to say that religious philanthropists of Mr. Hillocks' stamp are actuated by the basest motives: and, indeed, we are afraid that the Hillockses of this world are out of harmony with the admirable system of pauper protection established in our metropolitan workhouses."

"Nothing succeeds like success," so I found in this case, as in others of a like nature, not only in St. Pancras but elsewhere. At last the Government and Parliament of the day gave a helping hand. The change brought about was not such as I wished, but it not only turned the reigning enemies of the poor right about; the new arrangements have since made it difficult for such enemies of mankind to attain and retain place and power, and, for the poor, that was a gain.

The letters of congratulations which I received from all sorts and conditions of men, and women too, were hearty. Some enthusiastic as well as serious. For instance, in one letter there was this sentence, "Your writing direct to the Poor Law Board was a God-inspired act on behalf of the suffering and helpless poor." He referred to my letter in regard to "the child laid out alive," which letter, in the end, led up to the result just stated

Chapter VII.—Pastor or Evangelist?

An interesting memorial. Though this was not my only victory over Bumbledom, and several of its attendant evils, it proved to be the last of my more public efforts having reference to St. Pancras in its individual capacity. However, it brought upon me the curses of the wicked which happily could not injure me, they had done what injury they could before this. But it gained for me the blessings or good wishes of the poor, in which I rejoiced. In this I was the gainer.

Still these battles had been so long, and so hard, and against great odds, that they severely told against my health. The strain on body and mind was such that I broke down. This was something more added to my suffering of service; but what though one suffers, even a family, as it was in this case, if thereby many are saved from fearful suffering and premature death. And there was the cheering thought that I had been, by God, preserved so long "to do the good which was in my heart to do." However, let me confess, I was unwilling to yield, to cease, even when weakness called for rest. Hence, as far as my failing health permitted, I continued to labour as before, adopting all other possible means of helping the poor.

At this time, my attention was called to a matter which had about it a personal as well as a relative aspect. An affectionate and urgent memorial, signed by 254, was presented to me, asking if I would become the pastor of a church proposed to be formed by them and others, who had been helpfully interested in the work of my ministry among the people.

This was a matter not to be lightly put aside, for one reason, quite 200 of the memorialists had been rescued from sin and misery since I began to labour in St. Pancras, and many more of such were rejoicing in Jesus. And, besides, it was certainly pleasant to see so many so earnest, not only in regard to their own edification, but also interested in the welfare of others still in darkness and error. But I had first to settle in my own mind the question, Pastor or Evangelist?

This question, in turn, led me to look some facts in the face. One belonged to what by some is tauntingly called, "the bread and cheese matter." As things then stood, and as they still stand, the income of the Pastor is about two, three, four, five, even six fold that of the Evangelist, whilst the faithful Evangelist does three, four, five, even six times more work than the ordinary Pastor. This L. s. d. matter is important to all who have not an independent fortune to lean upon, and only a few of such have the disposition, and fewer still have the ability to be an Evangelist. Hence no man would be worthy of the humanity God had given if he thought lightly of these things. He has social claims to meet, and almost all have also domestic obligations pressing for consideration. And most of the wise and good believe that

The bread and cheese matter."

> "To make a happy fireside clime
>   For weans and wife,
> Is the true pathos and sublime
>   Of human life."

One of the great drawbacks on good work to an earnest Evangelist is to keep him and his family at the point of starvation. If he is worthy, he ought to be sustained; if not, he has no right to retain the place. To starve him is to rob those among whom he labours.

Another point at which I looked was the fact, that, unlike New Testament times, the Evangelist, as such, has no ecclesiastical standing in our churches. Too often

About ecclesiastical standing.

he and his family are looked down upon as belonging to the lower grade of Christian workers. I have seen him spoken of as "A lay agent," as if he dealt in coals or wood or straw. This being the case he cannot be trusted, so it is thought. He must be "superintended," that is watched, directed, upbraided—sometimes in biting, threatening words. And by whom? Possibly, very likely, by one described as "the Under-Shepherd," having the spiritual oversight of the flock. It is a matter of thankfulness that some "Superintendents" are good men and true, able in their way as preachers. But all are not good men, though some may be called learned men, many try to pass as such. At least very few have the ability and experience necessary to lead in the work outside their own little sphere of duty. And then, the most ignorant are the most conceited, and forward, and oppressive. Whether such is called a "Priest," or "Clergyman," or "Minister," or "Pastor," he is sure to damage any such work, and get rid of the Evangelist who would dare to think for himself in doing what is best. Trained apart from the people they neither know of their wants nor wishes. Their sympathy for the people is thiner than a shadow, because they do not see the people. And yet they will assume duties they cannot do. This they make out to do: by the power of use and wont—to bind the Missionary or Evangelist by red-tape till he becomes disheartened, if not disgusted. Finding their work thus retarded, and their peace broken, they reluctantly leave the field. Men of noble emotion and large sympathy—however good as Evangelists—have little countenance from our churches.

Compensation. But there was something *for* as well as much *against* being engaged in the work of the Evangelist. I look at that work in its widest sense, caring for the people in the physical as well as the spiritual sense, for body and soul. It is degrading to a man of spirit and power to be tied to a man who has neither, but the compensation comes in time. I never allowed myself to be fettered, if I had been so, the work which

God gave me to do would not have been done, if a sense of duty had not compelled me to rend asunder every hampering cord. But that work had enlightened me as to the nature and desire of the people in a way that could not have been, had I at first settled down in a quiet pastorate. And more, judging from other churches, it would have been a rare one that would have permitted me to become "the free lance," as I was called, and as has been indicated. Again, on the one hand the churches have ever been commissioned to evangelise the people, to care for the poor, as much as possible. And, with rare exceptions, they have failed to do either—not only in regard to those whom they designated "the masses," but also those called "the classes." This sad fact forced upon me the question, Is there not some better way by which to reach and raise the people? Results proved that, under God, I found the better way; but I could not have found it out had I not first been an Evangelist.

Therefore I was glad my lines had fallen in that course, and willing still to continue. But for the reasons stated, this memorial made me look on all sides as well as at what memorialists said. And in addition to that I felt sure that, in this case at least, a change of designation—from that of an Evangelist to that of a Pastor—would not entail a change of work, nor a change in the mode of working. The memorialists were of my own training. In spirit and in aim, we were one. Therefore I consented to their warmly expressed desire.

It was not to be in St. Pancras.

This gladdened the hearts of many, and a Committee was appointed, consisting of ministers and others to promote the object in view, particularly in the erection of a suitable building. But I became weaker and weaker; and every day's work tended to induce and increase the nervous exhaustion. And one day I felt as if I would have given the world for a day's rest, but I was asked to visit a sick mother in one of the fever dens. I could not say no, and I became a prey to infection. Because of the nature of the fever which laid me aside, and because of my weak state by overwork, the doctors regarded my condition as very serious. In the course of time, however, I once more rallied and hope revived.

A few weeks in the North of Scotland—together with the kind treatment of loving friends there—went far to restore my strength, and I returned home able for work, so I thought. But a few weeks made it too evident that I was mistaken. A serious relapse followed, and the doctor said it would be dangerous to persevere in the work on which I had set my heart.

It is said that history repeats itself. It is often so in human experience. This reminded me very much of the latter portion of my days in the Northern Capital. There, too, overwork made me to be all the readier to become a victim to infection.

But though like cause had led to like effect, I had more comfort during my illness and convalescence than we had in Edinburgh. Still the disappointment was about as trying. Only think of the doctor's words: "Even when you recover sufficiently it would be better to accept a country pastorate for a time, at least, until you become thoroughly invigorated."

Because of this I had most reluctantly to withdraw my consent to become the Pastor in St. Pancras of the proposed new church. The friends renewed their appeal to me in the hope I might once more recover strength. The words of this renewed appeal were very much like what was used in the memorial, but the circumstances rendered them even more impressive—reminding me of the necessity of my remaining amongst them should health at all permit.

"The thought of you leaving us is more than we can bear," they said, adding, "To all human appearance the vast and valuable machinery which you have put in motion for the social, intellectual, and religious well-being of the people, would be likely to stop. Our societies cannot well exist without your genial presence and careful superintendence. The happy change, arising from your noble defence of the poor, together with the fearless exposure of wrongs, has caused the poor and helpless to rejoice in hope. And are we to lose that protection which your presence here would secure? There are also the hundreds of children who, like those more advanced in years, have been under your care week-days and Sundays. You know how they love you and their cry is 'Do not leave us.' The young, too, who have been with you so long, are fast passing on to womanhood and manhood, are they to be left without your watchful care?"

It was a trying time. My spirit was willing to remain for the reasons therein urged. The pain of parting with a loving people was always sore to me; and then there was the giving up of my yet undeveloped plans. Still, remembering the physician's repeated orders, that for a time I *must* avoid every form of mental strain, I wrote thus in reply: "Most gladly would I have continued with you in the noble and ennobling work to which you refer, but I *must* yield, commending you and yours to the Good Shepherd, and praying that we may permit Him to lead us home to the fold where pain and parting are alike unknown."

"It was not to be," said a dear Scotch friend, "but something even better may be."

CHAPTER VIII.—A TWO YEARS' MINISTRY IN THE COUNTRY.

IN the latter part of this sentence there was something for hope, and I became more and more resigned. Some idea of the feeling occasioned by my having to seek renewed health in the country, and of the loving regard of the people towards me may be gathered by an extract from one of the newspaper notices: "The presentation consisted of a purse of money and an elegantly bound quarto volume entitled 'The Bible Album, or Sacred Truth Illustrated by the Poets.' The following inscription was inserted in the book—'Presented to the Rev. J. Inches Hillocks and Mrs. Hillocks, with a purse of money, as a token of hearty appreciation of their self-sacrificing, unsectarian, and useful labours in the cause of Christ in the physical, educational, and spiritual welfare of the masses—especially of the suffering poor in and round this district. This mark of affectionate regard was presented on the occasion of Mr. Hillocks resigning his duties here—because of failing health through over exertion in his arduous labours—by Christian friends, and those who have been benefited by his ministrations. This joint offering is accompanied by the earnest prayer that he may soon be completely restored to health and usefulness, and that the God of love and peace may be with him and his family wherever he may be called to labour.' Alexander Bremner, Esq., one of the deacons of Tolmer's Square Church, presented this testimonial in a short, warm and touching speech. Other friends took part in the meeting, expressing their joy that Mrs. Hillocks' name was connected with the testimonial—she having done so much, not only to encourage and help her husband, but also in feeding the poor and helpless in their own house."

Bidding adieu.

The news of the possibility of my accepting a country pastorate, as soon as I became strong enough, soon spread, and several invitations followed. I was emphatic not in regard to salary but on these two points; (1) That I would only accept a call as a minister of the gospel, and (2) That the invitation must be unanimous. The correspondence which had from me the most consideration was that from Darlington, which at the request of the Congregational Church there, I visited. In the letter accompanying that invitation occurred these sentences : " I hope you will be able to say 'Yes' to the accompanying call. . . Should you come, send notices to the *English Independent* and the *Christian World*. Also please to make the inquiries we thought desirable of Dr. Raleigh and Mr. (now Dr.) Allon. . . The unanimity among the officers and in the Church is very pleasing. . . The call at the Church Meeting was perfectly and heartily unanimous."

Another call.

I consulted my friends, and they, too, were unanimous in their advice to accept this call to the ministry. Among those who thus advised me was the late Rev. Dr. Thomas Guthrie of Edinburgh. He wrote :—" My dear friend, I know what such city work as yours is. I had years of it, and it is a burden both on mind and body, a strain on the nervous system greater than any one can stand beyond a certain limit. However, your London experience, as well as your training in Scotland, will prove of the greatest value, especially with your natural aptitude for the work of the pulpit and ministry. You know how much I have esteemed you. I think the people will be favoured who enjoy your services."

The Rev. Dr. Wilson also sent a few lines to me, saying, "London, with all its sins and sorrows, has a first claim on the best of talent and most earnest piety in the land; but, under the circumstances, I should say, go. If you come back you shall soon find another sphere in London."

I accepted the call to Darlington and entered upon my duties there in May 1868. I was heartily received by the ministers and other Christian workers, becoming a member of the Ministerial Association at its first meeting after my arrival. A note from my friend the late Lord Kinnaird introduced me to the late Sir Joseph Pease and other members of that worthy family, who continued to encourage me in my work, particularly that part of it which may be characterised by the word, "outside," I mean the undenominational labours.

First year's work in Darlington.

As was understood my duties were various, but stated, namely, preaching, visiting and taking oversight of the stations connected with the Union Street Congregational Church, particularly that at the north end of the town, with the view of ultimately forming a new church there as soon as all parties thought well.

This was accomplished in about a year. Then, as was agreed to, I resigned my responsibilities in connection with the Union Street Church, receiving a call to the newly formed church. This too was perfectly unanimous. The terms urging my acceptance of the pastorate were appropriate and affectionate. I consented.

This was on the 3rd of June, 1869. It would be a source of pleasure to record the fruits of my efforts up to this time. But they were noted by the press from time to time. Perhaps the Darlington papers paid all the more attention because of the nature and extent of my work in London. Be that as it may their notices were appreciative. For instance, summing up this first year's work, the *Darlington Telegraph*, in the course of a long report, said—

"As our readers are aware, about a year ago, the Rev. J. I. Hillocks came from London. Since then he has laboured successfully in our midst. It was perceived that it would be for the greatest good if his efforts were confined chiefly to the north end of our town, where there is a large population of ironworkers and others in want of help, which he, as a minister and social reformer, is able to render. This step in the right direction was taken on Thursday, by the formation of what is now known as the Northend Congregational Church, at a special meeting held at the usual place of worship, Albert Road. The Rev. H. Kendall and other office-bearers of the Union Street Congregational Church were present, to bid God-speed to the new cause. To the hearty invitation to become the pastor, Mr. Hillocks recorded his ready consent, and stated that with God's help he would, to the utmost of his ability, and to the full extent of his opportunity, attend to the feeding of the flock, to the advancement of the congregation, in knowledge and usefulness, and to the prosperity of the Sunday school, never for a day losing sight of the surrounding mission field, knowing that those who had already laboured with him in it would continue their efforts with increasing faith and energy. Most cordially do we join in wishing that Mr. Hillocks and his people may prosper, not only as a church and congregation, but also in the various useful movements with which his name is associated, and upon which he bestows much thought and effort for the general good."

More work. No more salary. But then I had become quite as strong as ever. The Congregational Church at New Sheldon was much in need of a helping hand. An appeal was made to me and I could not say, "No." I never could when extra work was asked of me. I consented, but only for a time, it being distinctly understood I meant to return to London as soon as I had all hands in working order. *A duel pastorate.*

The recognition services were held in due time, and this was the arrangement. On Sunday morning I conducted the service at the Darlington place of worship; in the afternoon I drove to New Sheldon—a distance of seven miles—conducted a service there, and after attending to other ministerial duties, returned in time for my evening service at Darlington. Unless there was special matter calling me to New Sheldon, I did not go there on the week day save once a month to conduct the evening service, and the monthly church meeting preparatory to the communion service on the next Sunday.

This worked fairly well, but my Darlington duties continued to increase. And anxious as I was to help the smaller town, I found the duel pastorate was too much for me. And, to the New Sheldon friends, I had to write:—"Ever since you called me to the pastorate of your church, I have been deeply interested in your welfare; but, as you know, similar duties at Darlington are requiring my close attention; and these have prevented me from doing all I desired for you. And, now that my duties here are daily increasing, I find it impossible longer to sustain the responsibilities connected with your church with credit to myself and benefit to you."

The Bud of Promise again. And with all this there was going on a somewhat extensive work not connected with the pastorate as such. It was that referred to at the close of the report from which I have just quoted—included in the words, "Efforts for the general good."

Of course, I carried my London experience with me. The Bud of Promise was an instance. Though the name implied work among the children, and that was really so, yet, here, my aim was also to interest and benefit children of larger growth. As in London, this Association was composed of boys and girls from six to sixteen years of age. It had in it several bands. Each band had a distinct aim, but all variously tending to the promotion of one common object—viz., the spread of Christian and general knowledge, and the cultivation of industrial and provident habits.

In a very short time it became a Darlington Institution, having the ready countenance and generous help of the most of those who were foremost in every good work. The Mayor, the late Henry Pease, J.P., presided over our first annual meeting. Almost all the ministers of the town were present, uniting with the chairman in hearty commendation of the work. The newspaper notices of this meeting went on to say—

"The first resolution was moved by one of the ministers—that 'the Bud of Promise is truly deserving of the practical sympathy of parents and all interested in the temporal, educational, and moral welfare of the young.' In supporting this resolution, the speaker said he wished to couple the name of Mr. Hillocks with it, as the founder and superintendent of the great and useful work. He was sure, from what he himself had seen, that Mr. Hillocks and his co-workers in this labour of love deserved the good wishes and the necessary help from all classes and all sects —the movement being quite unsectarian. In acknowledging a vote of thanks for his disinterested labours, Mr. Hillocks said he could not take all the praise to himself. 'There was God first and then the earnest helpers.'"

This work was connected with our church by one link only. That link was myself as the Superintendent of the former and the Pastor of the latter. Had the one been more directly connected with the other, perhaps I should not have been able to win so many workers for the general good. And yet the one assisted the other. Many of the Bud of Promise became members of our Sunday school, and occasionally they enlivened by sweet song the meetings held at the mission stations connected with our young church.

Closing months in Darlington.

So completely was my health restored that I was able to continue in such outside work and my church work without feeling more than being a little tired at night. This was genial work, and I felt happy in it. But this success all round also made me to begin to think of the time when I hoped to be able to leave every department of work in a flourishing condition. The happy results of the divine blessing were very pleasing to all of us.

Of course the church, in its membership, was not large to begin with, but before the first year of our existence, as a church, had ended, that membership had increased quite fifty per cent. The congregation and the Sunday school also increased. These cheering facts were stated and attested in the official report sent

P

to the Durham and Northumberland Congregational Association in a schedule sent to us for the purpose.

At last, however, the question, Is the time come when I should return to the Metropolis? claimed my consideration. There was something for and something against an affirmative answer. From the time of my going to Darlington, I was favoured with the countenance of pleasant friendships and the assistance of willing co-workers, but I longed for yet greater usefulness. This desire prevailed after I had taken all things into account. The Official Congregational Monthly, *The Northern Light*, had in it this announcement:—The Rev. James Inches Hillocks has resigned the pastorate of the Northend Congregational Church, Darlington.

CHAPTER IX.—SOME UNLOOKED-FOR EVENTS.

FULL of hope and vigour, I return to London on May 1870. That return was noticed by the press, and one of the comic papers, in a playful way, assured the St. Pancras authority of their safety, in as much as I had not taken up my abode in that parish.

Return to London.

This was very kind, but it would have been a source of gladness had I been assured that I was no longer needed to protect the poor in this or any other of the Metropolitan parishes.

During my conflict with evil and evil ways in the Metropolis before 1868, several incidents transpired which retained a place in my memory. Here is one. The late Sir Hugh Owen had frequently referred to the nature and extent of my labours in London. He had also spoken in appreciative terms in regard to what he was pleased to call my "organising powers," and "the art of leading others in good work."

On my return to London I would have accepted such an appointment readily, but other arrangements had been made in the meantime, so I thought of another sphere. To myself I said, "It may be some time before a suitable Pastorate opens for me; but, sooner or later, knowledge is necessary, and work is required."

That I might be the better prepared for whatever work God might have in store for me, I once more penetrated the great Metropolis to see how much improvement had transpired during the past two years. I found that thousands of houses had been added, and many thousands of people. The suburban aspect seemed to be greatly improved, but the most of the slimy slums still remained. The blazing gin palaces, and the filthy beer-shops, were as numerous as ever, and the fearful results were quite as evident. Some of the rescued whom I had known before, were joyful because they were still holding on in the right course. Some of the young whom I had also known, to their delight, were still resisting temptation. But almost everywhere, especially in the lowest localities, the horrible pictures were as horrible as I had seen them before I left. Many of the poor, oh, so many! were yet without God, and without hope.

What I once more saw moved me with intense pity for all concerned. Even the most wicked and wretched are our fellow-creatures. From my heart came the prayer, "God still help me to help the poor." And with the prayer came the determination to labour as before, but now with all the energy which renewed health and strength, knowledge and experience had given me.

Besides labouring as much as possible in London, I put myself in the way of supplying vacant pulpits, also of lecturing, and organising Christian work, wherever I was invited. An extract from an article in a London paper, may give you some idea of the extent and success of these efforts. Referring to my leaving a district, after labouring for a short time, the writer said, "The parting was a touching scene. Young and old, men and women, of all creeds and of none, were there, and had from Mr. Hillocks the promise to return as often as possible. Though it seems to him to be comparatively easy, it must be heavy to mind and body thus to put forth all his energies, mental and physical, wherever he goes; yet as it is evident this is one of the best ways by which he serves the Church and benefits the world, we hope churches and societies may avail themselves of his services before he again resumes the responsibilities of another pastorate."

But whilst thus "still achieving, still pursuing," we were sadly reminded that time is short. Our only son, and O, how well-beloved! left our home here below, for the Home of our Father above.

Our only son goes home.

I say, "*sadly* reminded," but perhaps I ought not to use the first of these two words; and yet in a sense it was severely true. It was well with the lad. We knew it and rejoiced in it. The "words of comfort" in the word of Life were known to us. They possessed a sustaining influence. But we were human, and before we had time to come to ourselves in the sight and love of our All-wise Father, we felt as if we could not part with George, so precious as a child, so loving as a brother, so noble as a boy, so devout as a Christian. We knew of a truth that Jesus came for His young and Faithful servant; and that on that very day—September, 16, 1870—he was with Jesus, in the place prepared for him. But we wept, Heaven was richer, but earth was poorer. Then came the thought, he has only gone a little before us, to be one more with Jesus to welcome *us* home when our work here is done. "Blessed are the dead that die in the Lord."

George had been a promising student, none gave greater promise, preparing to follow the great, good Livingstone as a Medical Missionary. And, during this preparation, his every word and way, as well as his every thought, kept him before us as he had been—a princely child, a princely boy, a princely youth, a princely son, a princely brother, a princely worker, so intelligent, so bright, so brave, so noble, so gentle, so heroic, a delight to see, a delight to meet, a delight to know, loving and beloved. But we knew all that was true and beautiful and noble in him on earth was now more completely beautiful in heaven, that he was better and happier than we could make him, yet, it must be confessed that our loss on earth was an indescribable blow, rending each heart, causing grief which for the time almost amounted to agony, till we thought again of our heavenly Father, and remembered that He was too wise as well as loving to do wrong, that George was with Him.

Generally one striking event is followed by another. Though, as a rule, I preferred to labour in London, yet I consented to run into the country to help Christian friends, if only for a day or two at a time. Being booked to preach at Atherston, near Rugby, on Sunday, November 27th, 1870, I left home on the afternoon of the day before. *In a railway collision.*

As a rule, some of my family saw me in the train when leaving home for the country. On this occasion, my youngest daughter, then a mere child, accompanied me to Dalston Junction. But when she returned home, she was almost distracted.

"Get a cab, mamma," she said, "you will be in time to prevent papa from leaving Euston Station. Something says to me you should prevent him. Do go, mamma. I'll get a cab in a few minutes."

The mother tried to soothe the troubled child, stating the fact that I had often gone by rail, and no harm had come thereby to me. It was about four o'clock when I left Dalston, and about an hour and a half after, "a strange something" entered the minds of her mamma and her sisters. They trembled, but they could not tell why. This feeling lasted all that night. On Sunday they attended public worship. Still, their minds were so troubled that they could not attend to the service.

This was at home. Something wonderful, to say the least, particularly when considered in relation to what had really taken place at Harrow. It is not much that I can tell you, but this I know:

I arrived at Euston Station from Dalston Junction quite in time for what was called, "The Irish Mail Express Train," timed to leave Euston at five o'clock. Before I entered the carriage, I purchased a newspaper. The name was new to me, and that attracted my attention to it. I think it was called the *London Scotsman*, a name which some of my more familiar friends give me; but I had not seen it in print before. We started in due time, and were soon up to full speed. We had not well passed Harrow Station when I heard some queer, confused noises, and felt as if our carriage had been lifted up. In a second this was followed by a tremendous crushing noise. After that I knew no more. But during that second or so, my son came to me, not in grave attire, but dressed as he used to be. He seemed as if overshadowed by a sweet melancholy, such as was natural to him when feeling for others, as was his wont when here below. Yet his countenance was lighted up by means of his usually soft, gentle smile. He was as an angel of mercy sent to me. "George," I said, but I remember no more.

I have no wish to harrow your feelings by any detailed account of this awful collision. I could not even if I would. Generally those who are overtaken in such a terrible calamity—especially those to whom it has proved to be almost fatal—must have their information from others who have hastened to see the wreck. But, depending on this information, I may briefly tell you that such was the force of the collision that some of the carriages were smashed, burying their mangled inmates in the blood-stained débris. Portions of the broken carriages had to be converted into fuel. By the aid of this fearful blaze, in the midst of surrounding darkness, "The Good Samaritans" of the neighbourhood searched for the dead and the dying. Many were more or less seriously injured, and the death roll was afterwards increased.

By some means or other I had left my card-case at home, hence there was no clue to my address. At last, however, about six o'clock on Sunday evening a railway porter was seen making inquiry from door to door. When he came to ours he was met with the question, "Is he killed?"

"He is not dead yet," was the brief reply.

My beloved was soon on the spot, but I knew her not. Then, and for some considerable time, my case was regarded as hopeless. I had to lie near to the station at which the collision happened for about three months before I could be taken home. And even then, such was the effect of the journey on my shattered frame, that I had a dangerous relapse—even though I was conveyed in an invalid carriage in the care of the nurse and one of the doctors.

During the time I was at Harrow, as well as after I was brought home the medical men held several anxious consultations.

"Poor man! His work here is over," said an aged physician, he himself being so overcome that he unintentionally allowed the words to escape his lips.

This was the general opinion, and all concerned were sad, but

Mrs. Hillocks found a glimpse of hope in a letter she received, and which she accepted as a smile from heaven.

Among the doctors none were more helpful than Dr. George Johnson, Professor of Medicine, King's College, London. So careful was he to know all about me—what I had previously endured, because of overwork and great distress—that he not only read "Life Story," a second time, but also my "Mission Life in London." And after doing so, he kindly wrote the letter referred to. In that letter he said, "Having seen he has recovered so often after being so near the grave, I feel almost sure—at least I can hope—that he may rally once more."

This hope was confirmed at the close of another consultation, not long before I was taken home.

"He may yet survive," said a far-famed physician—famed throughout the land as well as at Court—I mean Sir William Jenner, Bart.

Still the relapse checked the flow of the fondest hopes for several months. The tumult and noise which I supposed I saw and heard frightened me much. The pain all over the body was severe, but the brain pain was even more terrible. The sharp shots as from great guns, the awful thunder as if thousands of roofs were falling upon me; the terrible crash, as if a whole train rushed against an embankment; thrilling agony, as if the body had been torn to pieces, made me cry and pull the bedclothes over my head like a frightened child. At other times I felt as if the half of my head, the back half, was gone; as if one half, the right half, of my body had gone, save the right foot, which imparted a feeling as if it were a forty pound ball. Then a creeping sensation would crawl over me. Up and up, till it reached and overcame the heart. I knew no more for a time, till again I found myself surrounded by the nurse and my anxious family, some of whom were yet bathing my temples and using other means of restoration to consciousness.

But at last, by God's blessing on medical skill, and faithful nursing and loving watchfulness, these attacks, mental and physical, became less severe and less frequent, and at times the vague confusion would so clear off that I knew my dear ones. Our three girls were permitted to see me at times; once again I could intelligently look on those sweet smiles which had been the sunshine of my life.

It was a pleasant thing once more to know what was going on. At first the past was as a blank abyss. I made an effort to recollect, but for some time memory refused to help me. If I said it was like waking out of a fearful dream that would not be exactly correct, but I know not to what else to liken the return to life. Neither can I describe my feelings when, bit by bit, I was told what had happened, and how long I had been out of the world, so to speak.

CHAPTER X.—RENEWING THE WORK IN LONDON.

A glance at the past two years—from 1870.
As the fear subsided and the hopes again began to rise, in proportion as I gradually revived, some of the things which had transpired since November, 1870, were cautiously revealed to me, as my mind could take them in.

"It was a trying time for Mrs. Hillocks," said a lady friend in the course of a short conversation on this point. "Your only son having departed so short a time before, the young girls were the only source of domestic help and private counsel."

The lady was correct, but the dear children did their best, and that most wonderfully. Aggie being the eldest, was the only one who was in any degree able to take her late brother's place in anything of a public nature. In this, however, to the surprise of all around her, she leaped up into womanhood, and became her mamma's right hand supporter. One great help was in undertaking the necessary and pressing correspondence—to dictation of course. Copies of the most of her letters were kept, such as that sent to those friends of good work who had expected me at the dates previously arranged.

This was one: "I regret to inform you that dear papa was one of the sufferers in the serious railway collision at Harrow; and that consequently he will not be able to carry out the arrangements to be with you as he promised. I am sorry to have to add that papa is so seriously injured that he cannot be removed from Harrow."

There was another letter which was of still greater importance, informing me that the door of a suitable church had been opened for me. This letter had become the subject of anxious consideration. By the advice of the doctors, this was what was written in reply:—"Papa is so very ill that the doctors and mamma think it would be better that the church do not wait his recovery, which, at present, seems very doubtful. And the doctors believe that, even should he be spared to us, it must be some considerable time before he could undertake the oversight of another church."

Our conversations on these and other matters were not without their influence on our after life and efforts. Sometimes they proved too much for me, but then there was something so pleasing in the recovery, to find the watchful partner of my joys and sorrows so affectionately, tenderly, and skilfully applying the means used for my restoration. With one hand she would gently press my aching brow, and with a soft handkerchief in the other, she would gently wipe the tears away. Then she would turn the pillow and make it gratefully soft. And in all this she was kindly and skilfully assisted by the good nurse, and sometimes by one or other of our darlings. And, in all this I was more than once reminded of the precious promise in the first three verses of the forty-first Psalm:—

> Blessed is he that considereth the poor;
> The Lord will deliver him in the day of evil.
> The Lord will preserve him and keep him alive,
> And he shall be blessed upon the earth;
> And deliver not thou him unto the will of his enemies.
> The Lord will support him upon the couch of languishing:
> Thou makest all his bed in his sickness.

These conversations also revealed to me that I had no engagements, no charge, but the doctors said this was fortunate because having no responsibility, my chances of a more complete recovery were better. So I rested, waiting for returning health.

Perhaps I should also tell you that because of the interest manifested in us by our friends, the Right Hon. W. E. Gladstone, and the late Right Hon. the Lord Kinnaird, the matter of compensation for my suffering and loss was settled without bringing the case before a jury. This, too, was favourable. It not only let the mind rest as regard money matters, it enabled me the more freely to use the means to the regaining of strength.

Our stay in the country gave all of us new life and revived our hopes. Our girls and their mamma—all of whom were greatly in want of change of air—were greatly benefited, and this had a considerable reviving influence on me.

When we returned home I was able to receive friendly visits and deputations, congratulating me on my recovery. The following sentences from one of the addresses presented to me may indicate the nature of these greetings:—"Though we have to regret the consequences of the serious injuries you received in the lamentable railway collision at Harrow, depriving us of your valuable services; yet we rejoice and are thankful that your life has been spared to your beloved family. We would even yet indulge in the hope that the time of your enforced retirement may come to an end soon, and that we may see you in our midst again."

Reasoning together—the decision.

There was on my mind much that led me to join in the wish expressed in the last sentence. But it was an anxious time for us. As a family we were one in the opinion that I had been spared for some special work, and that the means now at our command—the price of much suffering—would greatly help us to make a good beginning. The only difference was as to the time. My family had on their side the opinion of the friends with whom I had consulted, explaining the nature of the work I meant to establish. "How," I was asked, "can you, only recovering, organise and carry on such a work, even with willing helpers waiting to rally round you?"

I was not insensible to this, seeing much common sense in it. I was yet very weak, but I had known that love lightens labour. Between one thing and another, the question, what would the Lord have me to do? was kept before my mind. For instance, other friends of good work called in the hope of securing the aid of my first utterances in public on behalf of the respective causes they represented. As soon as the doctors agreed that I might, for once at least, try to help in this way, I ventured to preach an anniversary sermon in the south of London. Happily, I was able to speak with considerable freedom, to the surprise and delight of all concerned, more particularly my medical friends, who to the last moment were afraid of the possible result of such an effort.

This effort was reported in the press, and the news resulted in my receiving several letters from those who were leading in vacant churches. Some of these I read to the friends who called, and to whom I could speak with confidence.

"Certainly," said one of them, "the best way is to accept of a quiet country pastorate. The salary might not be large, but the interest on your money would help you to keep the family comfortable, leaving the principal to keep them when you are gone to rest."

"That is true," chimed another. "Money is in demand, and a good investment might be made."

"All very well from a commercial point of view," said I to myself, "but I shall lend what I have to the Lord, and give myself with it for His glory and the good of my fellow-creatures, especially the poor. I have a plan as well as a plea, and this may help me, under God, to prove the plan to be in accordance with His will and way. And once this is proved, the generous, who are interested in the poor, may help me to continue."

On the principle I had bestowed much thought, and had frequently lectured on the same to Christian workers. And almost all agreed with me, but the difficulty was want of means, the well-known habit of even the best of givers of not supporting a new movement, particularly if its leading features were new to them. But now I had the means, and I felt sure that God would bless efforts properly made and based on the teaching and example of the Saviour, "the Healer of Men."

Still it must be admitted that these well-meaning friends, in course of consultation, touched a tender point when they feelingly referred to my family's comfort and rest. I knew what they had done in the past, but they too were anxious to do more. The arguments put forth in favour of less extensive work, of my falling in with old and ordinary ways, were strong when merely looked at from the quietude point. The family needs, as pointed out, were necessary, but there was also the necessity for more work, for better work.

So we thought. Earnest thought and frequent out-spoken conversations at the fireside, before God, confirmed us more and more in the righteousness of our first impulse—to remain in London, and work there. We could see the possibility of my frail frame having to yield before mental and physical strains; we could also see the possibility of our store running out before the friends of good work might see well to help; but we also knew that no good work is lost however little it may be, that every good effort, divinely directed, lives, and leads on to other good efforts; that good done, if it has a fair chance, is always prolific. God loves and fosters the good. It is His. Hence we had no difficulty in leaving ourselves and the future to God.

Work followed thought. It was but a simple incident that crowned our decision. One morning after a conversation on this important matter, one of our daughters suggested and led the hymn, "Onward, Christian Soldiers." That was the starting point, and from that day were renewed our efforts in behalf of those in need of help.

The work begun —first meetings. The first meeting of the friends, willing to co-operate with me in the work I had sketched, was held in our dining-room, Amhurst Road, N., on the evening of the first Sunday of November, 1872. It was held there because, as yet, I was not able to go elsewhere without the assistance of some conveyance, and I preferred, when possible, not to have such on Sunday.

As you have no doubt noticed, with me the month of November has been an eventful one. In November, I opened my first public school; in November, "Auntie Maggie" became Mrs. Hillocks; in November, we saw our first child and only son; in November, we received the Queen's letter; in November, I nearly lost my life in the Harrow Railway Collision.

Our Sunday gathering became one of those sweet hours of prayer of which we sing. The next meeting was held in the same place on the following evening, when I delivered the opening address, briefly referring to the nature and need of the work before us. I also stated the principles which were to be our guide, and the plan on which we meant to work.

My space being so limited, I cannot give the full text of that address, but I hope to refer to the whole matter in another series of "the battles." Here I cannot do more than indicate the fundamental principle, namely, The whole man for the loving God. This principle I regarded as divine, direct from heaven—suggested, fostered, and enforced by the word of God. I had been long convinced that we, as individuals, must freely, fully and affectionately dedicate our being to God, and that for His preservation and service. I also held that what was necessary for us to that end, was necessary on the part of those in whose case we are interested as Christian workers—That is not one element of being merely, but the whole man, spirit and soul and body; that no man can be regarded as rescued from death to life until the faculties of the spirit, the affections of the soul, and the powers of the body, are dedicated to God, not only wholly but also holy.

All this was heartily accepted, and many kind words were said, but one of the speakers seemed to wish to learn a few of the causes which led up to, and still continued to feed what he called "Pauline enthusiasm." Seeing this desire was general I give a sketch of some of the incentives. This is one, and I give it because it was still gently urging me on:

When, three months after the railway collision, I was brought home, the parlour was converted into a bedroom. It was larger, and was considered better suited for the frequent meetings of the doctors attending. Two companion pictures were left hanging on the wall facing me. These I recognised as soon as I was able to reflect on what I saw.

One was the representation of the cross, to which a human form was clinging with both hands, evidently to save herself from being carried away by the raging sea beneath. The other picture represented the same form, having increased confidence, but still clinging to the cross, but with one hand. With the other outstretched hand, the body bent downward, she held another woman who was being carried away by the swelling gulf which threatens her destruction.

Nothing could have been more suggestive and inspiring to me at that time, than those two pictures. In the first I saw personal safety in Christ. In the second I saw not only the same safety by the same means, but relative usefulness also; not only clinging to Christ, but working for Christ. Precious lesson, blessed reminder.

Chapter XI.—Something About the Work.

AFTER my short address, resolutions touching the constitution were submitted and carried unanimously. And soon after, some neighbouring Friends (Quakers), hearing of our aim, kindly offered such accommodation as they had in connection with their own work for our meetings and free of charge. This offer was gratefully accepted. It was so kind on their part and so helpful to us.

Rapid progress.

"God speed you," was the hearty expression of all who spoke to me of the work now commenced; and this prayer was soon answered. Christian workers—approving of our plan as well as our aim—rallied round us. Rejoicing in the evidences of success, and in the help so effectively rendered, we held on our own way; but were ever ready, on all suitable occasions, to co-operate with other good workers.

But the premises thus so kindly and generously provided for us, soon became too small, and we had to be on the look-out for larger. Every place of meeting became so packed, night after night, that we knew not what to do with the people. But in time we were fortunate in securing other premises. This building was old, but extensive. Some called it the "Manor House," others the "College," no doubt because it had been previously used as such. Having obtained a lease we soon finished the necessary alterations and repairs, and found ourselves in possession of the very accommodation we needed, under the name of the Christian Union Rooms. The class-rooms, the reading and consulting rooms, were opened as soon as possible. The services, the lectures, and the conferences, were held in the lower hall, known as Eden Hall. And whilst special attention was being paid to this centre of operation, the circumference was not forgotten. Auxiliaries were soon formed, and became very useful in their respective districts.

Of course, I brought my past experience to my help, both in the arrangements and efforts, adding to it, what I had longed to do but had been prevented chiefly from the want of means.

There were three distinct yet united elements in this work, the religious, the physical, and the educational. The first for the winning of souls, the second, the health department, for the care of the body, and the third for the enlightening of minds.

In all three—as throughout the whole of my work—I realised the benefit of my experience in the work of preparation in Scotland. For instance, though during my stay at the Normal Institution, Castle Hill, Edinburgh, I was not greatly advanced as a teacher of the young, yet what I did learn there was of great service to me in helping those of our assistants who wished to become preachers.

It has been asked, "what is in a name," "nothing," say some, "something," say others. I believe there is something, *if it is a good one*. So we tried to get a good one, one that would, if not perverted, speak for itself. THE CHRISTIAN UNION FOR CHRISTIAN WORK was the name by which we wished to be known. By it, we meant a Union of Christians *for* Work; and a Union of Christian Work for Christian ends—each department, with various sections, was made to run into each other, each helping the others.

Our name.

But simple and plain as this was to most people, there were some who put quite another construction upon it. They went out of the way so far as to declare I was a dangerous man because I was "forming a new sect." I pitied them because nothing was farther from my mind. I had no longing for something merely new, but I did long for something better, more in accordance with the recorded will of God. I was anxious to prove that Christian Work, carried on in the spirit of Christ, was, by the Spirit, made a means

Castle Hill, Edinburgh.

of Christian Union. The truth is, I was simply trying to lead on to what I conceived to be Bible lines—working for Christ, not for any sect.

But though some preferred to run on the old narrow gage, and did not see eye to eye with us in our wider range, and, in their ignorance, spoke against our mode, if not against our work; yet some of them have since learned that after all we were on the right rails. To some extent, they, with others, have followed on, to our delight. But, as you see, even then we were not without encouragement.

Encouragement.

Those who have read "The Condensed Record" of the first three years of this Institution, are aware that notes of approval and encouragement came from friends of such work in the country as well as in the metropolis. Such as came from my fatherly friend, the Rev. Dr. Thomas Guthrie, were very stimulating. The late Lord Kinnaird also thus wrote to me: "It is now many years since I became acquainted with your labours in the cause of our Divine Master, and I rejoice to think that after being laid aside for so long by the fearful accident you met with, you are able to resume the work on which your heart is set. You have my best wishes for your success."

The School of Medicine also extended its favours, speaking approvingly of our efforts. Here is a note from Professor George Johnstone:

"DEAR MR. HILLOCKS.—The Health Department of the Christian Union has for me an especial interest. As physician to a large London hospital, I have had abundant opportunities of learning how much preventable disease among the labouring classes is a disregard of obvious sanitary laws. Teach your disciples to acquire habits of cleanliness in their persons and in their dwellings, and to shun the abuse of alcoholic liquors, and you will diminish to an incalculable degree the demands for hospitals, prisons, and lunatic asylums. I heartily wish you God speed in the

Christian work in which you and your fellow-labourers are engaged."

The Council's appeal for funds. For quite two years after the date of the condensed Record the work progressed as rapidly as before, but I became straitened financially. That is, my own means were so reduced that I could not do more than continue to give my time without salary as I had done from the beginning.

The Council, which had been elected from among the co-workers, appointed two committees. The first was deliberative in regard to the work; the second was financial, concerned in the raising and distributing the necessary funds. The circular making an application for funds to those likely to be interested in such work was signed by the Hon. Secretary, and myself as the Hon. Superintendent.

Like the work, this appeal was heartily approved of by the press—local, general, and religious. A fair specimen is found in the kind words of the *Christian World:* "The object of 'The Christian Union for Christian Work,' is to reach and raise the poor by attention to their temporal and intellectual, as well as their spiritual, welfare. Many ministerial brethren have expressed their full appreciation of this Institution, and recommend the appeal for funds to the favourable notice of Christian philanthropists—a recommendation which we have great pleasure in endorsing."

The usual sources of such incomes were open to us, but our Institution was comparatively young, and therefore not so well known to the givers as to the hearers. And those givers who did know of us were confined to such as saw the necessity of a wider range of thought and action in such work.

This so hampered us that for the moment I was foolish enough to wish that all good work might be independent of money. But as things are, this is impossible. Whether we will or not, finance comes up, and we must look at it, think of it, and strive to keep the balance on the right side.

Such was their advice to me. On the other hand I ventured to advise them to this effect: That all the money *Mutual helpfulness.* kind friends may give for the work be entirely devoted to that purpose, for purely working expenses.

We agreed, but I was reminded that the work of securing the sinews of war must necessarily depend mostly on me. "True," said one, "the work is God's work, but you are at the head of it, we are helpers."

I knew what was meant, but, at first, could not see my way. "Perhaps, the worst collector that could be thought of," said I to myself, but something must be done soon, it would have been wrong to give up.

I did not know what was coming. Not long after, I was urged to take a few days' rest, and off I went, as usual to Bonny Scotland, to Blairgowrie, where I was the guest of my dear old friend the Rev. Dr. Baxter of the First Free Church there. And before leaving for home, I preached in his church. At his request I referred to our work in London. Again, at his request the congregation there and then gave a retiring offering to help the work.

This was suggestive. The Finance Committee united with the Work Committee in the suggestion that I might do so elsewhere. At their request, I wrote the following letter:—

"DEAR SIR.—Some time ago, the Finance Committee of this Institution, in addition to recommending an appeal for subscriptions and donations, suggested that I should ask the ministers of the Gospel likely to be interested in this work, to give me the opportunity of preaching in their pulpits in aid of its funds. In cases where it may be found impossible to give this privilege during the ordinary Sunday services, perhaps a week-day may be suitable as the next best. When it is possible to name several open days, it would be an additional favour to mention them, because then I could select that which might answer best. Being in the locality I could lessen travelling expenses."

Some ministers readily responded to this. In time, others followed their example, and such retiring offerings not only became helpful financially, I also had the pleasure of being useful in return by explaining our principle and plan to others. This twofold result induced me to leave home as often as my duties permitted. It also showed that man's extremity is God's opportunity, and that He is ever ready to turn every good effort to good account. For instance, one of the ministers, referring to the time I had an opportunity of preaching in his church, said, "If we were richer we would have you oftener with us. Since your visit, there has been in my church an increasing liberality and activity."

This was very encouraging, not only because it was helpful to the work in London, but also because to me it became a widening field of usefulness. Hence too, some time after, I was all the easier induced to occasionally extend this means of two-fold helpfulness to week-days as well as Sundays. At times I would take a day or two from home more or less as my duties permitted. The following is the substance of a newspaper report of "A week from home," as this effort was called:—

"On Sunday morning the Rev. J. I. Hillocks, of London, preached to Seamen in the Bethel. In the evening he also preached in the Free Church. On Monday he attended a conference of ministers and others, on Christian Work. In the evening he addressed a special gathering of the young. On Tuesday, he addressed the Christian Workers in conference. On Wednesday, he spoke specially to the Friends of Temperance. On Thursday, he delivered one of his Popular Lectures. And on Friday, he conducted a special Evangelistic service."

Chapter XII.—Seeking Health and Facing Figures.

These efforts—together with donations and subscriptions from individuals—enabled us to persevere. In time, however, the presence of serious symptoms reminded me that I had mis-calculated my renewed strength. *A visit to our kin beyond the sea.* The need of such work prevented me from listening to nature's warnings till almost too late. Because of the great and constant strain on mind and body, more than one of the alarming results of the railway collision persisted in threatening to return.

"Entire rest and complete change," were the doctor's imperative orders. But where to go was the question.

"A sea voyage and a winter in Canada are almost certain to do much good," was the guiding sentence.

And here again God in His Providence showed He was near, even at hand. It so happened that in past days I had been favoured with several hearty invitations to cross the Atlantic. And not many days after this advice was given, another invitation came. As soon as I was fit for the journey I sailed in one of the good ships of the "Allan Line" for Quebec City. Our voyage, I suppose, was very much like other voyages. Of the nine days' sail, six were as bright and beautiful as could be desired. This was beneficial and cheering to me.

At first, Canada was my resting-place. For several weeks it remained doubtful whether or not the expectations of the doctors and my other friends were to be realised. But when, at last, I began to get better, the improvement came rapidly.

As soon as I was able to read and inquire, I began to consider what means were most likely to further the restoration of my strength and the conformation of what was being regained. In this object and in the use of the means to gain this end, I was readily and greatly assisted by the marked kindness of "our kin beyond the sea," in the Canadas and the States. By God's blessing on this change, and rest, and kindness, I was able to return home after about a year's absence; prepared, as I thought, to carry the world before me, at least, as far as restoring the Institution to its former usefulness.

During this year, 1877-78, "Across the Atlantic," I saw not a little of life—being four months in Canada and the rest in the United States. Not long after my return home, my friends asked me to record in a volume what I saw and learned during my sojourn. To this I did not consent, but promised to compose and deliver four lectures based on the notes I had taken. The first was entitled, Some of the scenes I saw; the second, Some of the cities I visited; the third, Some of the people I met; and American women at work.

I have so much to say that it would be folly even to attempt to begin here. This, however, may be said, "our kin beyond the sea" have around them much external grandeur, and within them many undoubted blessings—the twin Continent because of the vast expanse and the evident great energy; but also, and chiefly, because of a beautiful spiritual vitality, manifest in the conduct and efforts of her noblest sons and the best of her daughters. This was evident also in the Institutions which abound—civil and educational as well as religious. Whatever fault and shortcomings, even wickedness, found, in the main, there was that Christian character which, under God, comes of the firm grasp of religious truth, and which enjoins honesty, prompts activity, regulates energy and lays the true basis of stability.

"God bless our kin beyond the sea, and continue to help them, with us, evermore to be a blessing to each other and to mankind." Such was my prayer when leaving for home.

The balance on the wrong side.

This visit was a source of great benefit to me. I enjoyed it immensely after I was able to find my way about. But beneficial as this journey was to mind and body, reviving, strengthening, and inspiring, I thought of home and the dear ones there, of London and what was being done to help the poor. I would not consent to remain on the other side of the sea, kind and encouraging as the friends were. For one reason I had promised to return home if I got better.

My friends and fellow-workers in London—particularly those of them who were more directly connected with the Evangelistic Department—had, before I left home, volunteered to do their utmost during my absence, and this proved to be no small consolation to me. But the financial statement for the year, ending October 31st, 1878, showed a balance on the wrong side of almost £200.

This had not been brought about by spending too much, but from the falling off of the income during my absence. For instance, there had only been a very few special offerings that year, there being only a few special sermons for that purpose. Again, the most of those who gave subscriptions or donations for the work, did so when I called or wrote. From my special connection with the work, as its originator and superintendent, these friends preferred to render help through me.

Comparatively speaking, this was not a large sum; under other circumstances it would have been a light burden, but many other things added to that obstructive weight. First, the demands made on my own resources in my search for health, made me unable to do more than I had been doing. Then, as may be remembered, the hard times were about the hardest, so that some of our friends could not continue their help, however willing: hence like many other Institutions at this time, ours suffered greatly, the educational and the health departments suffering most.

Thus we were prevented from doing much that was greatly needed. But now I was stronger than I had been since the railway collision, so I set to myself the task—an increasingly difficult one, of carrying on the work, and, by the help of friends, to lessen the debt.

This difficulty was all the greater because of what was called "The no salary matter." As before, so now, and ever since, this stood in the way of our domestic comfort, and consequently fettered my public efforts. I mention this here simply because a word of explanation in regard to the matter is due to the friends who co-operated with me.

"The no salary matter."

I know it has been said that the question of salary should have been considered from the beginning, and this is the mind of nearly all who have expressed themselves on the point. In ordinary circumstances, as well as from a sound commercial view, they are correct. But if there was blame, it should have been laid mostly at my door. The idea of salary was suggested by the late Lord Kinnaird as soon as he knew I was spending my means on the work. This he did lest my family should suffer in the end. He not only urged me to mention the matter to others, but also kindly offered to co-operate with them when action in that direction was taken. I could not very well do so for two reasons; one was we were all so engrossed in the work, the claims of which were many and increasing; the other reason was still stronger, namely, I was conscious that none were responsible to me for support in the work. As you know, I was not called to it by any society, nor by any church. My only call was a conviction that the work was needed and would be blessed. This call I obeyed, but not without counting the cost, and that with my family, who have been one with me in aim and effort.

Neither had this matter escaped the practical minds of my co-workers. The gentlemen were engaged in business in the daytime, and laboured with me in the evening after their city and other labours were done. They, with the ladies, came for the love of the work, *not to be responsible for the expenses*; but some of them, assisted somewhat to meet the expenses. All honour to them, they did what they could, and their work was considerable, and all without remuneration. They, however, thus spoke of the necessity of salary in a paragraph which appeared in the Council's appeal for funds :—

"It is our duty also to state that Mr. Hillocks, our Superintendent, has not had any pecuniary remuneration, though from the commencement he has devoted his means, time and energy to the work. His experience and efforts are still necessary to the further development of this work, the commencement of which is one of the happy results of his persevering efforts as a Christian worker, ever ready to co-operate with all such. But none, save those of independent means, could continue thus to labour without the necessary support."

In a foot note was stated the amount which I would have received had I been paid "the nominal salary of £200 yearly," and then added, "without having a penny of this, he continues to promote the objects of the institution and spread the principles upon which it is based. *All this he has done on the means he received as compensation for the fearful suffering he has endured caused by the railway collision in which he nearly lost his life.*"

To this I should also add that an effort was made to make this last as long as possible, not only by writing a little, but also by the assistance derived from some literary lectures during the lecturing seasons.

Still, those who think things should have been otherwise, so far as salary was concerned, have reason on their side. Without fear of being accused of egotism, I may admit that, no man ever laboured harder, that such a salary as that named would not have been too much, and that the amount (£2,600) would have added greatly to our public usefulness, as well as our domestic comfort. But I can only repeat that I was most to blame. And I offer no defence save this: "Not being untutored in suffering, we had learned to pity those in affliction." What has been done has been in the cause of God for the good of man, and we have His promises.

My friends mean well when they chide me for working when I ought to have been resting, for spending on the work when I ought to have invested, for not being sufficiently careful of my own and my family's comfort; but they do not know me who suppose I was forgetful of those whom God has given to bless my home, to strengthen and to encourage, and otherwise to be truly helpful to me in all good work. And let me add, though we may never receive a penny of this sum, we shall not be without reward. God's smile and blessing on the good work done are no small matters to those who desire to spend and be spent in His cause.

Chapter XIII.—The Sphere Still Widening.

EVERY conductor of good work, not having large wealth at command, will remember that up to 1885 and after, it was difficult to make ends meet. Yet between one thing and another—but particularly the kind help rendered by good friends, hard as the times were—we, on the 31st October of that year, were not only able to continue in well-doing, but enabled to reduce the debt to £13 6s. 5d. *Supplying vacant pulpits on Sunday.*

This was a triumph in regard to the work; but some of our more intimate friends, who knew how we were pressed at home, urged that one of two things must be done as early as possible. Foremost among these friends was the late Rev. Dr. Aveling, then the devoted and talented pastor of Kingsland Congregational Church. The alternative referred to was this:—Either to give up the work and put myself in the way of being called to the pastorate; or cease being responsible for the Sunday part of the work, and be thereby open to preaching appointments in vacant pulpits.

I elected the latter course, as then I could continue the work during the other six days of the week. But an unthought of difficulty arose from the fact that since I organised the Institution, my name had been more closely associated with evangelistic than pastoral work. But, to help to overcome this, a notice to Ministers and Churches was issued. The following are extracts from it:—

"Dear Friends—Because of new arrangements in connection with the Christian Union for Christian Work, which I have superintended since 1872, I am open to accept preaching appointments on Sundays."

My brethren in the ministry have been thus pleased to speak of my ministerial standing.

"We, the undersigned, have good knowledge of the Rev. James

Inches Hillocks, of 127 Stoke Newington Road, London, N., as a Congregational Minister of good repute."

"Here followed the Signatures, viz., that of the late *Thomas W. B. Aveing, D.D.*, Ex-Chairman of the *Congregational Union of England and Wales, and four neighbouring Congregational Ministers.*"

Hearing of this, the Rev. Dr. Donald Frazer, Ex-Moderator of the Presbyterian Church of England, was pleased to write to the Secretary, then the Rev. John Black, whose duty it was to see to the preaching appointments.

"Mr. Hillocks, who has a remarkable history, and who has been known to me for many years, is a true and earnest servant of Christ. He is free on Sundays for supply, and though he cannot go on your list, perhaps you will give him an appointment when you have not satisfactory appointments otherwise."

This notice became helpful, and, in the next issue, I was able to add—

"Should I be unknown to any of your friends to whom you may impart this information, please call their attention to the fact that my acceptance of preaching appointments is not confined to the denomination to which I belong. For instance, in London, I have accepted appointments in the Presbyterian Churches, such as Belgrave Church, the Rev. Dr. Saphir's; the Baptist Churches, such as Bloomsbury Church, as well as the Congregational Churches, such as Approach Road and Kingsland.

"The same remark applies to Appointments in Scotland and Ireland—such as the Established Churches, the Free Churches, the United Presbyterian Churches, as well as the Congregational Churches."

I was also glad to see several appreciative notices taken of these special efforts by the press, such as that from the *Dundee Advertiser*:—

"The Rev. J. I. Hillocks speaks, as he writes, with an ease and a fervour which never fail to command the attention of his hearers. It is delightful to see the cordial way in which he is received by the Ministers and other active Christians belonging to the various denominations."

Thus we continued till my health failed once more. However, a partial rest in Scotland restored me somewhat. But from this date, the extent of the extending work had to be considerably lessened. *The lost in London.* This was rendered imperative for three reasons: (1) The funds at my command were insufficient. (2) My strength, after years of hard fighting, was not equal to the strain on mind and body. (3) In the natural course of events during these years many of my co-workers had changed their residence; some had died, some had left London, and some had entered on Christian enterprises on the same principle, but on their own account. True, others had joined us—or rather were co-operating with us—but for all practical purposes the management, as well as the responsibility, had returned to me, as in 1873 before the council was elected.

This being the case, I thought it well to shorten the name under which we had laboured: "Christian Work" being the name adopted instead. I liked, and I still like, the fuller name. It bespoke the need of the time, most likely the need of all time, that is, whilst there is a sinner to be restored or a burden to bear. But I wished to speak in my own name only. However, though there was this change in the name, and a change in the plan, there was no change of aim. It was Christian in the widest sense. It is Christian still. Every effort put forth by me—whether visiting, teaching, preaching, or lecturing, in the Metropolis or in the Provinces, has the same object in view—to raise the poor to God and usefulness; to promote the divine principle, the whole man for the loving God; to enlighten minds, win souls and care for bodies.

Nor do I mean that co-operation with other good workers ceased, even for a day. My experience and co-operation is at the call of the churches and societies when I have the honour of an invitation. But apart from this, if something was in a manner lost, something was gained. I was abler to attend to other forms of the work, one of which may be mentioned.

The occasional preaching and lecturing in the country has brought me in contact with those who had relatives "lost in London"—lost to all that is good. In this way I learn much of the dark side of life, much that cannot be retold to others. My search for the "lost" is not an easy task, it is sometimes a dangerous one; but as a rule good fruit comes of it. The smile of God on it is at once a defence and an inceptive. In this way one might spend a life-time in London to good purpose.

"Pray number me among your scattered wayward flock," is a sentence the like of which is not new to me. The care taken of those restored to God, their relatives and peace, takes the form of frequent visits and much correspondence; but the re-unions are touching times. And what is also of importance, those thus restored generally become helpful in several ways—not only telling of others yet lost, but helping to rescue them.

Fruition at last. But I must also mention another important incident which happened about a year before the last mentioned date. It was a source of joy to me, and I wish you to look upon one of the proofs of my hearty co-operation with others in all good work.

The good work to which I now more particularly refer is an effort made on behalf of the physical health of the people. In this matter I had for long stood almost alone; being—as *The Sanitary Record* puts it—"one of the earliest pioneers in the agitation for the improvement of the dwellings of the poor." As the law stood, and stands, I had to fight against the power of local authority, which, as a rule, was on the side of the middlemen or house farmers, not a few of whom were vestrymen. Their kicking against this interference with their interest, and their influence with those around them, led some "very good" people to "think" and to say I should "leave the law of supply and demand to work its way." But I kept at it, always at it. Now appealing to the *local* authorities, generally in vain; now exposing in the press some of the more glaring of the disgusting and murderous spots in slumdom; and now appealing to the Local Government Board, not always in vain. In this I persisted because every special effort—though I did not always obtain for the victims what I wished—led a few here and a few there to think of the manner in which thousands of our poor were being murdered in slumdom.

Imagine then the feeling of triumphant gladness which filled my soul, when, at last, it became evident that something right and strong was about to be done in regard to the sanitary condition of the homes of the poor. I refer not to the effervescing enthusiasm which for the time made "slumming" fashionable and popular. I felt sure it would soon die away. I speak of that grand grip of the question which resulted in the foundation of "The Mansion House Council on the Dwellings of the People."

This Institution does not go as far in seeking to guard and promote the health of the people as I would wish, nevertheless I look upon its aim and efforts as, in a measure, the realization of what I had long desired. I look upon the organization as a pleasing proof that the public conscience was, in a measure, roused to a sense of the horrid cruelty endured by the poor in murderous dens called "homes." "Fruition at last," said I to myself.

In 1884, Alderman Sir R. N. Fowler, Bart., M.P., then Lord Mayor of London, with several gentlemen of a like philanthropic disposition, called a conference in the Mansion House on this subject. I was heartily invited to this important gathering, but remained silent, being anxious to hear others. My past utterances on this theme had, in some quarters, been characterised as "the exaggerations of a raving philanthropist," but now I was in the company of other "raving" friends of the poor. True, some statements made testified that the subject was new to the speakers, but they were evidently in earnest, and

The Mansion House Council.

deeds might follow words. I was glad that budding philanthropy had plenty scope.

However, I soon made up for my silence by means of my pen, in a series of letters addressed to some of our leading men who had freely expressed themselves in regard to the evils under consideration. The point of my letters was twofold. What are the causes of the evils, and what are the remedies. Each letter referred more particularly to the relative points most likely to be specially interesting to the person addressed.

The first letter was written to the Lord Mayor. And this was followed by others: To the Rt. Hon. the Earl of Shaftsbury; the Rt. Hon. Sir W. V. Harcourt, Bart., M.P., Secretary of State; the Right Rev. Dr. Benson, Archbishop of Canterbury; the Rev. Dr. Joseph Parker, Chairman of the Congregational Union of England and Wales; the Rev. Dr. Thomas W. Aveling, Hon. Sec., Reedham Orphan Asylum; the Rev. C. H. Spurgeon, president of the Pastors' College.

The replies sent were such as I expected to receive from intelligent gentlemen in earnest. In one case, it was *more* than I expected. I mean that of the Lord Mayor, as president of the Mansion House Council on the Dwellings of the People. From it I give the following extract:—

"I am directed by the Lord Mayor to acknowledge the receipt of your letter to him and to thank you for the same. The wide experience you have had, and the able manner in which you have grasped the difficult questions affecting the condition of the London poor, render it very desirable that this Council should have the benefit of your advice and co-operation, and I have to ask you to be good enough to allow me to add your name to the Council. I will, with your permission, retain your letter, as it will be useful to us in connection with the literature we shall have to produce and disseminate in connection with this movement."

To both requests I readily consented because I felt convinced that some good would be done, and that the Council might be able to do on a large scale what I had been endeavouring to do for more than twenty years previously, namely, to find out and enforce the best means of securing those improvements in the dwellings of the poor which are essential to the welfare of the nation.

As was to be expected, not a little of this "new-born enthusiasm" subsided, not being sufficiently grounded to withstand the test of hard and disagreeable work, yet during the first year upwards of two thousand five hundred cases were reported with the view to enforce those concerned to carry out the Sanitary Acts. And this work of investigation and reformation has been steadily progressing. In 1887 "More than 3,500 cases of insanitary conditions were brought to light and dealt with and remedied by the Council's Central office, and, in addition to these, there has been an enormous amount of work in almost every district in the metropolis by the local committees in connection with the council."

Into this work I entered most heartily as far as my other duties, my time and strength would permit. True, as has been said, reform in the spiritual and educational matters is higher than that which merely refers to the physical health of the people, but the enforced absence of the bodily health of the people goes greatly against every other reform, social and religious. John Hamer, Esq., the able and energetic Hon. Sec. of this Council, has said many things, true and strong, but there are none with which I more heartily agree than this:—"Healthy homes mean less drink, less profligacy, less disease, less death."

CHAPTER XIV.—CLOSING OF THE AUTOBIOGRAPHIC NARRATIVE.

ONE who knew something of this has deposed to "the comfort and blessing that literature can prove in sickness and sorrow." If by "intellectual pursuits" he includes the use of the pen, he assures us that it can powerfully keep "the head from crazing and the heart from breaking."

The pen as a relieving element.

Though compared with others eminent in literature I am a novice in that line, yet I have reason to believe that there is something, some truth, in what Thomas Hood says. At least I have known a little of the pen as a relieving element, from the day I wrote the lines entitled, "My Mammy's Awa'," even till the time when I made a little more effort in that way to help the work as well as my family. And I really found that such efforts, humble as they were, assisted in saving "the head from crazing and the heart from breaking."

Of course, I had no idea of becoming what is called "a literary man." My thoughts and hopes and efforts were in another direction. Still I was thankful when my pen was fortunate enough to bring in a little just in time to meet an approaching crisis. True, this would have been the case more frequently if I had been paid all the money I was promised, and which I had earned; but there seems to be drawbacks and broken promises in every line of life, and greedy people seem to make the most of poor people.

In this line I had some dealings with several kinds of people. Those who said what they wanted, and were able and willing and ready to pay for what they had from me. Those who really meant to pay what they promised but could not. And those who promised to pay but would not. With the first I had no trouble. The second I pitied, and would have helped them still more had

I been able. Of the third I would not trust myself to say what I thought of them. But this I would say to you, my reader, if you should ever wish in this way to earn an honest penny, be on your guard should you be brought in contact with those canting hypocrites who seek your time and efforts at reduced rates "for the benefit of the cause"—I found this to mean personal gain. Let no amount of whining hypocrisy draw you into their net.

I rejoice to know that some of our religious weeklies are conducted on sound commercial principles. Some have paid more than they promised, because I had been helpful to them. In other cases, however, my experience has been all the other way. For instance, a large sum is yet due to me for brain work. The last time I called on the trustee of the so-called "estate" I was told not to look for more than a shilling in the pound, if even that. But such losses, notwithstanding, my pen has not been altogether fruitless. Indeed, had it not been helpful now and then I could not have been able to carry on the work for so many years without salary.

"Hard battles" in the flames. When across the Atlantic my friends there, like my friends here, urged me to write the Story of my Life Work anew, carrying it on to the date at which I ended the writing of the narrative. This I had been doing at intervals, from 1878 to 1883, as far as my other duties permitted.

When it was known that these chapters were finished, several publishing firms expressed a desire to see the MS., with the view of publishing the book if thought well, and if the terms were agreeable. The work was put into the hands of a firm; but, unfortunately for the publishers, and for me, two days after the whole establishment—my MS., other MSS., and many volumes—were consumed in the flames, in one of those great fires which frequently startle London.

The fire assurance offices took no cognisance of MSS. Therefore the loss of my MS. fell on me. Of course I felt it deeply; but there was no use crying over spilt milk, so I began again.

About this time, or shortly after, there was a desire that I should publish the letters already referred to, addressed to the London Mayor and others. I did not consent, but promised to extend the proposed volume; and give their substance under the heading, "Roots and Remedies of London Miseries." In due time the work assumed the handsome form of a royal 8vo. volume of between three and four hundred pages. The price was 7s. 6d.

The reviews of this volume were such as might please any author; and the book became helpful in several ways.

A Postscript Chapter. "It reads like a novel, but does not end like one," said a critic referring to my Prize Autobiography, more than a quarter of a century ago. The same, for the same reason, is likely to be said of this volume, simply because it is not a novel, but "a piece of real life."

Had even one of two incidents transpired, it might have given the romantic ending which most novel readers like. For instance, had I become heir to a large fortune; had I said to those of my fellow-workers still willing to rally round me, "We need not now trouble ourselves about money, let our thoughts be all about the work." If I could have said and done this, such an ending would have been like a novel; but this is not my position yet.

Or if—what would have been nearly the same thing—if some rich lady or gentleman, as willing as able, had said to me, "Do not trouble about money. I shall see that you and your family are attended to, and that all necessary expenses connected with the work shall be paid. Go on, all of you, improving by your long apprenticeship. Keep your co-workers together, there is much need for all that can be done." But this has not yet come to pass.

Nevertheless, I promised my readers that I would add a postscript chapter to the volume should any event of this kind transpire. I do not know if this promise pleased all my readers, but I really meant to keep my word, if only to prove that fact is at least as strange as fiction.

"Though this is possible, it is not probable," I said to myself. But I am glad to gladden your heart by telling you that a postscript chapter was called for, to record an event of quite another kind, giving pleasure to many, my family and myself included. On the 16th of September, 1885, *The Times* and the other London Daily Papers stated the pleasing and encouraging fact that "The Queen has been pleased to confer a Civil List Pension on the Rev. J. Inches Hillocks, author of 'Hard Battles for Life and Usefulness.'"

About three years before this, some of my more appreciative friends, who knew of my work among the poor, spoke of calling Her Majesty's attention to these efforts. Then I did not consent, but after "Hard Battles" appeared and the volume was so well received, one of these same friends told me that he and others had resolved to take the initiative in communicating with Her Majesty's Ministers by Memorial. After careful reflection I wrote thus to him :—

"As you know, I entered into public life when a mere boy. From the first, my ambition has been that God would so own and bless my labours that they might become more and more helpful to my fellow creatures. It is possible you have seen the sentence, 'Not being untutored in suffering, I have learned to pity those in affliction.' This is my case, and the thought thereby conveyed has had no small share in urging me on in the midst of many difficulties. Coupled with a sense of my duty to God and man, it has also been to me one of the incentives to perseverance all through my 'Hard Battles for Life and Usefulness.' But the thought never entered my mind that even the most appreciative of my friends, private and public, would look upon these forty years, thus spent, as meriting the gratitude of my country. Now, however, since this is the opinion of those who are best acquainted with my 'Life Struggles,' and now that the matter has been mentioned to me more than once, I have simply to say that should our Sovereign and her Ministers be of the same opinion, I shall gratefully look upon Her Majesty's generous consideration as a helpful encouragement to go on in the same good work, if possible, with greater energy. One thing I ask, that the signing of the memorial be confined to representative gentlemen without regard to party, such as Chief and Ex-Chief Magistrates, and Members of Parliament."

There were thirty-one signatures including the Right Hon. the Earl of Aberdeen.

London, (to which I was called in 1860), was represented by Sir R. N. Fowler, Bart., Lord Mayor of London, M.P.; Alderman W. J. R. Cotton, Ex-Lord Mayor of London, M.P.; Alderman Sir William M'Arthur, Ex-Lord Mayor of London, M.P. for Lambeth; The Right Hon. C. T. Ritchie, M.P. for the Tower Hamlets.

Dundee (where I was born), by Provost Hugh Ballingall, Ex-Provost William Robertson, Ex-provost James Cox, Ex-Provost George Rough, George Armstead, M.P., and Frank Henderson, M.P.

Aberdeen, by Lord Provost J. Matthews, Ex-Lord Provost D. Esslemont, Ex-Lord Provost G. Jamison, and Dr. Webster, M.P.

Greenock, by Provost E. Wilson, Ex-Provost D. Campbell, Ex-Provost Abram Lyle, and Thomas Sutherland, M.P.

Glasgow, by Lord Provost W. M'Onie, Ex-Lord Provost John J. Ure, Ex-Lord Provost Sir William Collins, and Dr. Cameron, M.P.

Edinburgh, by J. R. Buchanan, M.P., and S. D. Waddy, M.P.

Also by H. W. Eaton, M.P. for Coventry, Provost R. Binnie, Gourock, B. Whitworth, M.P. for Drogheda, Joseph Cowan, M.P. for Newcastle, Right Hon. H. Campbell Bannerman, M.P. for Stirling, Right Hon. A. J. Mundella, M.P. for Sheffield.

From this you will see that both of the great parties in the State were represented. The statements contained in the Memorial were sustained by brief quotations from the Metropolitan and Provincial Press in regard to my past Life and Labours.

These need not be repeated here, but some of the publications then quoted from may be named, as they also indicate a representative character: the *Athenæum* and the *Scotsman*—the *Academy* and the *Glasgow Herald*—the *Christian*, the *Christian World*, the *Christian Age*, the *Christian Leader*, and the *Freeman*. Of the "Reviews" there were the *Saturday*, the *British Quarterly*, the *Scottish*, the *Contemporary* and others. Also *The English Churchman* and *The Nonconformist*. And with all this there were also quoted words of kindly commendation from the Rev. C. H. Spurgeon, Lord Mayor, Sir R. N. Fowler, Bart., M.P., and Dr. Smiles, the author of "Self-Help."

On the 6th of March, 1885, The Right Hon. W. E. Gladstone, (then Prime Minister and First Lord of the Treasury), acknowledged the receipt of the Memorial, at the same time stating that the claims would have careful consideration.

Not long after this there was a change in the Ministry, Lord Salisbury became Prime Minister and Lord Iddesleigh First Lord of the Treasury. On August 4th, 1885, I received the following —"Lord Iddesleigh has the pleasure to inform you that the Queen has been pleased to confer upon you a Civil List Pension of £75 a year."

For this I was, and still am, grateful for more reasons than one. One is, it is a recognition of good work as well as the humble worker. Another reason is it will help me to continue to help others with less anxiety concerning the dear ones at home. And I was all the more delighted when I learned that the honour was conferred upon me because of philanthropic labours as well as authorship. The first had led to ready sacrifices; the second had been the humble means of a little gain occasionally.

I must now end this Autobiographic narrative by one or two closing notes, notes of gratitude.

Grateful notes.

1. It would be wrong not to accord my hearty thanks to those who have, in this work, given unmistakeable evidences of good will, even of cordial friendship. This has been

done on the part of some by donations, some by subscriptions, some by working hand in hand with me, and some by fervent prayer. I rejoice in this helpfulness of all such assisting friends.

2. I may be pardoned if here I look at the matter nearer home. Without in any way lessening the force of the merited praise just expressed, I must add that without such a home as I have had I could not have so battled for Life and Usefulness. My beloved help-meet and our precious daughters wish me to say as little as possible on this point. And to this our noble son, had he been still with us, would have said, "Amen." But, as you know, in this respect, it is long since the "I" might, with all propriety, been changed into the "We." But for the fact that we looked upon the work as God's work, we, in a domestic sense, called it "*Our* Work." During these years of thought and effort, often in the midst of severe buffetings and frequent persecutions, my home influences have continued to be very helpful. Whatever the nature of duties before me; whatever the difficulties or dangers to be encountered, these influences have been with me, fostering courage and kindness, and imparting strength. Whatever good has been done, the "better half" of it is due to the care, devotion and prayer of that precious one whom God gave me as a loving help-meet—a devoted companion, a wise counsellor, a skilful nurse, and a fellow worker for the good of others.

3. But more and above all this, my Father in Christ has given me Himself with all His ready helpfulness. All along, from my first days, as now, He has been making all things work together for good. In His providence and by His grace He has inspired and equipt me for the work He has given me to do, not only blessing it, but drawing me nearer and nearer to Himself. His have been wondrous ways, and all for good. He has not only forgiven my mistakes and shortcomings, He has also assisted me to that devotion and endurance, which are essential to success in all works of faith and labours of love. Looking at the past and the present, we can say, "Thine, O Lord, is the greatness, and the power, and the glory, and the victory, and the majesty." In all that has been done by me, or through me, for His glory and

man's good, He has been first and last and all through. I know what it is to say, "I had fainted unless I had believed to see the goodness of God in the land of the living." But He strengthened my heart, saying, "Be of good courage." "Go forward."

4. And as to results, I cannot attempt to number them, and I can hope there are many more than are known to me. I mean such as are, under God, now rejoicing in enlightened minds, saved souls and healthier bodies. Work is ours, results are God's. If the work is of the right kind, and done in the right way, His blessing is certain—on earth and ascending to heaven. The Lord knows all and to me that is enough. Dr. Walter C. Smith, in his genial introduction, sums up in a few words. The kind-hearted poet, preacher, and popular author, says:—"And now Mr. Hillocks's only wealth is a burden of care for the London poor. Yet he is rich in the kindly feelings and abundant labours which he expends upon them. He, too, has conquered fortune, for he has won the place and power to do the good which it was in his heart to do. That is true success, and he fought gallantly for it."

5. This is the state of matters as these closing lines leave me. The battle is not yet over. Why should it, while strength of body and mind and heart remain? While there is wrong to right? While consolation and courage are needful on every hand? While the weak need strength, and the heavy-laden pant for rest?

Because of being so frequently nigh unto death, I am not so strong as I have been, save in the pulpit; but I am as anxious as ever to devote the remaining days for the good of others, particularly for those to whom this life is truly "a vale of tears." And, I think, I shall be all the happier if found in the harness when the Master calls me home.

As for the future that is His, and He will be there. To us—myself and my dear ones—that is enough. In our journey thus far, amid the varied maze of life, there have been showers and storms many, but we have not been without sunshine occasionally. From our limited point of view, we at times have thought that our triumphs have not been equal to our trials, but man is so shortsighted. Of this we are certain, the Lord has been our Shepherd. And we still believe His—

> "Love and mercy will
> Attend us on our journey still."

Reader, Adieu, until the Sequel to these "Hard Battles" appears, which I hope may not be long.

INDEX TO PART SECOND.

Sunday in London, 11; Greatly Disappointed, 14; Another Door Opened, 16; The Past becoming Useful, 17; My Family brought to London, 18.

A Fortnight in the Country, 21; Stealing a March on the Bishop, 23; With a full Robed Clergyman, 24; A Sojourn in Islington, 26.

My New Sphere, 29; A Friendly Glance at the Work, 30; Organising the Forces, 31.

Visiting the Poor, 33; Our Adult Meetings, 34; Caring for the Young, 37.

Open Air Preaching, 40; Three Opposing Classes, 41; My First Open Air Audience, 42; My Life Threatened, 44; An Easy Victory, 49; Kindred Fields of Labour, 50.

The Field as I Found it, 54; Workhouse Horrors, 58; About to be Buried Alive, 58; Aids to Triumph, 60.

An Interesting Memorial, 62; "The Bread and Cheese Matter," 63; About Ecclesiastical Standing, 63; Compensation, 64; It was not to be in St. Pancras, 65.

Bidding Adieu, 68 ; Another Call, 69 ; First Year's Work in Darlington, 70 ; A Duel Pastorate, 71 ; The Bud of Promise again, 72 ; Closing Months in Darlington, 73.

Return to London, 75 ; Our only Son goes Home, 76 ; In a Railway Collision, 77.

A Glance at the Past two Years, from 1870, 82 ; Reasoning Together—the Decision, 84 ; The Work Begun—first Meetings, 86.

Rapid Progress, 89 ; Our Name, 90 ; Encouragement, 93 ; The Council's Appeal for Funds, 94 ; Mutual Helpfulness, 95.

A Visit to Our Kin beyond the Sea, 97 ; The Balance on the Wrong Side, 98 ; The " No Salary Matter," 100.

Supplying Vacant Pulpits on Sunday, 103 ; The Lost in London, 105 ; Fruition at Last, 106 ; The Mansion House Council, 107.

The Pen as a Relieving Element, 110 ; " Hard Battles " in the Flames, 111 ; Postscript Chapter, 112 ; Grateful Notes, 115.

THE END.

www.ingramcontent.com/pod-product-compliance
Lightning Source LLC
Chambersburg PA
CBHW080511090426
42734CB00015B/3029